FORMS OF

Feeling in Victorian Fiction

BARBARA HARDY

Methuen & Co. Ltd

First published in 1985 by
Peter Owen Ltd

First published as a University Paperback in 1986 by
Methuen & Co. Ltd
11 New Fetter Lane, London EC4P 4EE

Printed in Great Britain by
Richard Clay (The Chaucer Press), Ltd
Bungay, Suffolk

British Library Cataloguing in Publication Data

Hardy, Barbara
Forms of feeling in Victorian fiction.
1. English fiction—19th century—
History and criticism
I. Title
823.8′09   PR871

ISBN 0-416-42640-9

To friends and former colleagues
at Royal Holloway College
and especially
Patricia Ball, Peter Caracciolo, Tony Davenport,
Martin Dodsworth, Joan Grundy, Tony Ladd,
Katie Wales and Katharine Worth
with love

Contents

Acknowledgements

I want to thank the following friends for help and advice: Barbara Brunswick, Dan Franklin, Diana Godden, Coral Howells, Andrew Sanders, and Michael Slater. My greatest debt is to Valerie Hall and Graham Handley, for their unflagging labours and good temper.

The first section of Chapter 2 draws on material published in 'The Complexity of Dickens', *Dickens 1970*, Michael Slater (ed.) (1970), and 'Dickens and the Passions', published in the Dickens Centenary Number of *Nineteenth-Century Fiction* (1970). Chapter 6 draws on an essay published in *Notes and Queries for Somerset and Dorset* (March 1978) and on the Introduction to the New Wessex Edition of *The Trumpet-Major* (1974). I am grateful to Macmillan Ltd for permission to use material from that Introduction.

B.H.

A Note on References

The editions used in the present work for the purpose of quotation are as follows:

Bunyan, John	*Grace Abounding and The Pilgrim's Progress*, Roger Sharrock (ed.), Oxford: Oxford University Press, 1966.
Defoe, Daniel	*Robinson Crusoe*, Oxford: Shakespeare Head Press, 1927.
Richardson, Samuel	*Clarissa Harlowe*, Oxford: Shakespeare Head Press, 1930.
Fielding, Henry	*Tom Jones*, M.C. Battestin and F. Bowers (eds.), The Wesleyan Edition of the Works of Henry Fielding, Oxford: The Clarendon Press, 1974.
Sterne, Laurence	*A Sentimental Journey*, I. Jack (ed.), Oxford English Novels, Oxford: Oxford University Press, 1968.
Brontë, Emily	*Wuthering Heights*, H. Marsden and I. Jack (eds.), The Clarendon Edition, Oxford: The Clarendon Press, 1976.
Brontë, Charlotte	*Jane Eyre*, J. Jack and M. Smith (eds.), The Clarendon Edition, Oxford: The Clarendon Press, 1969.
——	*Shirley*, H. Rosengarten and M. Smith (eds.), The Clarendon Edition, Oxford: The Clarendon Press, 1979.
——	*The Professor*, Oxford: Shakespeare Head Press, 1931.
——	*Villette*, Oxford: Shakespeare Head Press, 1931.
Dickens, Charles	*Oliver Twist*, K. Tillotson (ed.), The Clarendon Edition, Oxford: The Clarendon Press, 1966.
——	*Little Dorrit*, H.P. Sucksmith (ed.), The

	Clarendon Edition, Oxford: The Clarendon Press, 1979.
———	The New Oxford Illustrated Dickens, Oxford: Oxford University Press, 1947–58.
Thackeray, William Makepeace	*Vanity Fair*, G. and K. Tillotson (eds.), London: Methuen, 1963.
———	Centenary Biographical Edition of Thackeray's Works, London: John Murray, 1910–11.
Eliot, George	*The Mill on the Floss*, G.S. Haight (ed.), The Clarendon Edition, Oxford: The Clarendon Press, 1980.
———	The Cabinet Edition of George Eliot's Works, Edinburgh and London: William Blackwood and Sons, 1878–80.
———	*Quarry for Middlemarch*, A.T. Kitchel (ed.), Berkeley: University of California Press, 1950.
Hardy, Thomas	The New Wessex Edition, London: Macmillan, 1974.
James, Henry	*Roderick Hudson*, Harmondsworth: Penguin Books, 1969.
———	*The Novels and Stories of Henry James*, P. Lubbock (ed.), London: Macmillan, 1921–3.

INTRODUCTION

The novel generates forms of feeling, for writer, characters, and reader. As it creates, it inquires and analyses. Novelists often insist that the attempt to know our feelings is fraught with difficulty, not many sharing the assurance of Jean-Jacques Rousseau, who begins *Les Confessions*, 'Je sens mon cœur, et je connois les hommes'. Proust, as intent as Rousseau on examining the heart, sees the strenuousness of rejecting emotional certainty, stereotype, and 'our most cherished illusions, ceasing to believe in the objectivity of our own elaborations'. We have to use intelligence, 'to distinguish, and with how much difficulty, the shape of that which we have felt' (*Remembrance of Things Past*; *Time Regained*, Chapter 3). The enterprise demands 'sentimental courage'.

D.H. Lawrence, in 'The Novel and the Feelings',[1] also admits the obscure shape of personal feeling, the inaudibility of 'the cries in our own forests of dark veins'. He shifts the Dantean darkness and search to our intimate but arcane interior life. Introspection may not clarify affective experience and, since Lawrence has little faith in science, he concludes that we have scarcely begun to 'educate ourselves in the feelings' – a usefully ambiguous phrase which brings out the possibility of knowledge and improvement. He asserts the value of looking 'in the real novels', where we may 'listen in' more easily than to our own heartbeats. It is not an exclusively twentieth-century proposal; it echoes John Stuart Mill's *Autobiography*, with its record of arid education, breakdown, and recovery. Mill claimed poetry as a means of affective education,[2] Lawrence proposed fiction.

Lawrence mocks one traditional form of emotional expression, the figure of personification. He sees that it can represent a dangerous taxonomy: 'We see love like a woolly lamb, or like a decorative panther, in Paris clothes, according as it is sacred or profane. We see

11

fear, like a shivering monkey. We see anger, like a bull with a ring through his nose, and greed, like a pig' (op. cit.). This traditional bestiary is dangerous and convenient, implying control, knowledge, system; Lawrence uses an arbitrary, but useful, distinction between emotion and feeling, meaning by emotion a feeling which has been classified, named, limited, and falsified. His satiric zoology has the ring of personal polemic, but refers to a faculty psychology as old as Sophocles and as new as Freud. It also derives from traditional rhetoric. The figures of personification, and its narrative extension, allegory, of course much older than the novel, occupy a central place in English fiction. As forms for feeling they may imply a systematized moral and psychological knowledge, like that distrusted by Lawrence, but even in Bunyan, where allegorical simplicity is a functional dogmatic form, it is occasionally amplified by other modes. In later novels, from Defoe and Fielding to George Eliot and Henry James, allegory either criticizes fixity and definiteness, or appears in combinations with other figures which qualify and transform its simplification.

This book deals with the attempt made by the major Victorian novelists to discover 'the shape of that which we have felt'. Their effort can be polarized in terms of the figure of personification, with its claim to definition and analysis, and its opposite, the figure of incapacity, or what Ernst Robert Curtius called 'the topos of inexpressibility' (*European Literature and the Latin Middle Ages*, translated by W.R. Trask, London, 1979). This is the device which in one stroke expresses powerful feeling, and the impossibility of expressing it: 'I cannot tell you how much', 'I cannot say what', 'Words fail me.' The figure is a cliché of everyday speech, an intensifier, and a denial of stereotype. It is as central in fiction as personification, which is also a cliché, an intensifier, and a satire of stereotype. The topos of inexpressibility is a key figure in Defoe, whose simple characters utter their strong and unutterable fears, longings, faiths, and joys, as it is in George Eliot, whose narrators and dramatized characters recognize the limits of emotional clarity and comprehension. It is present in the sophisticated dumbshow of *The Golden Bowl*, where Maggie Verver, for example, discovers and communicates feelings, not by words but by actions, as she goes to meet her husband at home, instead of her father's house. It appears in an elaborate, sometimes sentimental use, in the deadpan stoicisms of Hemingway, and other modern masters of understatement.

Personification and the topos of inexpressibility are twin aspects of a mimetic representation of emotional crisis, conflict, and continuity. They also form part of the self-conscious narrative medium which moves from particularity to generalization. Personification may figure conflict, dislocation and resolution in character, or an image offered in the narrator's discourse. The expression of incapacity can show the characters' frustration, rapture, and powerlessness, or the narrator's admission of doubt and difficulty. My brief sketch of pre-Victorian models from Bunyan to Sterne is a reminder that the eighteenth-century novel is more conspicuously self-analytic and reflexive than Victorian forms of fiction. The early novels show, in origin and resemblance, those non-realistic, even anti-mimetic, procedures which are prominent but sometimes neglected features of the so-called period of realism.

In Victorian as well as eighteenth-century fiction, the forms and languages which represent affective experience break with – and break – mimesis. The narrative medium in all the major Victorian novelists is reflexive, constantly diverting attention from verisimilitude to analysis. It is discursive, constantly drawing attention to its own fictitious form. Literary history is less tidy than we might wish: although the great eighteenth-century novelists are predominantly unrealistic, placing fictions in a comic or discursive medium, there is the exception of Richardson, as interested as any Victorian novelist in representing individual characters in depth and flux. Fielding, like Jane Austen, anticipates both the comic fragmentations of Thackeray and the tentative realism of Charlotte Brontë and George Eliot, who combine discursive analysis of feeling with the particularized representation of characters. The great Victorians are never simply mimetic. The formal collaboration of narrator and character, in Dickens, Thackeray, and George Eliot, makes for an open and overt analysis of feeling, moving beyond the limits of realistic representation to register an admission of fictional effort, author's awareness, and reader's response. When we examine the representation of feeling in fiction, we find the assertion of artifice placed in realistic character, and in reflexive narrative. Victorian novelists are fully aware of the response of the reader, and build the awareness into their medium. They see the response as created and structured by the text, and, less conventionally, as actively creating that text. What is apparent in Dickens, Thackeray, and George Eliot, is the manipulation of the readers' feelings, and a sense of the multiplicity of response. Thackeray and George Eliot, like Sterne and Diderot, admit the existence of a reader and set tests and exercises which reveal an awareness of this multiplicity. They can force the reader to see the difference between responding to novels and responding to experience outside novels. Emma Bovary tries to make life as fresh, intense, renewable, and particularized as fiction, imposing its structures and languages on what Flaubert splendidly calls 'the eternal monotony of passion'; the reader ironically contrasts her loss of distance and Flaubert's expectation of a cold response to unfictionalized, but fictionalizing, emotions. Dickens, in *Bleak House*, makes the reader stop weeping for Jo; Thackeray, in *The Newcomes*, makes the reader stop longing to console Clive and Ethel; George Eliot, in *Middlemarch*, makes the reader stop sympathizing with Dorothea Brooke. As they do so, they insist on the manipulative power of art, and make us judge our response to fiction. The earnest Victorian realists, like the comic jugglers who precede and succeed them, experiment with sleights and shifts of emotional language.

The major Victorian novelists show anger, desire, jealousy, anguish, pity, terror, joy, and love. So of course do the minor and popular novelists, but through crude, manipulative and stereotyped forms which we call sentimental, pornographic, or gothic. Bad novels represent the affective experience falsely, through lies and mistakes, while good novels try to know and understand. In practice, however, we find profound inquiries into emotion and passion which lapse into sentimentality and sensationalism. But the Victorian novel, at its best, does not represent the passions simply or singly, bringing them on one at a time, but carefully shows the company they keep. The complexity of affective experience can be analysed even in forms which are lyrical and condensed, like the novella or short story. Twentieth-century novels, like *Jacob's Room* or *Mrs Dalloway*, tend to be more emotionally selective than Victorian narratives, but they still blur and blend emotions and passion. George Orwell's *Nineteen Eighty-Four* is centrally concerned with the conditioning and crippling of feeling, but dramatically illustrates its emotional theme by showing a movement from familiar norms to a 'world [where] there will be no emotions except fear, rage, triumph and self-abasement' (Part 3, Chapter 3). Samuel Beckett's *How It Is*, a novel of remarkable emotional reduction, pierces a muddy darkness to show nostalgic glimpses of joy and love, not to raise false faiths, but to keep suffering familiar, as well as strange.

These modern instances make a special thematic emphasis, in concentrated forms rather different from the typical comprehensive stretch of the Victorians. The few comparable examples in the last century always combine the variety of emotional experience with images of distortion, like that of Esmond in *Henry Esmond*, Arthur Clennam in *Little Dorrit*, and Gwendolen Harleth in *Daniel Deronda*. These novels are thematically concentrated, but they are not exclusively concerned with single or simple passions. They show a restriction or obsession of feeling as deviant; the argument depends on a sense of norms. In *Daniel Deronda*, for instance, where there is an unusually specialized drama of fear or dread, the emphasis is placed on the movement and growth of feeling. George Eliot never concentrates on one passion, unlike contemporary scientists, from whom she clearly derives support and knowledge. Darwin's *Expression of the Emotions in Man and Animals* (1872) deals with the emotions one at a time. Not so the novelist. Daniel tells Gwendolen to transform her dread, and the analytic allegory which presents his model, and Gwendolen's experience, shows emotional conflict and complexity.

The question of scientific influence on the art of affective representation is a difficult one. We know that Shakespeare is likely to have read Timothy Bright's *Treatise of Melancholy*, that George Eliot studied Darwin,[3] that D.H. Lawrence was introduced to Freudian ideas by his wife; but Hamlet, Gwendolen, and Paul Morel are more complex, in their dynamism and particularity, than the classified illustrations of Bright, Darwin, and Freud. Emotional experience precedes scientific and artistic taxonomy, though the scientist and the artist provide forms and languages which influence and direct our feelings by affecting our ways of thinking about feelings. In *Middlemarch*, George Eliot cleverly makes Casaubon feel disappointed by his lack of rapture because his reading in poetic precedent invokes invidious comparisons. He is not stupid, however, in his consoling reflection that the poets probably exaggerate the force of masculine passion. Nor is he alone in being betrayed by poetry. Will Ladislaw is potent enough to beget children, if not to please Henry James, who understandably thought that after Casaubon Dorothea needed a trooper, but he is persuaded by love-poets to underestimate the pains of courtly love. As George Eliot uses literature to investigate the emotional life, she prudently draws attention to the limits and dangers of literary knowledge, like Cervantes, Jane Austen, and Flaubert before her.

Novelists draw on personal as well as literary and scientific sources in their representation of feeling. Biographical evidence tempts us to speak of *The Newcomes* and *Henry Esmond* as products of Thackeray's unhappy affection for Jane Brookfield, though he himself spoke only of the latter novel as uttering his 'Cut-throat melancholy', and melancholy marks all his work. When George Eliot in *Middlemarch* creates images of withered dying and infertile waste, we remember how Thornton Lewes was slowly dying as she wrote, and that it was a novel conceived in her middle age, with years of voluntary sterility behind and involuntary sterility ahead. But the sense of dreariness and self-negation was a common experience of her early womanhood, before she wrote novels; its imagery permeates her fiction from beginning to end.

George Eliot acknowledged an ancient and distinguished tradition when she told R.C. Jebb, the great Sophocles scholar, that Sophocles had influenced her 'In the delineation of the great primitive emotions',[4] confirming his previous impressions. It is an emphasis which must be remembered when we attend to the context of scientific psychology and physiology with which she was well acquainted. Before twentieth-century scholars had drawn attention to Sophocles' primitivism, she felt it. Like Jebb, she must also have felt the combination of primitive emotion with what P.E. Easterling, in her edition of *The Trachiniae*, calls 'subtle and highly sophisticated' forms and language. When Jebb observed the influence he may have been directed by George Eliot's clear comparison of primitive passions on the Floss and in Middlemarch to those in Sophoclean Corinth and Thebes. Sophocles shows civilized people driven out of their minds and their societies: by pain and revenge in *Electra* and *Philoctetes*, by jealousy, desire, and pain in *The Trachiniae*, by anger and revenge in *Ajax*, and by dread and pity in the two Oedipus plays. The same passions ravage characters and institutions in the novels of George Eliot. (And also in the Brontës, Dickens, and Hardy.) Sophocles shows transformations of emotion, when the self-pity and guilt of Oedipus change into dignified self-defence and holy dread. George Eliot also shows passions interacting and developing. Maggie Tulliver's intelligence is overpowered by passion, and Tom's less susceptible response is registered with a measure of sympathy. Like Electra and Antigone, Dorothea has a less subversive and less passionate sister. Sometimes direct comparisons are made mock-heroically, as when the anger of Maggie and her father is amplified by a context of Greek drama, but the irony is deceptive, bracketing and not belittling. Sometimes the reference is cunningly tangential, as when Philip Wakem consoles the wounded hero Tom by telling him the story of Philoctetes, which has a deeper, more secret, reference to his own wound and bow.

An obvious technical link between George Eliot and Sophocles, in their representation of emotions, is their flexible narrative, which both intensifies and distances the impassioned conflicts and outcries of the *dramatis personae*. What is more profoundly important is their ritualizing of feeling. Sophocles takes us to the primitive origins of passion by rites and ceremonies which enlarge and deepen human experience, placing particulars of passion in the context of religious vision and belief. George Eliot generalizes emotional experience, through her anonymous but impassioned choric voices which make resonant allusion to other cultures and other literature.

All the great Victorian novelists perform something like this act of emotional deepening. Whether through analysis, allusion, imagery or direct address, they do more than dramatize emotional conflict and crisis. Movements from the particular to the general can create intensification; such acts of emotional enlargement are tests of imagination. They are, however, not always easy to achieve. Dickens and Hardy succeed in defamiliarizing the act of reading, and refamiliarizing the act of sympathy, as they show the deaths of Jo and Henchard. Dickens, however, falls into a stock request for a stock response when he shows the rituals of Nell's holy dying. Even the great artist has lapses, especially in this dangerous area. If I have emphasized success, it has not been because I have taken sentimental courage for granted.

NOTES

1 Lawrence's essay, reprinted in *Phoenix: The Posthumous Papers of D.H. Lawrence* (London, 1936), is a discussion of emotion, rather than of the representation of emotion in fiction. He mentions the subject frequently in many essays, and the famous defence of the novel in *Lady Chatterley's Lover* (London, 1960) is relevant:

> It is the way our sympathy flows and recoils that really determines our lives. And here lies the vast importance of the novel, properly handled. It can inform and lead into new places the flow of our sympathetic consciousness, and it can lead our sympathy away in recoil from things gone dead. Therefore, the novel, properly handled, can reveal the most secret places of life: for it is in the *passional* secret places of life, above all, that the tide of sensitive awareness needs to ebb and flow, cleansing and freshening. (Chapter 9)

2 Mill's 'Essay on Poetry' (1833) makes a provocative comparison between what he

judges to be the immature and extrovert genre of narrative, and the emotionally expressive and analytic one of poetry.

3 See Gillian Beer, *Darwin's Plots* (London, 1983), Chapter 7, for an excellent discussion of *Daniel Deronda* and Darwin.

4 See Gordon S. Haight, *George Eliot: A Biography* (Oxford, 1968), pp. 463–4, for a full account of the occasion.

1

FEELING IN FICTION

Some Pre-Victorian Models

The novel is an affective form. Not wholly so, or simply so. While it expresses, shapes, and analyses feelings and passions, it also expresses, shapes, and analyses ideas and arguments. In *Daniel Deronda* Gwendolen Harleth wonders at Daniel's caring for feelings as well as 'ideas, knowledge, wisdom, and all that', and he replies, 'But to care about them is a sort of affection' (Chapter 35). From Bunyan to Beckett, the novel delineates the feelings of fictitious characters, but in many different ways – mimetic, stylized, symbolic, analytic, and reflexive. Fiction draws on the conscious and unconscious affective life of its author, and seeks in various direct and indirect ways to move the reader. If the author loses control of his feelings, as Dickens and Lawrence sometimes do, the result is unbalanced or self-indulgent. If the author takes his eye off the subject of feeling, to solicit the reader boldly and crudely, the result is didactic, pornographic, or sentimental. At its best, the novel uses emotion to investigate emotion, in many forms.

The great English novelists move our feelings not through gross stimulus or the sentimental offer of blanks for us to fill, but through impassioned particulars. They have no simple or single commitment to psychological realism. Victorian novelists use complex and dynamic units of character, together with functional stylization, mixing the modes. The Victorian novel is less conspicuously reflexive than its eighteenth-century ancestors or its twentieth-century descendants; it does not offer illusions of a closed fictitious world of persons and events, but a characteristic multiplication of narrative, which has room for direct as well as indirect appeal, for emotionally charged generalizations as well as for particulars. It is hard to find flawless works; control neighbours excess, profound analysis lapses into superficial fantasy. Novelists are particularly alive to the dangers of affective form: Sterne and Richardson, for instance, recognize and articulate problems of emotional distance and generality, even though both novelists are often uncontrolled and mawkish. The novel's formal mixture of dramatic, narrative, and discursive forms equips it to reflect on its own analysis and emotion. One of its great subjects has been the affective life.

John Stuart Mill's 'Essay on Poetry', written in 1833, before the rise of the Victorian novel, proposes poetry, not fiction, as the medium for the delineation of feeling. But fiction had already refined forms and conventions for the representation and analysis of feeling. Bunyan initiated the mixed medium, which is narrative and discursive, typological and particularized. Though his invented characters are types, and his invented action is an allegory, *A Pilgrim's Progress* already offers a variety of emotional experience. Its main mode of characterization is that of personified attributes, but the central figure, Christian, has emotional and moral complexity. Like Everyman and Faustus, he is an illustrative figure; he stands at the centre of an imagined population whose members relate to him as characters and personifications of his faculties and moods. In expressing emotion through realism and symbolism, Bunyan is a model for the novelists who were to succeed him. The tradition of allegory and personification which he inherits is as old as literature and drama; he uses it to create forms that were to be developed and made subtle by the Victorian novelists.

Bunyan can combine and relate different modes of character. Christian is a complex being, both faithful and wayward, Faithful is only faithful, Evangelist and Giant Despair are magnified images of vision and mood. The characters are set in an action which enlivens and substantiates illustrativeness with emotional detail and nuance. Such detail is most common in the complex characters, but even the simple ones are endowed with emotions and passions. The allegorical landscape and journey, too, express and generalize the feelings of despair, depression, inertia, sloth, fear, rest and joys. The representation works through scenes and objects, as well as people. Just as Spenser – another model for the mixed mode of representing emotion – uses emblems, personifications, and allegories of action and event which are warmed and enlivened by feelings, so Bunyan develops a form which is clearly schematic, yet affectively particularized. At the beginning of *A Pilgrim's Progress*, the author's verse 'Apology' acknowledges the devious techniques of fictional persuasion. It promises that the reader shall be 'diverted from melancholy', 'be pleasant', 'laugh and weep together', 'read' himself, 'read thou know'st not what,' and lay 'heart and head together'. The formula applies to many succeeding entertainments and persuasions in the genre of prose fiction. Within the convoluted structure of the story, the dreamer imagines the allegory and its persons. These are set in motion to behave as type determines, but with some measure of naturalism; the characters are endowed with emotions and passions, which may be demonstrated and explicated, as Passion and Patience are. Moral analysis and dramatic versatility go hand in hand. Bunyan creates an emotional continuity which becomes the norm in most later prose fiction. *A Pilgrim's Progress* begins with passion, as Christian asks his great agonized question, 'What shall I do?' It will be echoed passionately, especially by women, in the Victorian novel. Christian's distress is described, uttered, and set in active relationship with the feelings of other characters:

and as he read, he wept and trembled: and not being able longer to contain, he brake out with a lamentable cry; saying, *What shall I do?*

In this plight therefore he went home, and refrained himself as long as he could, that his Wife and Children should not perceive his distress; but he could not be silent long, because that his trouble increased: wherefore at length he brake his mind to his Wife and Children; and thus he began to talk to them, *O my dear Wife*, said he, *and you the Children of my bowels, I your dear friend am in my self undone, by reason of a burden that lieth hard upon me: moreover, I am for certain informed, that this our City will be burned with fire from Heaven, in which fearful overthrow, both my self, with thee, my Wife, and you my sweet babes, shall miserably come to ruine; except (the which, yet I see not) some way of escape can be found, whereby we may be delivered.* At this his Relations they were sore amazed; not for that they believed, that what he said to them was true, but because they thought, that some frenzy distemper had got into his head: therefore, it drawing towards night, and they hoping that sleep might settle his brains, with all hast they got him to bed; but the night was as troublesome to him as the day: wherefore instead of sleeping, he spent it in sighs and tears. So when the morning was come, they would know how he did; and he told them worse and worse. He also set to talking to them again, but they began to be hardened. They also thought to drive away his distemper by harsh and surly carriages to him: Sometimes they would deride, sometimes they would chide, and sometimes they would quite neglect him: wherefore he began to retire himself to his Chamber to pray for, and pity them; and also to condole his own misery.

Passion sets the action in motion, and animates the whole story. Though the characters are personifications, they are roused and activated in a fluent and unpredictable track of feeling. Experiences develop, change, stimulate and generate fresh emotions. Even undeveloping types like Evangelist respond with intensity. Evangelist shows 'a severe and dreadful countenance' when Christian is diverted from the Strait Gate by Mr Worldly Wiseman, but after delivering a homily, 'Evangelist, after he had kissed him, gave him one smile'. Forgiveness is there, physical and warm. When Faithful tells Christian about his meeting with Shame (aptly and not predictably 'bold-faced'), he says that Shame fetched up the blood in his face. In the stinking prison of Giant Despair, Hopeful argues (hopefully) against suicide, but a touch of nature makes him feel 'sad and doleful', almost hopeless. The lesson is animated by particularities of emotion. The allegory moves about, leaving its moorings from time to time.

This tradition is the inheritance of the novelists. Daniel Defoe's voyages, storms, shipwrecks and desert island are allegorical, and his Robinson Crusoe is a more complicated Christian. The emotional action of the novel shows the mark of Bunyan's personifications, though Defoe's story projects an elaborate emotional continuity, linking external action with internal, and retarding events to take us into the mind and heart of the character. It is both mind and heart we see, for Defoe not only creates intense emotional episodes, but draws attention to the complex nature of emotional experience. One of his favourite figures for representing strong feeling is the topos of inexpressibility:

> It is impossible to express here the Flutterings of my very Heart, when I look'd over these Letters, and especially when I found all my Wealth about me; for as the *Brasil* Ships come all in Fleets, the same Ships which brought my Letters, brought my Goods; and the Effects were safe in the River before the Letters came to my Hand. In a Word, I turned pale, and grew sick; and had not the old Man run and fetch'd me a Cordial, I believe the sudden Surprize of Joy had overset nature, and I had Dy'd upon the Spot. (Vol. 2)

This characteristic episode marks cause and effect: Robinson Crusoe is overcome by wealth and goods. It is concerned with physical response, using the image 'Flutterings', a favourite of Defoe's, to blend emotion with sensation and to suggest feeling which cannot be named.

The explicit 'it is impossible to express' articulates intensity of experience and the naivety of character. Other instances are more complex:

> I cannot explain by any possible Energy of Words what a strange longing or hankering of Desires I felt in my Soul upon this Sight; breaking out sometimes thus: O that there had been but one or two; nay, or but one Soul sav'd out of this Ship, to have escap'd to me, that I might but have had one Companion, one Fellow-Creature to have spoken to me, and to have convers'd with! In all the Time of my solitary Life, I never felt so earnest, so strong a Desire after the Society of my Fellow-Creatures, or so deep a Regret at the want of it.
>
> There are some secret moving Springs in the Affections, which when they are set a going by some Object in view, or be it some Object, though not in view, yet rendred present to the Mind by the Power of Imagination, that Motion carries out the Soul by its Impetuosity to such violent eager embracings of the Object, that the Absence of it is insupportable.
>
> Such were these earnest Wishings, That but one man had been sav'd! *O that it had been but One!* I believe I repeated the words, *O that it had been but One!* a thousand Times; and the Desires were so mov'd by it, that when I spoke the Words, my Hands would clinch together, and my Fingers press the Palms of my Hands, that if I had had any soft Thing in my hand, it would have crusht it involuntarily; and my Teeth in my head wou'd strike together, and set against one another so strong, that for some time I could not part them again.
>
> Let the Naturalists explain these Things, and the Reason and Manner of them; all I can say to them is, to describe the Fact, which was even surprising to me when I found it; though I knew not from what it should proceed; it was doubtless the effect of ardent Wishes, and of strong Ideas form'd in my Mind, realizing the Comfort which the Conversation of one of my Fellow-Christians would have been to me. (Vol. 1)

The use of two tenses, the doubling of expressive language, the quoted apostrophes from the past, and the articulation of inexpressibility, marked by the epithet 'strange', denote the strength and mysteriousness of emotion and perhaps also its supernatural prompting. The observation about energy of language underlines the figures of exclamation and repetition; such generalization marks the religious interpretation typical of this Providence novel, but draws attention to the need for a style appropriate to 'violent embracings of the object'. There is an acute observation about language as cause, as well as effect,

of feeling, 'the Desires were so mov'd'. Defoe blends his expression of
feeling with an analysis alive to the relation between feeling and
language, and to the generative power of language. The accompanying
details about gesture and body-language speak for themselves.

In the famous incident where Robinson Crusoe finds the single
footprint in the sand, the novelist uses an objective detail which excites
through its simplicity and oddity. Both character and reader are
'exceedingly surprised':

> It happen'd one Day about Noon going towards my boat, I was
> exceedingly surpriz'd with the Print of a Man's naked Foot on the Shore,
> which was very plain to be seen in the Sand. I stood like one Thunder-
> struck, or as if I had seen an Apparition; I listen'd, I look'd round me, I
> could hear nothing, nor see any Thing; I went up to a rising Ground to look
> farther; I went up the Shore and down the Shore, but it was all one, I could
> see no other Impression but that one. I went to it again to see if there were
> any more, and to observe if it might not be my Fancy; but there was no
> Room for that for there was exactly the very Print of a Foot, Toes, Heel, and
> every Part of a Foot; how it came thither I knew not, nor could in the least
> imagine. But after innumerable fluttering Thoughts, like a Man perfectly
> confus'd and out of my self, I came Home to my Fortification, not feeling, as
> we say, the Ground I went on, but terrify'd to the last Degree, looking
> behind me at every two or three Steps, mistaking every Bush and Tree, and
> fancying every Stump at a Distance to be a Man; nor is it possible to
> describe how many various Shapes affrighted Imagination represented
> Things to me in, how many wild ideas were found every Moment in my
> Fancy, and what strange unaccountable Whimsies came into my thoughts
> by the way. (Vol. 1)

The image of fluttering is intensified by 'innumerable', and the
detail, 'like a Man perfectly confus'd and out of my self', fixes the sense
of strangeness through a naive and careful comparison. The movements
of Robinson's puzzled search also intensify feeling through repetition.
There is conscious generalization about words, 'not feeling, as we say,
the Ground I went on', and the excitement of discovery is blended with
a conscious record of imagination and its creative fantasies, which are
strange, wild, and fearful, like their cause. Once again, what seems at
first sight a naive and bewildered effort of language is complex and
analytic, characteristic of the sustained dramatization of fear, surprise,
joy, sadness, and longing which generates inner and outer action in
Robinson Crusoe.

Richardson's *Clarissa* is one of the great novels of passion. It is subtle when compared with *Pamela*, whose appeal is both pornographic and loftily moral, though occasionally showing an analytic depth when Pamela is surprised by love. It is complex compared with *Sir Charles Grandison*, which evades all problems of feeling in its treatment of Charles's love for Harriet and Clementina, and falls into monotonous raptures of high-toned, didactic congratulation. But in *Clarissa* there is a depth and continuity in Richardson's inspection of passion, sustained over the longest narrative stretch in English fiction. He finds a form for episodes of strong feeling, and for development and growth.

Lovelace abuses passion. He constantly refers to the oscillation of 'REVENGE' and 'LOVE', and the upper case marks his emotional simplification and confidence. He stereotypes the passions, in a style both crude and corrupt. His poetic diction ('my charmer' and 'frostpiece') and his selected quotations from the poets are both over-excited and conventional:

> But couldst thou have believed that I, who think it possible for me to favour as much as I can be favoured; that I, who for this charming creature think of foregoing the *life of honour* for the *life of shackles*; could adopt those over-tender lines of Otway?
>
> I check myself, and leaving the three first Lines of the following of Dryden to the family of the whiners, find the workings of the passion in my stormy soul better expressed by the three last:

> > *Love various minds does variously inspire:*
> > *He stirs in gentle natures gentle fire;*
> > *Like that of incense on the altar laid.*
> > *But raging flames tempestuous souls invade:*
> > *A fire, which ev'ry windy passion blows;*
> > *With Pride it mounts, and with Revenge it glows.*

> And with REVENGE it *shall* glow! – For, dost thou think, that if it were not from the hope, that this stupid family are all combined to do my work for me, I would bear their insults? – Is it possible to imagine that I would be braved as I am braved, threatened as I am threatened, by those who are afraid to see me; and by this brutal Brother too, to whom I gave a life (A life, indeed, not worth my taking!); had I not a greater pride in knowing, that by means of his very Spy upon me, I am playing him off as I please; cooling or inflaming his violent passions as may best suit my purposes. (Vol. 1, Letter 31)

In the first three lines, which Lovelace significantly rejects, Dryden refers to gentle loving, and to the variousness of love, subjects close to Richardson's heart and far from Lovelace's. (Lovelace rapes, and is blind to complexities of love.) He talks about playing on the brother's passions and this is his special talent. He also plays on Clarissa's feelings, even though he grossly simplifies them. In Letter 35 (Vol. 1.) he writes to Belford that he will assume humility 'To dissipate her fears, and engage her reliance upon my honour'. The next letter (36), from Clarissa to Anna, begins with fear: 'I have been frighted out of my wits – Still am in a manner out of breath'. She describes her fear at an unexpected appearance of Lovelace, then tells how 'his respectful behaviour soon dissipated these fears'. Her words are a frightening echo of his, and confirm his success.

His simplifications trap her complexities. He did not notice Dryden's complex analysis. However, Clarissa is fully alive to the variety of emotion. Her analysis, like Crusoe's, tries to understand and admits the difficulty of understanding. Her heart-searchings are serious and urgent investigations, matters of life and death. *Clarissa* is the first novel of heart-searching in English: its epistolary form makes a passionate analysis of the passions. Crusoe looked back to relive past emotion, but Clarissa speaks in and for the present. Her questioning is not solitary, but collaborative, worked out in the long correspondence with her bosom-friend, Anna Howe. The conventional question-and-answer of personal letter-writing creates a new form for feeling. Clarissa's niceties are juxtaposed with Lovelace's stereotypes, but also contrasted with Anna's lively probing. Anna's letters extend and contemplate Clarissa's meditation, provoking and encouraging renewals and revisions. Clarissa sets the pattern for many later heroines who mistake their feelings, and who are misled or corrupted by the dominant masculine language of feeling. Clarissa's errors are different from those of Emma, Emma Bovary, Maggie Tulliver, and Eustacia Vye; she is not limited, as they are, by fantasy, literature, and ignorance. Hers is the error of fine intelligence, which plays persistently and scrupulously on experience; she feels and narrates with immediacy. Richardson locates error in the experience of a woman capable of understanding herself, but arriving at understanding slowly and painfully. We see her step-by-step pondering, as she writes from sequestration. Her imprisonment, first by family and then by seducer, is an environment from which the only release is language, though language constricted, thwarted, and almost destroyed. The desperate woman, shut in by patriarchy, is intent on making out the meanings of the emotional life. At first she is helped by Anna, a sister-victim also vigorously aware of the language of feeling. Anna picks up, considers, and concentrates Clarissa's words, such as the 'throbs and glows' of agitation, and the phrase 'a conditional sort of liking' which crystallizes the subject of many of the letters. 'Nothing less than the knowledge of the inmost recesses of your heart', writes Anna in Letter 37 (Vol. 1), 'can satisfy my Love and my Friendship.' Clarissa probes those recesses, which cannot simply be plumbed for her friend, since they are not wholly accessible even to herself. But as her name tells us, she is clear and candid as she reflects on what she feels.

In Letter 40 (Vol. 1) she writes both from a sense of the fluidity of emotion, and from a sense of the conventional language which denies such fluidity: 'I never was in *Love* as it is called; and whether This be *it*, or not, I must submit to *you*.' They discuss the phrase 'conditional liking', which Anna 'humorously raillies' but takes seriously. Clarissa conducts her analysis by imaginatively recapitulating and revising her own and Anna's words, inventing dialogue in order to elucidate and question:

> From these considerations; from these *over-balances*; it was, that I said in a former, that I would not be in Love with this man for the world: And it was going further than prudence would warrant, when I was for compounding with you, by the words *conditional liking*; which you so humorously railly.
>
> Well but, methinks you say, what is all this to the purpose? This is still but reasoning: But, if you *are* in Love, you *are*: And Love, like the vapours, is the deeper rooted for having no sufficient cause assignable for its hold. And so you call upon me again, to have no reserves, and so forth.
>
> Why then, my dear, if you will have it, I think, that, with all his preponderating faults, I like him better than I ever thought I should like him; and, those faults considered, better perhaps then I *ought* to like him. And I believe, it is possible for the persecution I labour under, to induce me to like him still more – Especially while I can recollect to his advantage our last Interview, and as every day produces stronger instances of *tyranny*, I will call it, on the other side. – In a word, I will frankly own (since you cannot think anything I say too explicit) that were he *now* but a moral man, I would prefer him to all the men I ever saw.
>
> So that This is but *conditional liking* still, you'll say. – Nor, I hope, is it more. I never was in *Love* as it is called; and whether This be *it*, or not, I must submit to *you*. But will venture to think it, if it be, no such *mighty* monarch, no such unconquerable power, as I have heard it represented; and it must have

met with greater encouragement than I think I have given it, to be so *absolutely* unconquerable – Since I am persuaded that I could yet, without a *throb*, most willingly give up the *one* man to get rid of the *other*. (Vol. 1, Letter 40)

Uncertainties, scruples, and development are products of a familiar, intimate, and impersonalizing discourse. It questions, admits, and sets the experience of feeling against tradition, knowledge and usage. Its frequent italics are scrupulous and precise, not simply emphatic. Clarissa refuses to use the conventional hyperboles and personifications of Lovelace, saying that if what she feels is what is called love, it is 'no such *mighty* monarch, no such unconquerable power, as I have heard it represented'. After the rape, when letter-writing and self-scrutiny have been broken, like her virginity, the forms of feeling become agitated and fragmented; the analytic mode is ruptured, rationality disturbed, continuity undermined, and straight speaking replaced by the innuendo of metaphor and allegory. Language is polluted, losing its openness and power to examine passion.

Clarissa's letters are suspended during Lovelace's hour-by-hour narration of the day's events leading to the rape (Vol. 3, Letter 28). Her topos of inexpressibility, in a torn letter, is a travesty of her normally earnest language of rational effort. She whose periodic style was elegant and controlled writes in exclamations, repetitions, and disjointed words like 'dreadful' and 'vile, vile', and fails to narrate events or emotions:

> I sat down to say a great deal – My heart was full – I did not know what to say first – And thought, and grief, and confusion, and (O my poor head!) I cannot tell what – And thought, and grief, and confusion, came crouding so thick upon me; *one* would be first, *another* would be first, *all* would be first; so I can write nothing at all. (Vol. 5, Letter 36)

The failure to tell is articulated as a failure to order, to discriminate, to make priorities, to take those formal decisions she has formerly managed so logically and sensitively. (At the beginning of the novel her style is ironically contrasted with the uneducated or falsely educated styles of masculine oppressors, including that of her university-educated brother.) The figures of metaphor and personification which she uses after the rape are new and uncharacteristic. They begin, here, to figure incoherence. In Paper 3 she re-invents a beast fable in which she hesitates between a choice of figure: 'Lion, or a Bear, I forget which – But a Bear, or a Tyger, I believe, it was.' In Paper 7, where there is a partial return to the ordering of periodic style, she shifts between images of caterpillar, moth, and canker-worm. Paper 10 lapses into poetry, and is textually disordered; it has typographical confusions of format, its verses are fragmentarily disposed in the margins, and it adopts Lovelace's habit of pastiche and collage. What is called her 'divided Soul' is expressed through disjunctions of form and style. The communications are called 'Papers', in a significant refusal to call such scraps letters. There is a refusal to order the fragments, on the part of author and character. Before transcribing the papers, Lovelace mentions what he receives first but the reader sees last: an 'odd letter', which he is not immediately capable of copying, ''tis so extravagant'. It bears the marks of stylistic confusion, syntactical repetition, interruption, breaks, and colloquialism like 'good, now, Lovelace'. There are suggestive, clandestine metaphors of locks and keys: 'But when all my doors are fast, and nothing but the key-hole open, and the key of late put into that, to be where you were, in a manner without opening any of them'. Incoherence is a vehicle for agitation and an exact image for rape and loss of self-possession. Towards the end of the letter there is a space, marking what Clarissa calls 'a little interval' which 'seems' to have been lent her, after which she speaks of an act of partial reperusal. As usual in the novel, every physical detail of these letters is expressive; some of the papers are torn, and the long letter has its paper blistered and ink blurred by 'the tears even of the harden'd transcriber'.

A little later in Letter 36, which encloses these fragments, Lovelace discusses her failure to conform to his expectations of passionate response: 'My Charmer has no passions; that is to say, none of the passions that I want her to have.' The significant discrimination of 'that is to say' marks his apprehension of failure, loss of assurance, and an awareness of the arbitrary and authoritarian take-over of language. In Letter 38 his discomfiture is expressed in terms of expectation and frustration. He anticipates a convenient and conventional response, of the kind he has known, which he could meet with a matched violence, but what he meets is a recovered composure of feeling. He reads it correctly as inexpressible grief, which defeats him, putting his emotions and style in disorder:

As I told thee, I had prepared myself for high passions, raving, flying, tearing execration: These transient violences, the workings of sudden grief, and shame, and vengeance, would have set us upon a par with each other, and quitted scores. These have I been accustomed to; and, as nothing violent is lasting, with these I could have wished to encounter. But such a majestic composure – Seeking me – whom yet, it is plain, by her attempt to get away, she would have avoided seeing – no Lucretia-like vengeance upon herself in her thought – Yet swallowed up, her whole mind swallowed up, as I may say, by a grief so heavy, as, in her own words, to be beyond the power of speech to express – and to be able, discomposed as she was, to the very morning, to put such a home-question to me, as if she had penetrated my future view – how could I avoid looking like a fool, and answering, as before, in broken sentences, and confusion?

What – What-a – What has been done – I, I, I – cannot but say – Must own – Must confess – Hem – Hem—Is not right – Is not what should have been – But-a – But – But – I am truly – truly – sorry for it – Upon my soul I am – And – And – will do all – do everything – Do what – What-ever is incumbent upon me – all that you – that you – that you shall require, to make you amends! (Vol. 5, Letter 38)

Clarissa cannot always defeat his style with hers; the language of his passion invades and contaminates hers. In the final episodes of slow dying, she resorts to the equivocal allegory of her father's houses, excused by Belford as innocent artifice, and attacked by Lovelace as a lie. Clarissa feels it to be a significant failure of candour, and her judgement is a sign of sincerity and of a scrupulous self-examination. Before the rape, she criticizes her own self-scrutiny, looking back to the ignorance and pride of the discussion with Anna, to blame her 'own inclination'. What Clarissa sees, as Richardson insists, is not only the simplifications of Lovelace, but the limits of her own rational analysis of feeling. It was less composed and detached than it seemed. Character and author share an awareness of the difficulty of controlling passion by well-intentioned intelligence. The novel voices a suspicion of emotional language, perhaps most clearly articulated in feminist terms in Vol. 8, Letter 49, where Anna attacks the affective language of men. Anticipating Mary Wollstonecraft's rejection of a periodic style and flowery diction in *Vindication of the Rights of Women* (1792), Anna attacks many aspects of men's language, including a style 'spangled' with metaphor, a sublime 'lying in *words* and not in *sentiment*' whose authors 'sit . . . fully satisfied with their own performances, and call them MASCULINE'. Clarissa's own periodic style is conventionally masculine, but here praised as a correlative for the 'discriminating faculty', and earlier attacked by her sister Arabella as 'affected' (Vol. 4, Letter 58). It represents an educated ideal which the heroine succeeds in reaching. Exact punctuation and orthography are defended by Clarissa (as quoted in Anna's analytic letter) as 'a proof that a woman understood the derivation as well as sense of the words she used', and the pen is said to be 'next to the Needle, of all employments, the most proper, and best adapted to their genius's'. The woman's genius is explicated in terms of affective superiority: 'The gentleness of their minds, the delicacy of their sentiments (improved by the manner of their education) and the liveliness of their imaginations.' The defence is conventional and limited, but the novel's differentiations and developments are not. Clarissa is not praised for gentleness and delicacy, but for order, candour, and the ability to discriminate her own defects.

Richardson's suspicion of allegory is not shared by Fielding, who uses it as a dominant comic figure. In Book 4, Chapter 12 of *Tom Jones*, he describes Sophia's love for Tom through personification, 'a secret Affection for Mr *Jones* had insensibly stolen into the Bosom of this young Lady', where it had 'grown to a pretty great Height before she herself had discovered it'. This gives way to a medical metaphor, 'When she first began to perceive its Symptoms', which develops into psychological analysis in 'the Sensations were so sweet and pleasing, that she had not Resolution sufficient to check or repel them; and thus she went on cherishing a Passion of which she never once considered the Consequences'. Fielding continues the metaphor of disease, in comic anecdote and generalization which deflect us from the passions of the central characters:

> The Diseases of the Mind do in almost every Particular imitate those of the Body. For which Reason, we hope, That learned Faculty, for whom we have so profound a Respect, will pardon us the violent Hands we have been necessitated to lay on several Words and Phrases, which of Right belong to them, and without which our Descriptions must have been often unintelligible.
>
> Now there is no one Circumstance in which the Distempers of the Mind bear a more exact Analogy to those which are called Bodily, than that Aptness which both have to a Relapse. This is plain, in the violent Diseases of Ambition and Avarice. I have known Ambition, when cured at Court by frequent Disappointments, (which are the only Physic for it) to break out again in a Contest for Foreman of the Grand Jury at an Assizes; and have

heard of a Man who had so far conquered Avarice, as to give away many a Sixpence, that comforted himself, at last, on his Death-bed, by making a crafty and advantagious Bargain concerning his ensuing Funeral, with an Undertaker who had married his only Child. (Book 4, Chapter 12)

After this mock-apology, with its serious awareness of metaphor, we return to Sophia, in a new metaphor: 'That Passion which had formerly been so exquisitely delicious, became now a Scorpion in her Bosom.' This preserves a grotesque continuity with the earlier images through the common indeterminacy of metaphor and personification in 'stealing into and growing'. The 'secret affection' is a technical but punning term linking the verbal acts of metaphor. We return to the medical image, by a neat transition from the scorpion to implied malady:

She resisted it, therefore, with her utmost Force, and summoned every Argument her Reason (which was surprizingly strong for her Age) could suggest, to subdue and expel it. In this she so far succeeded, that she began to hope from Time and Absence a perfect Cure. (Ibid.)

This mixed mode is characteristic of Fielding's comic representation of the passions. His chapter titles speak of them with ironic irreverence, as in Book 5, Chapter 2, which is advertised as including 'some fine Touches of the Passion of Love, scarce visible to the naked Eye', a joke about the passions and the language of passion, which plays on the convenient ambiguity of 'fine Touches'. As Sophia plays the harpsichord to the convalescent Tom, the narrator observes, 'Love may again be likened to a Disease in this, that when it is denied a Vent in one Part, it will certainly break out in another' (Book 5, Chapter 2). Tom becomes alive to the disturbance 'in the tender Bosom of *Sophia*', insight cures his diffidence, effects 'a Perturbation in his Mind' and reveals that 'he had a much stronger Passion for her than he himself was acquainted with' (Ibid.). The analysis is serious and comic; the very continuity of metaphor is punctuated by self-conscious references and makes a cool commentary. There is discontinuity as well as continuity, as Fielding mixes the medical with the legal metaphor, in mocking collisions of language. Tom's growing passion for Sophia is distracted by compassion for Molly Seagrim: 'his own Heart would not suffer him to destroy a human Creature who, he thought, loved him, and had to that Love sacrificed her Innocence. His own good Heart pleaded her Cause; not as a cold venal Advocate . . .' (Book 5, Chapter 3). Fielding's comic analysis insists on the complexity of the passions, as 'His own good Heart' artfully calls in the assistance of another passion, and desire comes to compassion's help. The observations of affective activity, through logic and fancy, are sardonically comic. Fielding likes to hold the passions at an ironic distance, while scrupulously insisting on their powers. His comic refusal to simplify is made in the interests of psychological and moral accuracy. It is a refusal to simplify or flatter. Sophia's filial love is seen as pious and self-sacrificing, and piety and sacrifice are coolly inspected:

> The Idea, therefore, of the immense Happiness she should convey to her Father by her Consent to this Match, made a strong Impression on her Mind. Again, the extreme Piety of such an Act of Obedience, worked very forcibly, as she had a very deep Sense of Religion. Lastly, when she reflected how much she herself was to suffer, being indeed to become little less than a Sacrifice, or a Martyr, to filial Love and Duty, she felt an agreeable Tickling in a certain little Passion, which tho' it bears no immediate Affinity either to Religion or Virtue, is often so kind as to lend great Assistance in executing the Purposes of both.
>
> *Sophia* was charmed with the Contemplation of so heroic an Action, and began to compliment herself with much premature Flattery, when *Cupid*, who lay hid in her Muff, suddenly crept out, and like *Punchinello* in a Puppet-shew, kicked all out before him. (Book 7, Chapter 9)

Here the action of personification is aptly complicated. The comic action of Cupid cunningly judges Sophia's self-love and mimes the action of emotional surprise. At times the personification is subdued, suggested through metaphor rather than acted out in full-scale action, as in Book 6, Chapter 12, when the debate between reason and passion which runs through the novel is described through comic gesture and straightforward inventory: 'he presently fell into the most violent Agonies, tearing his Hair from his Head, and using other Actions which generally accompany Fits of Madness, Rage, and Despair.' Tom then cools down to reason with his passion:

> And now the great Doubt was how to act with regard to *Sophia*. The Thoughts of leaving her almost rent his Heart asunder; but the Consideration of reducing her to Ruin and Beggary still racked him, if possible, more; and if the violent Desire of possessing her Person could have induced him to

listen one Moment to this Alternative, still he was by no means certain of her Resolution to indulge his Wishes at so high an Expence. The Resentment of Mr *Allworthy*, and the Injury he must do to his Quiet, argued strongly against this latter; and lastly, the apparent Impossibility of his Success, even if he would sacrifice all these Considerations to it, came to his Assistance; and thus Honour at last, backed with Despair, with Gratitude to his Benefactor, and with real Love to his Mistress, got the better of burning Desire, and he resolved rather to quit *Sophia*, than pursue her to her Ruin.

It is difficult for any who have not felt it, to conceive the glowing Warmth which filled his Breast, on the first Contemplation of this Victory over his Passion. Pride flattered him so agreeably, that his Mind perhaps enjoyed perfect Happiness; but this was only momentary: *Sophia* soon returned to his Imagination, and allayed the Joy of his Triumph with no less bitter Pangs than a good-natured General must feel, when he surveys the bleeding Heaps, at the Price of whose Blood he hath purchased his Laurels; for thousands of tender Ideas lay murdered before our Conqueror. (Book 6, Chapter 12)

Once more Fielding describes passion and division though his narrator's irony and mock-heroics. Impassioned self-flattery is represented as unflatteringly as possible. Fielding loves to cut his characters down to size at the peak of self-sublimation.

He can use plainer language. In Book 5, Chapter 4, he describes Tom's perplexity after the squire throws Sophia's muff (a sacred object in the amorous drama) into the fire; Tom's love revives, the hero's 'Citadel' being 'taken by Surprize'. Love and War join mock-heroically as the 'God of Love marched in in triumph', to conclude chapter and conflict. But in the next chapter, the narrator lays 'aside all Allegory' to reflect, seriously, on Tom's honest conflict, in an analysis which matter-of-factly names passions, 'Compassion instead of Contempt succeeded to Love'.

Fielding's allegory of passion claims the virtue of moral realism. He refuses to draw class-distinctions between his characters, all of whom submit to forces beyond class. The inner theatre of the major characters dominates, but the minor characters are occasionally made to play parts. When Mrs Honour wavers between loyalty to Sophia and to Squire Western, her conflict is mostly, but not entirely, materialistic; she balances self-interest against self-interest, throws 'her love to her Mistress' into one scale, but after apparent victory, more scruples enter, and the allegory becomes blended with the larger action (Book 7, Chapter 7). When Black George hovers between keeping Tom's purse or returning it, his conflict is shown as a debate between avarice and conscience:

> His Conscience, however, immediately started at this Suggestion, and began to upbraid him with Ingratitude to his Benefactor. To this his Avarice answered, 'That his Conscience should have considered that Matter before, when he deprived poor *Jones* of his 500*l*. That having quietly acquiesced in what was of so much greater Importance, it was absurd, if not downright Hypocrisy, to affect any Qualms at this Trifle.' In return to which, Conscience, like a good Lawyer, attempted to distinguish between an absolute Breach of Trust, as here where the Goods were delivered, and a bare Concealment of what was found, as in the former Case. Avarice presently treated this with Ridicule, called it a Distinction without a Difference, and absolutely insisted, that when once all Pretensions of Honour and Virtue were given up in any one Instance, that there was no Precedent for resorting to them upon a second Occasion. In short, poor Conscience had certainly been defeated in the Argument, had not Fear stept in to her Assistance, and very strenuously urged, that the real Distinction between the two Actions did not lie in the different Degrees of Honour, but of Safety: For that the secreting the 500*l*. was a Matter of very little Hazard; whereas the detaining the Sixteen Guineas was liable to the utmost Danger of Discovery.
>
> By this friendly Aid of Fear, Conscience obtained a compleat Victory in the Mind of *Black George*, and after making him a few Compliments on his Honesty, forced him to deliver the Money to *Jones*. (Book 6, Chapter 13)

Allegory emerges from the dialogue form in which the faculties converse. Conscience is weakened by the feminine pronoun 'her', and the adjective 'poor', and given legalistic rather than moral arguments. As usual, there is the comic exposure of self-congratulation. Fielding is as devastatingly suspicious of virtue as Freud.

Fielding's allegory punctuates narration, action, and dialogue. It brings us close to feelings but withholds sympathy, because comic analysis coolly reveals a consistent descent from the ideal. The method is continued through the formally discursive parts of the novel, often entirely engaged in the analysis of the passions. The commentator discloses actions and characters, but occupies a space of his own. In a discursive analysis of love he continues to use dominant images, like food ('the Desire of satisfying a voracious Appetite with a certain quantity of delicate white human Flesh'); theatre ('The Passions, like the Managers of a Playhouse, often force Men upon Parts without

consulting their Judgments'); and law ('Examine your Heart, my good
Reader'). As in the last instance, the reader is set a test of self-scrutiny,
appropriately comic and serious, and asked to stop reading if he fails
the test. In Book 6, Chapter 13, the reader is dramatized as a member
of a critical audience, and called in to discuss the episode of Black
George's conflict. Some readers refuse to give their opinions, because
they are not attending or want to hear the opinion of the best judges.
Fielding not only jokes about the reader's response, but invites its
collaboration as part of his loose, reflexive form. He requires us not
only to attend, but to resist the temptations of responding too excitedly
or too coldly. We must not identify with the characters, and we must
not take the reading experience too lightly. The novelist insists on
examining us while he jokes. In Partridge's response to *Hamlet*, he loses
all distance, 'the same Passions which succeeded each other in *Hamlet*
succeeding likewise in him', but subsequently refuses to praise as art
what he mistakes for nature. He is Fielding's paradigmatic bad
spectator of art. Fielding's affective form inhibits identification and
rapture, and encourages a balance of sympathy with analysis.

The two greatest novelists of their period, one tragic and one comic,
both use reflexive forms, which merge representation with analysis.
Laurence Sterne conflates their methods, and devises fresh means of
combining pathos and comedy. In *A Sentimental Journey* there is an
elaborate commentary on the representation of fictional feeling;
Sterne uses comic analysis to present and permit the pathetic story of
the caged starling who was taught to mimic the words appropriate to
his condition. Travelling in France without a passport, in wartime,
Yorick is shaken when told that the Lieutenant de Police has called.
He tries to reason himself out of a fear of imprisonment in the Bastille.
The first stage in emotional analysis and control is a recognition of the
power of language. The next stage is an act of demolition:

> – And as for the Bastile! the terror is in the word – Make the most of it you
> can, said I to myself, the Bastile is but another word for a tower – and a
> tower is but another word for a house you can't get out of – Mercy on the
> gouty! for they are in it twice a year – but with nine livres a day, and pen and
> ink and paper and patience, albeit a man can't get out, he may do very well
> within – at least for a month or six weeks; at the end of which, if he is a
> harmless fellow his innocence appears, and he comes out a better and wiser
> man than he went in.
>
> I had some occasion (I forget what) to step into the courtyard, as I settled
> this account; and remember I walk'd down stairs in no small triumph with

the conceit of my reasoning – Beshrew the *sombre* pencil! said I vauntingly –
for I envy not its powers, which paints the evils of life with so hard and
deadly a colouring. The mind sits terrified at the objects she has magnified
herself, and blackened: reduce them to their proper size and hue she
overlooks them – 'Tis true, said I, correcting the proposition – the Bastile is
not an evil to be despised – but strip it of its towers – fill up the fossè –
unbarricade the doors – call it simply a confinement, and suppose 'tis some
tyrant of a distemper – and not of a man which holds you in it – the evil
vanishes, and you bear the other half without complaint. (Vol. 2, 'The
Passport: The Hotel at Paris')

The magnifying power of word and image is put into reverse, by a
revisualization and reconstruction: 'suppose 'tis some tyrant of a
distemper'. But the soliloquy is arrested by an 'actual' event; a voice,
'which complained that it could not get out'. Yorick first puts fear
aside in order not to worry La Fleur, and, when left alone to feel freely,
is surprised to find the gaiety remaining:

Is it folly, or nonchalance, or philosophy, or pertinacity – or what is it in
me, that, after all, when La Fleur had gone down stairs, and I was quite
alone, I could not bring down my mind to think of it otherwise than I had
then spoken of it to Eugenius? (Ibid.)

He has deliberately assumed a mood, which is actualized and
sustained. Smiling, he becomes cheerful.[1] But the recovery of self-
possession is followed by a real example of imprisonment, lamenting its
lot.

The starling in the cage is not offered as an object of pathos to the
reader, but as the means of destroying Yorick's insouciance and
contributing to his sentimental education:

I vow, I never had my affections more tenderly awakened; nor do I
remember an incident in my life, where the dissipated spirits, to which my
reason had been a bubble, were so suddenly call'd home. Mechanical as the
notes were, yet so true in tune to nature were they chanted, that in one
moment they overthrew all my systematic reasonings upon the Bastile; and
I heavily walk'd up stairs, unsaying every word I had said in going down
them.

Disguise thyself as thou wilt, still slavery! said I – still thou art a bitter
draught; and though thousands in all ages have been made to drink of thee,
thou art no less bitter on that account. – 'tis thou, thrice sweet and gracious

goddess, addressing myself to LIBERTY, whom all in public or in private worship, whose taste is grateful, and ever wilt be so, till NATURE herself shall change – no *tint* of words can spot thy snowy mantle, or chymic power turn thy sceptre into iron – with thee to smile upon him as he eats his crust, the swain is happier than his monarch, from whose court thou art exiled – Gracious heaven! cried I, kneeling down upon the last step but one in my ascent – grant me but health, thou great Bestower of it, and give me but this fair goddess as my companion – and shower down thy mitres, if it seems good unto thy divine providence, upon those heads which are aching for them. (Ibid.)

The tender affections are not awakened to evoke compassion, but return the Traveller to a proper appreciation of fear and liberty. At first, pity is briefly touched: 'slavery . . . thou art a bitter draught' and 'though thousands in all ages have been made to drink of thee'. The impassioned apostrophe is undermined by the comic over-particularizing detail of kneeling 'upon the last step but one'. The next chapter, 'The Captive', begins with another comic detail: 'The bird in his cage pursued me into my room'. This is a reflexive joke about rhetoric, made by combining the literal fact of the caged bird with the metaphor of motion, a novel dislocation, fluently and smoothly fracturing the distinction of vehicle and tenor. The image establishes passionate motivation, as the analysis emphasizes excited creativity:

I sat down close to my table, and leaning my head upon my hand, I begun to figure to myself the miseries of confinement. I was in a right frame for it, and so I gave full scope to my imagination.

I was going to begin with the millions of my fellow creatures born to no inheritance but slavery; but finding, however affecting the picture was, that I could not bring it near me, and that the multitude of sad groups in it did but distract me. –

– I took a single captive, and having first shut him up in his dungeon, I then look'd through the twilight of his grated door to take his picture. (Vol. 2, 'The Captive: Paris')

The first instructive detail insists on particularity and intimacy. The imaginative Traveller accordingly revises the first conception, and brings a particular feeling close by setting creativity in a particular place. Having established person and locality, he begins to enlarge and develop: 'I then look'd through the twilight of his grated door to take his picture.' This is another grotesque movement from imagined image to 'actuality', as the look through the door, a fair emblem for the

artist's contemplation of work in progress, is uncomfortably made part
of the fable. The literalization brings in not only the contemplative
aspect of art, but the fictional elaboration: physical details are
completed, emotion imagined, and history filled in. But the particulars
come too close, and break down at the too painful detail of 'his
children', which makes the artist's 'heart bleed' and forces him to 'go
on with another part of the portrait':

> He was sitting upon the ground upon a little straw, in the furthest corner
> of his dungeon, which was alternately his chair and bed: a little calender of
> small sticks were laid at the head notch'd all over with the dismal days and
> nights he had pass'd there - he had one of these little sticks in his hand, and
> with a rusty nail he was etching another day of misery to add to the heap. As
> I darkened the little light he had, he lifted up a hopeless eye towards the
> door, then cast it down - shook his head, and went on with his work of
> affliction. I heard his chains upon his legs, as he turn'd his body to lay his
> little stick upon the bundle—He gave a deep sigh - I saw the iron enter into
> his soul - I burst into tears - I could not sustain the picture of confinement
> which my fancy had drawn. . . . (Ibid.)

The circumstantiality of the prison cell is first specified and then
approved by the artist. The artist's revisionary activity, 'As I darkened
the little light he had', is a plausible representation of making stories
and images. It also draws attention to the oddity of creating victims in
order to rouse compassion. There is a blurring of distinctions between
artist and art, as the deep sigh of the fictional character provokes the
tears of his creator. The quotation, from the Book of Common Prayer,
invoked as the sublime last straw, 'I saw the iron enter into his soul',
breaks up the artist and his work.

Sterne uses the starling to introduce the serious political subject of
slavery, and to analyse fictional pathos. Discourse is combined with
the image; the creative underdistancing of emotion which is described
places the subject at a comic, but instructive, distance from the reader.
The passive and active elements in the creative process are dramatized,
with special relevance to the subject of the emotional journey, and the
passage of emotion. The failure of distance is exemplified in the way
the images come too close, in the description of art and artist, and in
the sigh and tears, which firmly fix the inset exercise of fancy as image
and microcosm of the novel in which it plays its part.

In the next chapter, 'The Starling', we are also told that the starling
has only been taught four words, which it utters and repeats; and the

information itself is repeated: 'four simple words – and no more'. But earlier (in 'The Passport') the novelist makes the Traveller add one word, 'No', to the starling's speech, which beautifully destabilizes the narrative: as an additional detail invented in resistance to mere mimesis, and as a false memory. It is the one word which imputes feeling to the bird, who, as the Traveller says, 'I cannot set thee at liberty', speaks non-mechanically: '"No," said the starling – "I can't get out. . . ."' The taught phrase is made to do what parrot-talk cannot do, to generate dialogue, in fresh blurring of what purports to be truth and what is presented in art. Pathetic description fictionalizes memory, and varies fictional effects.

In another variation the bird appears as a visual image, in the illustration of the Traveller's crest, interestingly out of his cage, but textually paralysed. After the emblem the chapter ends with one more flouting of the dividing line between art and what is outside art: 'And let the heralds officers twist his neck about if they dare.' Even the heralds cannot twist the two-dimensional image: Sterne's joke marks the distance we have travelled in the story of the starling. It is his achievement to overcome sentimentality, in the pejorative sense of the word, but to see and analyse its dangers and temptations.

Yorick's journey, as Sterne explains, is a voyage of the heart, 'in pursuit of nature, and those affections which rise out of her, which make us love each other'. There are many episodes where the comic control of sensibility is released, to demonstrate and celebrate the capacity for 'generous joys and generous cares' beyond the self. Bursts of compassion, kindness, and tenderness subdue character and action and concentrate on the analysis of sensibility. When Yorick pities Maria, for instance, in the chapters called 'Maria Moulines', 'Maria' and 'The Bourbonnois', Sterne indulges and criticizes sympathetic melancholy. He brings out the narrator's delight in sentimental adventures, which he seeks 'like the Knight of the Woeful Countenance', rejoicing when he becomes 'entangled in them' because they make him most 'perfectly conscious of the existence of a soul within'. The encounter with Maria has its ridiculous side, though it is not presented to us just for mirth: Maria has lost lover, father, and goat, and is left with a little dog, to whom she says, 'Thou shalt not leave me, Sylvio'. She is sitting under a tree, head on one side, supported by her hand, and hair dishevelled, like an image of the Elizabethan melancholic lover. The image is summary and strong, precipitating Yorick's sentimental response. In the lachrymose scene in which they dry each others' tears (like Daniel Deronda and Gwendolen), Yorick uses the topos of inexpressibility, 'I felt such undescribable emotions within me, as I am sure could not be accounted for from any combinations of matter and motion', to conclude, 'I am positive I have a soul', and dismiss materialistic explanations. Tristram Shandy's handkerchief, a relic sacred to characters, novelist, and loyal readers, comes in usefully to mop up the tears provoked by Maria's account of her wanderings, when Yorick's sensibility overflows: 'Nature melted within me'. He longs to comfort and place her in his bosom 'as a daughter', but has to leave and does not shed his sorrow till just before he gets to Lyons, where he casts 'a shade across her'. There follows the celebrated address to sensibility:

> – Dear sensibility! source inexhausted of all that's precious in our joys, or costly in our sorrows! thou chainest thy martyr down upon his bed of straw—and 'tis thou who lifts him up to HEAVEN - eternal fountain of our feelings! – 'tis here I trace thee – and this is thy divinity which stirs within me – not, that in some sad and sickening moments, *'my soul shrinks back upon herself, and startles at destruction'* – mere pomp of words! – but that I feel some generous joys and generous cares beyond myself – all comes from thee, great – great SENSORIUM of the world! which vibrates, if a hair of our heads but falls upon the ground, in the remotest desert of thy creation. – Touch'd with thee, Eugenius draws my curtain when I languish – hears my tale of symptoms, and blames the weather for the disorder of his nerves. Thou giv'st a portion of it sometimes to the roughest peasant who traverses the bleakest mountains – he finds the lacerated lamb of another's flock – This moment I behold him leaning with his head against his crook, with piteous inclination looking down upon it – Oh! had I come one moment sooner! – it bleeds to death – his gentle heart bleeds with it –
>
> Peace to thee, generous swain! – I see thou walkest off with anguish – but thy joys shall balance it – for happy is thy cottage – and happy is the sharer of it – and happy are the lambs which sport about you. ('The Bourbonnois')

'My design', wrote Sterne on 12 November, 1767, 'was to teach us to love the world and our fellow creatures better than we do.' He always tests the efficacy of feeling in action. The pathetic or tender episodes in *Tristram Shandy*, like the Maria story, or the Le Fever passage, or Uncle Toby's address to the fly, are instances of sympathy rapidly converted to comedy, while those in *The Sentimental Journey* are precisely what have come to be called sentimental – blanks to be filled by personal but uncommitted response. Sterne's sentimental scenes and stories are undramatized, stylized, directed towards lyric and moralizing. They pose as affective failures but they are parodic exercises in sentimentality, even though Sterne's account of his intentions in his *Letters* may sound more naive than the novels themselves. No great novelist is as daringly sentimental as Sterne, and probably no great English novelist, except perhaps Thackeray and Joyce, so brilliantly defines the limits of sentimentality. At the beginning of the novel, Yorick feels benign and buoyant, after food and wine, and reflects indulgently that now would be the time 'for an orphan to have begg'd his father's portmanteau of me!', only to disperse and disprove the generous upsurge when a monk comes to beg and is arbitrarily turned away. The track of feeling is exactly traced: sympathy disappears, heartless refusal is followed by remorse, and remorse puts Yorick in 'an excellent frame of mind for making a bargain'. Twists and turns of uncontrollable and unpredictable emotion frame the moments of love and sympathy. Maria is a sentimental object in an object-lesson demonstrating the isolation and abstraction of charity. Yorick is all sympathy and benevolent aspiration, but he is safe. He cannot give her a cottage in his country, there is really no question of taking her to his bosom instead of Eliza. Charitable impulse is released but placed; self-interest rules, not sympathy.

There is a further analytic implication. The character of Maria is joined by the image evoked in the rhapsody (in the passage quoted on p. 41) of the rough peasant and his lacerated lamb, an image generated by feeling and generating fresh feeling. It underlines the isolation of sympathy, and makes an aesthetic analysis. Yorick's feeling for the shepherd and his lamb places sympathy within sympathy, to intensify and parody. He duplicates, on rhetorically separate planes, the image of afflicted Maria and the goat, to create a linguistic and fictional model for stimulus, response, and inaction. The reader is distanced further from the primary example of Maria, and forced to recognize the isolation of strong sympathy for fictional character. Sterne analyses the sentiments and sentimentality of imagination, in and outside texts.

The tender passions dominate, but they are not the only ones. In the third Chapter entitled 'The Remise Door', Sterne uses an allegory, very like Fielding's, to dramatize emotional conflict and arbitrary resolution. Yorick is tempted to offer a lady a share of his chaise, but is resisted by 'every dirty passion, and bad propensity' in his nature: Avarice, who counts the cost, Caution, who reminds him that he does not know the lady, Cowardice, who anticipates 'scrapes', Discretion, who expects scandal (''twill be said you went off with a mistress'), and Hypocrisy, Meanness, and Pride, who lend their aid. The passions are simply answered by the residual self, 'But 'tis a civil thing'. He explains that he generally acts from impulse, and 'therefore seldom listen[s] to these cabals, which serve no purpose, that I know of, but to encompass the heart with adamant'. But as usual Sterne surprises us, and the cabal lasts long enough to settle the question, since the lady 'glided off unperceived, as the cause was pleading'. The conflict of feeling, so seriously analysed before and after Sterne, by Richardson and Fielding, Charlotte Brontë and George Eliot, is demonstrated as a psychological curiosity, put in its place by comedy.

Sterne's *Sentimental Journey* offers a summary analysis of the rhetorical methods of representing feeling, but holds them in dissolution. The novelists who developed Victorian forms of the novel of sensibility learnt from him, as from the comic and tragic writers who came before him, but they developed more holistic structures. Still, the analytic method of Sterne, which anticipated so much of modernist dislocation and dilapidation, draws attention to the complexity of affective form in his successors. The classic Victorian novel is never a simplistic mimetic representation of feeling and passion, but conducts its analysis in discontinuity as well as continuity, through discursive as well as dramatic and narrative means. The analysis is often subdued, but displacements and stylizations of affective form are functional in Victorian novelists as well as in their more conspicuously reflexive predecessors. The obvious link between the centuries is Jane Austen, whose *Northanger Abbey* looks back to Sterne and Fielding in its continual assertion of fictionality, and whose other novels subdue comic self-consciousness in the course of an affective analysis as introspective and subtle as Richardson's, though quietly worked out through irony and litotes. From *Northanger Abbey* to *Persuasion*, Jane Austen contrasts public scenes, where the passions are shown obliquely, with private monologues, like those of Catherine Morland, Elinor Dashwood, Elizabeth Bennet, Fanny Price, Emma, and Anne Elliott, whose agitations and self-analysis look ahead to Henry Esmond, Lucy Snowe, Dorothea Brooke, and Isabel Archer.

NOTE

1   A small example of the novelist anticipating academic psychological discussion.
    Sterne makes Yorick generate emotion by miming appropriate behaviour. The
    production of emotion by performance is more extensively dramatized and analysed
    by Flaubert in *L'Education Sentimentale*, Stendhal in *Le Rouge et le Noir*, and
    Thackeray in *The Newcomes*. The novelists are dealing empirically with the subject of
    the well-known James–Lange theory of emotion. See especially W. James, 'What Is
    an Emotion?', *Mind*, Vol. 9, 1884, and two articles by W.B. Cannon, 'The
    James–Lange Theory of Emotion: A Critical Examination and an Alternative
    Theory', *American Journal of Psychology*, Vol. 39, 1927, and 'Again the James–Lange
    and the Thalamic Theories of Emotion', *The Psychological Review*, Vol. 38, 1931.

2

DICKENS

1 The Passions: Surfaces and Depths

> There was a fiction that Mr Wopsle 'examined' the scholars, once a quarter.
> What he did on those occasions, was to turn up his cuffs, stick up his hair,
> and give us Mark Antony's oration over the body of Caesar. This was
> always followed by Collins's Ode on the Passions, wherein I particularly
> venerated Mr Wopsle as Revenge, throwing his blood-stained sword in
> thunder down, and taking the War-denouncing trumpet with a withering
> look. It was not with me then, as it was in later life, when I fell into the
> society of the Passions, and compared them with Collins and Wopsle, rather
> to the disadvantage of both gentlemen. (*Great Expectations*, Chapter 7)

This is one of the observations often flung out by Dickens, comically
conspicuous at the moment of utterance but setting up no subsequent
references or resonances which are obvious or explicit. It can be seen as
a neglected text. Dickens never entirely discards the crude flourish of
blood-stained sword and war-denouncing trumpet which he ridicules
and enjoys in Wopsle's histrionics and Collins's all-too-performable
Passions, but even when he simplifies, the exaggeration often disguises
or accompanies subtle nuance and detail. From *Pickwick Papers* to
Edwin Drood the behaviouristic rendering is central: the characters
rant, rave, groan, sigh, weep, laugh fiendishly, heave bosoms, flourish
sticks and umbrellas, toss heads, strike breasts, hit stones, cast
themselves down, and writhe, as if only pantomimic violence could
utter intensities of feeling. The disadvantages of such hyperbolic
external signs are clear. The passions seem to be always expressible,
never inward and secret, and they appear atomized, coming on one at
a time, as in Collins's 'Ode'. The tossings and turnings are misleading.
Edith Dombey throws herself about as much as any of Dickens's
suffering men and women, but hers is a subtle case of pride, torment,
jealousy, effort and destructiveness: the complexity of her inner life has

45

little relation to the simple and crude actions of her head, hands, and bosom.

Dickens borrows conventional theatricalities, but has access to novelistic means of interiorizing the emotions and passions. Louisa Gradgrind tries to express her fears, frustrations, and emotional needs to her father through the metaphor of the smothered fires of Coketown, but he is unable to penetrate surfaces and read symbols. Oliver Twist almost succumbs to Fagin's brainwashing alternation of neglect and sociability. Dombey self-destructively bottles up love and hate. Arthur Clennam becomes so practised in self-control and self-denial that he smothers impulse and sympathy. All these characters can express some feelings but must repress or hide others, and in portraying them Dickens sets up a significant tension between the public display and the private or unconscious movement of inner feeling. For the expressible feelings he employs a simple language and gesture, but for the inner currents he devises complex forms of representation, which are reflexive and analytic.

Pickwick Papers isolates and departmentalizes the passions more than any other Dickens novel, formally dividing dark melodrama from bright comedy, and simplifying character and event. In the grim inset stories, the characters tell all. In the comic scenes, the characters have no inner life; Dickens is using a strongly visual and dramatic method which expresses no psychological problems. But from *Oliver Twist* onward he begins to use a greater variety of method. Sometimes the external rendering is crude, and the passion simply performed, but at times the passion is too deeply and complexly rooted to be represented in a simple notation of physical energy. And the analysis of feeling is not only presented through a division between suffering character and reflecting narrator, but also becomes a part of organically sensed integrity of thought and feeling.

The jealousy of Bill Sikes is of the more developed kind, though it expresses itself in clusters of physically violent metaphors, 'I'd grind his skull under the iron heel of my boot into as many grains as there are hairs upon his head', and in the simplicities of body language:

> Without one pause, or moment's consideration; without once turning his head to the right, or left, or raising his eyes to the sky, or lowering them to the ground, but looking straight before him with savage resolution: his teeth so tightly compressed that the strained jaw seemed starting through his skin; the robber held on his headlong course, nor muttered a word, nor relaxed a muscle, until he reached his own door. (Chapter 47)

And it is expressed in action, in the murder of Nancy, and the flight in fear and panic which follows.

In his Preface to the Third Edition of *Oliver Twist* (1841), Dickens describes Sikes as a hardened character, reflecting, 'Whether every gentler feeling is dead within such bosoms, or the proper chord to strike has rusted and is hard to find, I do not know'. In this generalized critical speculation about environment and feeling, there is doubt and questioning, but the novelist does know about the particularities of his invention, and the novel forms his answer. The violence of language, gesture, and event represents a character driven to extremes, but shown unsentimentally, through suggestion, as remaining in touch with human norms of feeling. In the flight of Sikes, Dickens succeeds in showing a totality of human response in which the passions are strong, but mingled, unclassified, and ultimately unnamed because unnameable. Sikes has always been presented as a simple brute, in spite of the implications of his relationship with Nancy. (She is a censored version of a prostitute, and he of a pimp, but the censorship has a simplifying tendency, sentimentalizing the figure of the fallen woman with a heart of gold, and depriving both characters of sexual nuance.) After the murder the interest in the criminal action concentrates on the solitary and inarticulate Sikes, whose character is enlarged through a prolonged psychological melodrama.

The outer events are strong and exciting: the pursuit, the flight, the fire, the trap, the death. The inner register is strong and unexpected. Dickens is not just eliciting horror for a murderous brute, or compassion for a hunted man, but is keeping character and reader in touch with common human feelings of loneliness, alienation, repression, energy, and fear. He combines and compresses these emotional experiences, using a range of external effects which includes the grim comedy of the cheapjack and the bloodstain on Sikes's hat, and the compressed terror of the fire, a focus which registers emotions without naming them. Dickens makes Sikes seize on the fire as an opportunity to join other people as emphatically as by murder he repudiated them. He is released into a rudimentary innocent pleasure, familiar in guilty or alienated states, in which impersonal participation in action gives relief or distraction. Dickens also shows the solace of sheer physical energy, which is destructive and constructive in turn. The effect of the unnamed, mixed, and private passions involved keeps us - in Coleridgean words - in the 'highroad' of human experience. We are induced to feel a form of sympathy, *Mitleid* rather than pity. At the same time the violent action is endowed with the inner life of sensation and emotion. At first, the notation of feeling is straightforward and central:

> For now, a vision came before him, as constant and more terrible than that from which he had escaped. Those widely staring eyes, so lustreless and so glassy, that he had better borne to see them than to think upon them, appeared in the midst of the darkness: light in themselves, but giving light to nothing. There were but two, but they were everywhere. If he shut out the sight, there came the room with every well-known object – some, indeed, that he would have forgotten, if he had gone over its contents from memory – each in its accustomed place. The body was in *its* place, and its eyes were as he saw them when he stole away. He got up, and rushed into the field without. The figure was behind him. He re-entered the shed, and shrunk down once more. The eyes were there, before he had lain himself along. (Chapter 48)

Guilt and remorse here find their language. The involuntary imagery realizes and re-enacts the murder through obsession. Memory acts as hallucination, the loved one's body is no longer 'hers' but 'its'. The same precision recurs in the analysis of Fagin's sharpened visual perceptions, in the catalogue of Jonas Chuzzlewit's terrors, and in Scrooge's nightmare of death. In *The Dickens Theatre* Robert Garis, one of the few critics to pay attention to the representation of feelings in fiction, suggests that Dickens is especially good at showing the passion of anger. He is also good at guilt, fear, and guilty fear. But he is exceptionally good at mixing the passions. As Sikes's isolation increases, Dickens blends the ordinary with the extraordinary in the episode of the fire. He begins in cliché, then suddenly catches the doomsday rhythm. There is analysis of excitement, as well as excitement:

> And here he remained, in such terror as none but he can know, trembling in every limb, and the cold sweat starting from every pore, when suddenly there arose upon the night-wind the noise of distant shouting, and the roar of voices mingled in alarm and wonder. Any sound of men in that lonely place, even though it conveyed a real cause of alarm, was something to him. He regained his strength and energy at the prospect of personal danger; and, springing to his feet, rushed into the open air.
>
> The broad sky seemed on fire. Rising into the air with showers of sparks, and rolling one above the other, were sheets of flame, lighting the atmosphere for miles round, and driving clouds of smoke in the direction where he stood. The shouts grew louder as new voices swelled the roar, and

he could hear the cry of Fire! mingled with the ringing of an alarm-bell, the fall of heavy bodies, and the crackling of flames as they twined round some new obstacle, and shot aloft as though refreshed by food. The noise increased as he looked. There were people there – men and women – light, bustle. It was like new life to him. He darted onward – straight, headlong – dashing through brier and brake, and leaping gate and fence as madly as the dog, who careered with loud and sounding bark before him.

He came upon the spot. There were half-dressed figures tearing to and fro, some endeavouring to drag the frightened horses from the stables, others driving the cattle from the yard and outhouses, and others coming laden from the burning pile, amidst a shower of falling sparks, and the tumbling down of red-hot beams. The apertures, where doors and windows stood an hour ago, disclosed a mass of raging fire; walls rocked and crumbled into the burning well; the molten lead and iron poured down, white-hot, upon the ground. Women and children shrieked, and men encouraged each other with noisy shouts and cheers. The clanking of the engine-pumps, and the spirting and hissing of the water as it fell upon the blazing wood, added to the tremendous roar. He shouted, too, till he was hoarse; and, flying from memory and himself, plunged into the thickest of the throng.

Hither and thither he dived that night: now working at the pumps, and now hurrying through the smoke and flame, but never ceasing to engage himself wherever noise and men were thickest. Up and down the ladders, upon the roofs of buildings, over floors that quaked and trembled with his weight, under the lee of falling bricks and stones, in every part of that great fire was he; but he bore a charmed life, and had neither scratch nor bruise, nor weariness nor thought, till morning dawned again, and only smoke and blackened ruins remained. (Ibid.)

The episode presents feeling less explicitly than in the earlier episode of guilt. The scene is painted vividly, and the fusion of comment with description is not immediately apparent. The narrator tells us plainly that Sikes is energized and renewed at the thought of personal danger, which provides an escape from obsessive memory and the sense of self, but something is left to the action's eloquence. The events show us Sikes escaping from one torment to another, responding to other human presences momentarily released by a delirious energy. Dickens contrives and works up an improbable event, but it acts as a carrier of plausible passion. Not inertly, however: the scene generates new passion. We see guilt and fear joined and enlarged by needs, sensations, and perceptions which link Sikes with common humanity. Dickens works action into symbol, not symbol into action: the fire-fighting is an extreme image of violence, destructiveness, desperation, and ruin. Sikes needs the fire, and is like the fire, burning, raging, and rocking.

In *Nicholas Nickleby* the character of Ralph Nickleby shows another facet of Dickens's awareness of nature and social shaping. We may take Ralph's initial dislike of Nicholas for an instinctive loathing of goodness by evil, but the novel eventually reveals the causes of a re-awakened sexual and moral jealousy, once felt for a brother, then transferred to a nephew. Ralph is slowly disclosed as a man made into a monster by his environment. Like Sikes, he is described as a man whose heart has rusted, 'only a piece of cunning mechanism, and yielding not one throb of hope, or fear, or love, or care, for any living thing'. Slowly, it turns out to be capable of a throb or two.

Chapter 19 ends with a sentimental incident: Kate has just got into the coach after the menacing dinner-party at Ralph Nickleby's, and as the door closes, a comb falls out of her hair. As Ralph picks it up, he sees in the lamplight a 'lock of hair that had escaped and curled loosely over her brow', and moved by 'some dormant train of recollection', he is reminded of his dead brother's face 'with the very look it bore on some occasion of boyish grief'. The language is packed with banalities as it mounts its appeal:

> Ralph Nickleby, who was proof against all appeals of blood and kindred – who was steeled against every tale of sorrow and distress – staggered while he looked, and went back into his house, as a man who had seen a spirit from some world beyond the grave.

But Dickens has already shown the survival of some susceptibility in Ralph, and with a finer touch both of observation and technique. At the end of the dinner-party where she has been displayed and humiliated, Kate is weeping, and the narrator observes a transient release of sensibility when Ralph's ruling passion is off-duty:

> Ralph would have walked into any poverty-stricken debtor's house, and pointed him out to a bailiff, though in attendance upon a young child's death-bed, without the smallest concern, because it would have been a matter quite in the ordinary course of business, and the man would have been an offender against his only code of morality. But, here was a young girl, who had done no wrong save that of coming into the world alive; who had patiently yielded to all his wishes; who had tried hard to please him – above all, who didn't owe him money – and he felt awkward and nervous. (Chapter 19)

The language is matter-of-fact and directed to its task of explanation. Touches like the jocular parenthesis create an illusion of emotional density and continuity even in these simplified characters, and show vital remnants of nature not wholly perverted. This observation is unsentimental; it quietly arouses contempt and understanding for the denatured man and simply explains the benign surplus of nature. Unlike the genre-piece of the hair in the lamplight, this scene is serious and analytic. Once again the privacy and secrecy of feeling leads the novelist to analysis.

In *Dombey and Son* two instances of affective symbolism, locally strong, set up streams of feeling for the whole book, and link the private passions of Dombey with the private passions of Carker, the false husband and false lover, apparent cuckold and apparent rival, victims of Edith's self-punishing and man-punishing honour. The fire in *Oliver Twist* only exists to render the passions of Sikes; it is attached to no before-and-after realities in the characters or the action, and has the status of sensitive scenery. Not so with Dombey's train journey. The image of the railway is connected with the industrial portraiture in the novel, animated and documented in particularized detail. It is a metaphor for Dombey's passions, but Dickens draws attention to the gap between the symbolic interpretation and the larger historicized 'reality' proposed in the novel, picking up the violence of the train's noise, the iron way, and the speed which 'mocked the swift course of the young life that had been borne away so steadily and so inexorably to its fore-doomed end'. He makes it clear that Dombey's stricken and active imagination is selecting the symbolic material, while the train, the journey, and the landscape are larger than the act of interpretation:

> He found no pleasure or relief in the journey. Tortured by these thoughts he carried monotony with him, through the rushing landscape, and hurried headlong, not through a rich and varied country, but a wilderness of blighted plans and gnawing jealousies. . . .
> Away, with a shriek, and a roar, and a rattle, from the town, burrowing among the dwellings of men and making the streets hum, flashing out into the meadows for a moment, mining in through the damp earth, booming on in darkness and heavy air, bursting out again into the sunny air so bright and wide. . . . (Chapter 20)

The descriptions of Dombey's journey emphasize the mythopoeic act: he chooses the dark and does not see the light. There is a wilderness outside like the wilderness inside, but there is also opulence, variety, and change. When Dombey moves through the industrial horrors, Dickens makes explicit what has been implicit; the railway is approved by the narrator, though not by the character:

> There are dark pools of water, muddy lanes, and miserable habitations far below. There are jagged walls and falling houses close at hand, and through the battered roofs and broken windows, wretched rooms are seen, where want and fever hide themselves in many wretched shapes, while smoke and crowded gables, and distorted chimneys, and deformity of brick and water penning up deformity of mind and body, choke the murky distance. As Mr Dombey looks out of his carriage window, it is never in his thoughts that the monster who has brought him here has let the light of day in on these things: not made or caused them. It was the journey's fitting end, and might have been the end of everything; it was so ruinous and dreary.
>
> So, pursuing the one course of thought, he had the one relentless monster still before him. All things looked black, and cold, and deadly upon him, and he on them. He found a likeness to his misfortune everywhere. (Ibid.)

This episode is more elaborate than the scene of the fire in *Oliver Twist*. Dickens is using the vehicle of appropriately violent object and action in order to delineate the passions, but also to analyse the symbolism and selectivity of passion. The whole episode cunningly emphasizes the relation of this tiny human figure to its vast historical background.

By the time the railway is used to render Carker's passions of fury and fear, it has picked up resonance from these earlier scenes and has come to stand for a monstrous Death. The episode following Edith's disclosure in the Dijon hotel is telling in its obscurity. Carker's fear of Dombey at first seems excessive. From the moment Edith warns him, 'Look to yourself!', saying that she has seen her husband in the street, Carker is blanched and shaken by terror. A bell rings and goes on ringing, and it is used to initiate a state of terror which continues throughout the next chapter (55) and is marked by superstition and confusion. Carker's emotion seems disproportionate as fear of Dombey, but Dickens cleverly accounts for this, at least partially, by relating it to the sexual humiliation Carker has just suffered, which seems to have 'rent and shivered all his hardihood and self-reliance'. The traditional bestiary is brilliantly evoked, even though there is some crudity of diction:

> Spurned like any reptile; entrapped and mocked; turned upon, and trodden down by the proud woman whose mind he had slowly poisoned, as he

thought, until she had sunk into the mere creature of his pleasure; undeceived in his deceit, and with his fox's hide stripped off, he sneaked away, abashed, degraded, and afraid.

The fear and panic are extended beyond the obvious and immediate cause. But they are further extended. Like the emotions of Dombey in the earlier journey they are particularized and generalized through the use of the railway. On this occasion the symbolic resonances (of rushing, sweeping, and trembling) appear before the train itself, to increase the irrational, blurred force of Carker's feelings, and to play mysteriously on the expectations of the reader:

> Some other terror came upon him quite removed from this of being pursued, suddenly, like an electric shock, as he was creeping through the streets. Some visionary horror, unintelligible and inexplicable, associated with a trembling of the ground, - a rush and sweep of something through the air, like Death upon the wing. He shrunk, as if to let the thing go by. It was not gone, it never had been there, yet what a startling horror it had left behind. (Chapter 55)

Carker is not afraid of death, but of an unintelligible and inexplicable 'horror' associated with sensations which are 'like Death'. During his flight Dickens incorporates the unknown object of the fear into the fear itself. He invokes irrational fear but also goes on accumulating the minutely comprehended social apparatus of fear: Carker feels alienated because he has been mortified and shocked where he felt most confident, in his sexual vanity, and because he is alone in a foreign country. Dickens perceptively makes self-consciousness deepen the sense of dissociation:

> The dread of being hunted in a strange, remote place, where the laws might not protect him - the novelty of the feeling that it *was* strange and remote, originating in his being left alone so suddenly amid the ruin of his plans. (Ibid.)

His claustral character opens out in precisely rendered fresh feeling. The emotional continuity and variety is beautifully done. The episode is also an inner drama of violent and desperate turmoil: the violence is right for Carker, as it was for Sikes, and similarly keeps us on the highroad of normal experience. Dickens devises the symbol's pre-echo: the push, the bell, the sweep of 'something through the air' are only explained when Carker – like other strong characters in nineteenth-century fiction – is destroyed by the train. Dickens describes his journey as he does Dombey's, inner feelings expressed by outer landscape, and imaginative selectivity brought out. The journey is 'like a vision, in which nothing was quite real but his own torment'. There are pages of compressed and incantatory summary where the rapidity and crowdedness of generalization conveys featureless motion, monotony, haste, change, and painfully incessant travelling. Descriptive details blur and whirl into a correlative for emotion. Like Sikes and Dombey, Carker is possessed and obsessed: he has to keep in motion, 'riding on nevertheless, through town and country, light and darkness, wet weather and dry, over road and pavement, hill and valley, height and hollow, jaded and scared by the monotony of bells, and wheels, and horses' feet, and no rest'. He forgets the day and the time, increases his 'disorder' with wine, is lured down to the railway, sees the train as Devils, is fascinated and terrified, holding on to a gate 'as if to save himself'. Derangement is dramatized, but it is finally neither the lure of the train nor his fuddled mind which brings him to his death. He meets the eyes of Dombey, then slips to meet the red eyes of the train.

In these bold set-pieces, where Dickens slowly swells the action to fix and mobilize the inner action of passion, the violence within and without gradually connect. In the later novels, Dickens becomes interested in strong feeling that cannot be suitably expressed in external events of this kind, because of a lack of outlet. Although Dombey does a lot of secret thinking and feeling, and his silence and stillness are eloquent of repression and reserve, when he suffers on the railway journey, there is a correspondence of action with passion. In Sir Leicester Dedlock's suffering, Arthur Clennam's depression, and Pip's misery there is no such outlet; the strong feeling cannot get expressed or acted out even symbolically, but leads its quiet life which is narrated or imagined by appropriately quiet means.

In *Bleak House*, the sick-bed of Sir Leicester Dedlock is a triumph of reticence:

'My lady is too high in position, too handsome, too accomplished, too superior in most respects to the best of those by whom she is surrounded, not to have her enemies and traducers, I dare say. Let it be known to them, as I make it known to you, that being of sound mind, memory, and understanding, I revoke no disposition I have made in her favour. I abridge nothing I have ever bestowed upon her. I am on unaltered terms with her, and I recall – having the full power to do it if I were so disposed, as you see – no act I have done for her advantage and happiness.'

His formal array of words might have at any other time, as it often had, something ludicrous in it; but at this time it is serious and affecting. His noble earnestness, his fidelity, his gallant shielding of her, his general conquest of his own wrong and his own pride for her sake, are simply honourable, manly, and true. Nothing less worthy can be seen through the lustre of such qualities in the commonest mechanic, nothing less worthy can be seen in the best-born gentleman. In such a light both aspire alike, both rise alike, both children of the dust shine equally.

Overpowered by his exertions, he lays his head back on his pillows, and closes his eyes; for not more than a minute; when he again resumes his watching of the weather, and his attention to the muffled sounds. In the rendering of those little services, and in the manner of their acceptance, the trooper has become installed as necessary to him. Nothing has been said, but it is quite understood. He falls a step or two backward to be out of sight, and mounts guard a little behind his mother's chair.

The day is now beginning to decline. The mist, and the sleet into which the snow has all resolved itself, are darker, and the blaze begins to tell more vividly upon the room walls and furniture. The gloom augments; the bright gas springs up in the streets; and the pertinacious oil lamps which yet hold their ground there, with their source of life half frozen and half thawed, twinkle gaspingly, like fiery fish out of water – as they are. The world, which has been rumbling over the straw and pulling at the bell 'to inquire', begins to go home, begins to dress, to dine, to discuss its dear friend, with all the last new modes, as already mentioned.

Now, does Sir Leicester become worse; restless, uneasy, and in great pain. Volumnia lighting a candle (with a predestined aptitude for doing something objectionable) is bidden to put it out again, for it is not yet dark enough. Yet it is very dark too; as dark as it will be all night. By-and-by she tries again. No! Put it out. It is not dark enough yet. (Chapter 58)

This is mature Dickens, controlled and subtle. Wit and hyperbole are subdued to the occasion. In a clever twist, he creates the gentleman with a heart of gold. Sir Leicester's gentlemanliness and formality (images of the legal and legalistic forms which colour the language of the novel) are expressed in his controlled and elaborate crescendo, parenthesis, inversions and legal phrases. It is not a dead or deadlocked language any more; Dickens uses it to express a 'manliness' that is larger than 'gentlemanliness', a nobility that has nothing to do with pedigree. The words 'noble', 'gentle', and 'man' are delicately weighed. A sense of loyal and loving feeling is given by precise and careful statement, exactly as Dickens tells us it does, shining through the 'formal array' of words that might have seemed 'ludicrous'. The caricature of style is subdued, and with it, the caricature of formality in the man. The wit that is so obtrusive and exuberant at the beginning of the novel is quietened, flashing out only in the vividly precise description of the oil lamps, as he explains the literal source (whale-oil) of the conceit, 'fiery fish out of water – as they are'. It is also subdued in the satirical collocation, 'to discuss its dear friend, with all the last new modes'. The world has been 'to inquire', and has put its friend before the 'last new modes', even if the subjects insensitively share a sentence.

Pathos and moral exaltation are also subdued. Sir Leicester's formal style is used for the words of loyalty, forgiveness, generosity, and love. It controls and individualizes the moral climax. His pathetic struggles with his illness are substantiated by the comic presence of Volumnia. His character is not transformed. There is the assertion of his old authoritarian peremptoriness, suddenly mobilized by the free indirect style, 'for it is not yet dark enough', as he tries to deny the coming of darkness and orders the candle to be put out. Such fusion of comedy, earnestness, and pathos is certainly not the rule in *Bleak House*, where there are plenty of passages of unrelieved sentiment and crude moral uplift. In this sick-bed scene, there is a fine co-operation of humour, pathos, solemnity, and quiet. The performer's brilliance is dimmed, like the lights, and his loudness softened, like the street noises. Dickens is acquiring the arts of decorum.

In *Little Dorrit* Dickens shows Arthur's depression continuously but again quietly. The portrayed environment is the perfect theatre for the passions of the hero; miserable city buildings, dark houses, dank weather, and prison climate provide the sustained expressive material. The prevailing passion of the chief male character is a variant of the prevailing passion of the novel:

> It was a Sunday evening in London, gloomy, close and stale. Maddening church bells of all degrees of dissonance, sharp and flat, cracked and clear, fast and slow, made the brick and mortar echoes hideous. Melancholy streets in a penitential garb of soot, steeped the souls of the people who were condemned to look at them out of windows, in dire despondency. . . . Nothing to see but streets, streets, streets. Nothing to breathe but streets, streets, streets. Nothing to change the brooding mind, or raise it up. Nothing for the spent toiler to do, but to compare the monotony of his

seventh day with the monotony of his six days, think what a weary life he led, and make the best of it - or the worst, according to the probabilities. (Book 1, Chapter 3)

The anonymous example of 'the brooding mind' exactly anticipates and heralds the character who is just about to arrive on the scene. The correspondence of environment and character, which is a prominent linking device in George Eliot's commentary and particularization of character, is much rarer in Dickens. But *Little Dorrit* is most conspicuously a novel with unity of feeling. The locally happy ending for Arthur and Amy fits modestly and suitably into the desolation of the larger scene, as it does not do in *Bleak House*. Even Flora Finching's amorous gush is a sad business, in its middle-aged self-knowledge, its undeceived hankerings after romance, and its sober acceptance of the second-best. 'It was not ecstasy but it was comfort,' she says of her marriage, while her young love was 'the morning of life it was bliss it was frenzy it was everything else of that sort in the highest degree'. A good comic example of the refusal to pin down the passions by classification.

Serious representation of tenderness and desire is not Dickens's strong point. He is better on jealousy, pride, revulsion, fury, fear, gluttony, and sloth, than on love. But as cheerfulness begins to ebb out of the novels, a change for the better comes about in his treatment of love. It is true, as Garis observes, that Arthur Clennam's subdued love for Pet Meagles is archly shown, but the later love for Little Dorrit, which is never treated archly, shows up the earlier archness as suggestive of something less than mature and solemn attachment. Moreover, a tender but untragically unrequited love is right for Arthur's middle-aged control and self-doubt. The feeling for Pet also allows him to suffer the right kind of blindness to Little Dorrit, more plausibly and quietly indicated than David's blindness to his love for Agnes. A mild amorous thwarting keeps him in a depressed but not heartbrokenly humourless state. His positive assaults on the Circumlocution Office and his partnership with Daniel Doyce continue the presentation of energy and depression. Arthur can't be a cynic, because Dickens thought cynicism too wicked to let his heroes feel it, though of course his villains can. But Arthur verges dangerously on world-weariness. His energetic depression is imaged and illustrated by the larger backcloth and argument of the novel, and is itself an image and illustration of the big social themes. His disappointment and gloom are consistent but overcome by the energy of his social helpfulness, quietly shown not as a saintly but as a temperate urge.

Arthur is a striking and central example of reserve, but not the only one. Dickens says that his history must sometimes see through Little Dorrit's eyes, and so it does. As Arthur understands, Amy is not used to dwelling on her emotions, and the most conspicuous instance of her stoical reserve illustrates the reserve of her author. The novel is not always reserved in its expression of feeling. In Chapter 31, for instance, where the Dorrit family rebuke Little Dorrit for walking arm-in-arm with Old Nandy, we find the characters starting, firing off words, head-shaking, trembling and turning pale, passing a handkerchief over the face, grasping convulsively, clenching, weeping, gasping and crying (as Fanny does) 'half in a passion and half out of it'. Unlike Arthur's depression, Amy Dorrit's secret love, like Dombey's, finds a symbol, even a communicable one. In 'The Story of the Princess' Dickens shows in the story-telling how fictions are used to express wish-fulfilment or life-as-it-is, to relate passion obliquely or directly. Amy tells the story of a Princess because Maggie needs to hear stories about Princesses, 'beyond all belief' and with 'lots of hospitals, because they're so comfortable', and because she herself needs to tell a story, neither beyond belief nor comfortable, about a 'poor tiny woman'. The woman's secret place – like the story and like the novel – has a shadow in it. The shadow is the image and the story is a reserved expression of Dorrit's secret passion. The episode is not entirely free from archness, but there is not enough to soften the quiet melancholy which belongs to the character and the novel named after her.

Quietness and reserve are also present in *Great Expectations*. Loving is less simple than in the earlier novels: Pip insists unromantically on the misery of his loving, and with restraint and humour. Even sensational episodes show some muted effects. Pip feels amazement and 'even terror' when Miss Havisham begs his forgiveness on her knees. He leaves her, goes down 'into the natural air', walks round the wilderness of rotting casks, the cold, lonely and dreary yard, and the ruined garden, sees the image of Miss Havisham hanging from the beam, then comments that 'the mournfulness of the place and time, and the great terror of this illusion, though it was but momentary, caused me to feel an indescribable awe as I came out between the open wooden gates where I had once wrung my hair after Estella had wrung my heart' (Chapter 49). The small joke is melancholy but substantiates and relieves nostalgia and awe; the account of Pip's fancy is cooled and elucidated. The word 'indescribable' is exact.

The passions are controlled and mixed. In the grim account of Orlick's attack in Chapter 53, Pip submits a mixture of pain, religiously 'softened' thoughts, detestation, despair, terror, and considerable mental activity. The varying passions are linked and rendered by an insistence on the 'inconceivable rapidity' of the mind's action. Pip repeats the phrase, outlining the range of subject-matter covered by inner action during one of Orlick's short speeches; he is caught up in the kind and quality of his imagery, admires the speed of imagination, and all the while is intent on his attacker:

> My rapid mind pursued him to the town, made a picture of the street with him in it, and contrasted its lights and life with the lonely marsh and the white vapour creeping over it, into which I should have dissolved.
>
> It was not only that I could have summed up years and years and years while he said a dozen words, but that what he did say presented pictures to me, and not mere words. In the excited and exalted state of my brain, I could not think of a place without seeing it, or of persons without seeing them. It is impossible to over-state the vividness of these images, and yet I was so intent, all the time, upon him himself – who would not be intent on the tiger crouching to spring! – that I knew of the slightest action of his fingers.

Here is excitement, control, restraint, and self-analysis. The interest in shifts and shades of feeling is not confined to crises in external action. At the dinner-party at Jaggers's house, Pip comes to suspect that Molly is Estella's mother, and realization dawns in a slow but sure associative process. Jaggers predicts that the Spider will make Estella a husband who will beat or cringe, and with the subject of marital brutality in mind, Pip notices Molly making a knitting movement with her hands, then remembers Estella's fingers moving as she knitted. Involuntary discovery is accompanied by a gathering up of previous feelings of inexplicable connection, and once again there is the rendering of strong feeling in an explicit and self-conscious comment:

> I thought how one link of association had helped that identification in the theatre, and how such a link, wanting before, had been riveted for me now, when I had passed by a chance swift from Estella's name to the fingers with their knitting action, and the attentive eyes. And I felt absolutely certain that this woman was Estella's mother. (Chapter 48)

This sense of reserve and passion continues through a conversation with Wemmick, the next interview with Miss Havisham, and breaks into social communication through the culminating dialogue with Jaggers.

The narrator draws attention to relaxed and stimulated feeling. Pip's appearance, with his arm bandaged and his coat over his shoulders, and the subject of the fire at Satis House, make for a promising informality, 'caused our talk to be less dry and hard' (Chapter 51). There is a spurt of wit in the image of the two murderers' casts 'congestively considering whether they didn't smell fire at the present moment'. Then Pip tells Jaggers that he has asked Miss Havisham about Estella, and discloses his guess; Jaggers still tries to turn back to business, but Pip makes 'a passionate, almost an indignant appeal to him to be more frank and manly with me'. As he appeals to Jaggers he uses the ironic phrase, 'little as he cared for such poor dreams'. There follows the high point of narrative and emotional discovery. In telling Estella's story, Jaggers – so hard, so unconfiding, so cautious – reveals his other self, the side not shown, though occasionally faintly hinted at. The language of his disclosure is legal, his narrative punctuated by the formal hypothesis of a barrister's refrain, 'Put the case'. It is cautiously impersonal, referring to himself in the third person, and avoiding names. The neutral language makes an ironic medium for the sympathy and generosity disclosed in the story, but there are telling breaks, when he picks up Pip's assumption that he would not care for the 'poor dreams':

> Mr Jaggers nodded his head retrospectively two or three times, and actually drew a sigh. 'Pip,' said he, 'we won't talk about "poor dreams"; you know more about such things than I, having much fresher experience of that kind.' (Chapter 51)

And in the middle of his chronicle:

> 'But, add the case that you had loved her, Pip, and had made her the subject of those "poor dreams" which have, at one time or another, been in the heads of more men than you think likely, then I tell you that you had better – and would much sooner when you had thought well of it – chop off that bandaged left hand of yours. . . . .' (Ibid.)

These implications of reserve, together with the actual history of reserve, disclose the unjagged side of Jaggers. In an inventive stylization for a divided life, Dickens makes Jaggers split the compromised social being from the unconditional 'natural' self. For Jaggers there is a division into public surface and secret depth, for Wemmick the divisions into the clerk of lawyer's chambers and the loving son of 'the Aged'. But the affinity is made plain and recognized by the character himself without as much surprise as he assumes, after Pip argues from Wemmick's natural self in order to prise open Jaggers's natural self:

> 'What's all this?' said Mr Jaggers. 'You with an old father, and you with pleasant and playful ways?'
> 'Well!' returned Wemmick, 'if I don't bring 'em here, what does it matter?'
> 'Pip,' said Mr Jaggers, laying his hand upon my arm, and smiling openly, 'this man must be the most cunning impostor in all London.'
> 'Not a bit of it,' returned Wemmick, growing bolder and bolder. 'I think you're another.' (Ibid.)

The doubling of a divided self is emphasized at the climax of this scene, when the professional world resumes its power, and Wemmick challenges the client Mike:

> 'A man can't help his feelings, Mr Wemmick,' pleaded Mike.
> 'His what?' demanded Wemmick, quite savagely. 'Say that again!'
> 'Now, look here, my man,' said Mr Jaggers, advancing a step, and pointing to the door. 'Get out of this office. I'll have no feelings here. Get out!'

The structure of the chapter itself is another model of restriction and release, juxtaposing and contrasting the world of private passions with that of public repressions.

Characters and scenes are analytic. Forms of division represent and examine the nature of character and environment and speculate about freedom and conditioning. Dickens is creating forms which excite the reader's expectations, curiosity and sympathy, but he is also trying to know and comprehend. The inquiring spirit is easier to spot in conceptually sophisticated languages like those of George Eliot and Henry James, sustained speculative and often discursive styles, in which questions about the affective life are formulated, discussed and worked out within the fiction. Dickens's psychological inquiry into emotion, as of other subjects, is embodied and embedded in structures of character and event, and assimilated to his sensational and openly manipulative styles. But an inquiry is being conducted. Its presence becomes clearer as his art develops; apparently casual or accidental effects become deliberate, intuition passes into conscious awareness, restoring to the art a clarity and strength of intellectual recognitions. In Sikes and Ralph Nickleby Dickens embodies insights into the mingling and divisions of feeling, but in the twinning of Jaggers and Wemmick the insights have become formulated and generalized, though through models which possess the force of particularity. As Dickens grows more experienced in presenting human nature he joins action with analysis. In the Preface to *Oliver Twist* there is a suggestion that 'such men as Sikes . . . closely followed through the same space of time and through the same current of circumstances, would not give, by one look or action of a moment, the faintest indication of a better nature'. It is true that the fire-fighting episode doesn't precisely indicate a 'better nature', but it certainly embodies feelings and needs which show Sikes as other than a simple brute. We can see in the reflective tones of the Preface, written some two years after the novel was completed, the consequence of a meditation on the character he has created; he speaks of *fearing* that 'there are in the world some insensible and callous natures that do become, at last, utterly and irredeemably bad' and adds, 'But whether this be so or not'. The novel itself is wiser than the critic, tentative though he is, showing not only the affective surplus value in Sikes's perverted human nature but the actual process of emotional destruction in permutations of social conditioning – in Sikes, Fagin, Nancy, the Artful Dodger, Charley Bates, and Oliver himself, in whose history an experiment in corruption is imagined, however imperfectly. In *Great Expectations* the awareness of determinism has made changes in characterization, and the subject itself is presented more centrally and more subtly. The awareness of deteriorations and constrictions of feeling has become embodied in the characters themselves, explicit in Jaggers's knowing irony and Wemmick's calculated segregations of style. Some changes took place quickly: in *Oliver Twist* Dickens set a house on fire to show the complex passions of fear, remorse and loneliness; in *Dombey and Son* he constructed a railway with historical and symbolic dimensions and showed his characters symbolizing their passions. The imaginative simplifications the novelist once created are formulated as simplifications in the fiction-making of his fictitious characters.

One development in Dickens's handling of feeling and intelligence is clear: he makes his characters more imaginative, more like himself. Thackeray once privately suggested that Boz might have learnt something from his own unexaggerated characters. This may well be true, but Dickens also learnt from his own art. Although he continues to need and use caricature as well as character, his presentation of both seems to derive from his own experience as he created and reflected on his creatures and on his own creativity. This is clear, both in the Prefaces and – more important – in the characters and the caricatures. The distinctive style for creativity in late Dickens – Flora's monologues, Esther's and Pip's languages, Jaggers's and Wemmick's divided life-styles – is that of the first-person meditative narration. Passion becomes contemplative. It is as if the complexity, as well as the intensity, of emotional process is first registered, then contemplated, to make the author articulate the process and embody it with greater profundity and precision in fresh images of impassioned contemplation. He manipulated the emotions of his readers, making their flesh creep, making them laugh, cry, and wait. He created characters who forced him to meditate more finely and more analytically on the emotional life, as his art grew.

2   *A Question of Sentimentality*

Dickens, then, is pursuing an inquiry into the affective life, while manipulating the responses of his readers, sometimes most blatantly. There are emotions which present special difficulties for the artist, and his age; Dickens and the Victorians found it notoriously hard to distance and particularize feelings of morbid pathos. As with his handling of the passions of guilt, fear, love, and sympathy, Dickens's representation of death-bed passions evolves, but he never entirely gets over a tendency to oscillate between crude rhetoric and subtle drama. His powers of affective control, expression, and analysis change and strengthen. What is stereotyped, mawkish, and overdone in the deaths of Smike and Nell becomes particularized, controlled, and economical, though the novelist persists in accumulating pathetic stimuli in a way uncongenial to modern tastes. Thresholds of emotional response vary from period to period, and from person to person, but Dickens's movement away from sentimentality can be judged by his own standards. Like all great artists, he repeats certain themes and forms, and through repetition and permutation, revises, corrects, and develops. Dickens can, early on, write about death with great control and finesse, as he does in the brilliant summary narration of the death of Godfrey Nickleby, the father of Nicholas:

> 'The very house I live in,' sighed the poor gentleman, 'may be taken from me tomorrow. Not an article of my old furniture, but will be sold to strangers!'
>
> The last reflection hurt him so much, that he took at once to his bed; apparently resolved to keep that, at all events.
>
> 'Cheer up, sir!' said the apothecary.
>
> 'You mustn't let yourself be cast down, sir,' said the nurse.
>
> 'Such things happen every day,' remarked the lawyer.
>
> 'And it is very sinful to rebel against them,' whispered the clergyman.
>
> 'And what no man with a family ought to do,' added the neighbours.
>
> Mr Nickleby shook his head, and motioning them all out of the room, embraced his wife and children, and having pressed them by turns to his languidly beating heart, sunk exhausted on his pillow. They were concerned to find that his reason went astray after this; for he babbled for a long time about the generosity and goodness of his brother and the merry old times when they were at school together. This fit of wandering past, he solemnly commended them to One who never deserted the widow or her fatherless children, and smiling gently on them, turned upon his face, and observed that he thought he could fall asleep. (Chapter 1)

This is an instance of Dickens's capacity for emotional modulation. He takes us smoothly but startlingly from comedy to solemnity in twenty-two lines, which present a motive for death, a choric response of some satiric force, a brief and vivid death-bed scene which tempers nostalgia with irony, and a restrained religious peroration. Even more admirable than the condensation and the emotional mixture is Dickens's scrupulous dramatization of Christian associations, presented briefly, lucidly, and individually through the dying man's point of view. The vagueness, gentleness, feebleness, and sanguine optimism which Godfrey shares with his more illustrious widow, Mrs Nickleby, are comically and seriously imprinted in his brief death-scene. The unusual control and restraint were assisted by the wish to get Godfrey out of the way as economically and rapidly as possible, but the success shows what Dickens can do. When he is working without such fruitful constraints, his handling of death is less happy, and raises the problem of sentimentality in the representation of feeling.

Smike's first appearance in Chapter 7 of *Nicholas Nickleby* is stamped
with appropriately morbid words and images. His hope is 'sickly', his look
'very painful', his garment 'a skeleton suit', his frame 'attenuated', and
he has a limp. He is 'eighteen or nineteen' but his innocence brings him
close to Dickens's other delicate children. His death is handled quietly
and briefly, in comparison with Nell's, but anticipates hers in several
ways. It is set in a sympathetic natural setting, quiet, tranquil,
autumnal and mild. It is prepared and intensified by the accumulation
of several sources of pathetic appeal, nostalgia, religion, nature, and
hopeless love. Although compressed into a page at the end of Chapter
58, its short space offers considerable emotional variety. In the early
parts of the chapter there is fear as well as pathos, uncertainty,
curiosity and tension as we share Nicholas's doubt about the source of
Smike's terror. The narrative dwells on images of deaths and graves.
Dickens took some time to learn that one death and one grave were
enough, at least for one chapter. In the deaths of Smike and Nell no
source of pathos is neglected, and Dickens intensifies morbidity by
having the dying person contemplate other deaths and tombs. The last
moment of Smike's dying is enlivened by the confession of his love for
Kate, and grimly particularized by a detail about the love-token,
Kate's ribbon, which he asks Nicholas to take off after his death and
replace when he is in the coffin. This dying request creates a tiny
morbid gap in which we realize he is thinking about his corpse being
laid out, and so provides an interesting mix of grisly and romantic
feeling in both author and character. The religious imagery is handled
briefly at the end, though it has been lavishly prepared. Smike wakes
from his last slumber to tell his paradisal dream of 'beautiful gardens,
which he said stretched before him, and were filled with figures of men,
women, and many children, all with light upon their faces; then,
whispered that it was Eden – and so died'. There is a slight but clear
emphasis on the frequency of child-death and the predominance of
child-virtue in the differentiation of 'many children', which helps to
particularize the dream. So does the plural form, 'gardens', with the
visual detail 'stretched', suggesting a vast and various landscape for
Smike's single-minded Eden. The men and women 'with light upon
their faces' are presented as angelic human beings rather than angels.
The slight delay in identifying the place as Eden and his choice of the
moment of recognition for the moment of death, shows that Dickens
has his eyes on the event, and is not simply writing excitedly and
solemnly in order to make us feel excited and solemn. He is imagining

and dramatizing the death-bed from a double point of view, that of the observer, and that of the dying person, though the presence of Nicholas is not vivid.

I do not want to exaggerate the control here, but the scene of dying is more restrained and particularized than the preceding episodes. Dickens rises to the challenge of the climax.

When we come to *The Old Curiosity Shop*, there is no such generation of particularity, and no restraint. The process found in Smike's death-scene is reversed, and the pathetic effects accumulated and intensified right up to the moment, at the end of Chapter 71, when Nell's death is discovered. Unlike Smike, she is the heroine, so it is not surprising that Dickens is less economical with his effects. (He may also be tempted into a special celebration because this is a woman's death.) Once more we find the combination of religious, aesthetic, and ethical appeal. Once more there is a gentle death (from consumption), once more there is preparatory morbidity, with other child-deaths, many child-graves (tidied up by Nell and her grandfather), and once more there is an elegiac pastorial setting. There is nothing concrete or individual: those details which are mentioned, like the winter berries and green leaves placed on Nell's 'couch' in response to her request to have something 'near' her 'that has loved the light', are not made specific, but left general and unvisualized, like all botanical detail in Dickens. The imagined need of the dying child for a link with life, in itself a specific and sensitive insight, is weakened by the portentous repetition, as the request for 'something that has loved the light' is unnecessarily underlined by 'These were her words'. The failure to give body and activity to insights is typical of the whole scene: the observation about the way inanimate objects pain the bereaved – 'every household god becomes a monument and every room a grave' (Chapter 72) – is left in lyrical abstraction and generality. (Lisbeth Bede's poignantly specified household gods come irresistibly to mind.) Here nothing is in sharp focus. The language takes on archaic syntactical forms which Dickens so frequently overworks for solemn occasions. In *Nicholas Nickleby* there were traces of these, when Smike is said to have 'lain him down to die', for example, but in *The Old Curiosity Shop* the style is in mourning throughout Chapters 71 and 72. The grandfather 'thees' and 'thous' the dying child, as he has not done before, Nell is 'fair to look upon', the old man presses her hand to his lips 'ever and anon' and 'the paths she had trodden but yesterday – could know her no more'.

But the structure is artful. Dickens has performed a sleight of hand,

and prepared a shock, as he loves to do. The reader comes into the death-chamber with Kit, and is at first kept within his limited and ignorant point of view. Kit has already encountered the dreaming child, whose thrilling voice speaks 'a meaning . . . hidden from him'. Both Kit and the reader take the old man's delusions for truth, accepting his report that Nell is only sleeping. Even when Garland, the schoolmaster, and the bachelor come in, their words are carefully kept ambiguous, 'It would pain her very much to know that you were watching' and 'You would not give her pain?' Then references to the 'good' sleep and the 'happy' waking begin to assert a metaphorical dimension. Traditional euphemisms of sleep and waking are exploited by Dickens as he retards the climax and accentuates shock and pathos.

The construction is devised for teasing deception, hint, and surprise. It also tells twice over the story of Nell's death. The climax in Chapter 71, 'She was dead', is a double climax, not only reporting the death, but also revealing and dispelling the ambiguity, and re-emphasizing the pathos of the old man's crazed grief. In the next chapter the story starts again; the death is narrated in retrospect. It begins with the information, 'She had been dead two days', and winds about in a disinclination to finish the story. After Nell (like Smike) has woken from a last quiet sleep, she asks for the watchers to kiss her, then clings to her grandfather, and dies: 'They did not know that she was dead, at first.' But we have not finished; the past-perfect takes us back: 'She had spoken. . . .'

It is hard to accept Huxley's comment in *Vulgarity in Literature* (1930) that Dickens's sentimentality is caused by a failure to think, 'just to overflow, nothing else'. On the contrary, he seems in full control of a quasi-biblical style and a manipulative structure. A recent critic, Malcolm Andrews, in his introduction to the Penguin English Library edition of the novel, is also misleading when he speaks of 'the quieter tone of Dickens's anthem for departed innocence' and says it would be pointless to persuade Huxley 'to respond more fully to the general momentum of feeling'. The 'general momentum' is too complicated to be referred to briefly. Andrews attributes Dickens's 'overcharged' language (specifically in the speech of the schoolmaster) to the author's 'obvious' compensation 'for the lack of secure conviction'. The causes of stylistic excess seem matters for conjecture only, though it is true that Dickens usually over-reaches himself when he expresses religious sentiment. The 'momentum of feeling' in the death-bed scene of Nell is not artless. I do not suggest that we can always put our finger on artifice: it seems impossible to decide whether the gross repetitions and solemn appeals in these episodes from *The Old Curiosity Shop* are the accumulated and overcharged results of self-indulgence, or arrangements made in the hope of wringing readers' hearts. There seems to be indulgence and persuasion here. Malcolm Andrews gives up as impossible the interesting fancy of converting Macready from lachrymose susceptibility[1] and Huxley from contemptuous rejection. (He shrewdly observes the 'highpitched' response of both readers.) Such critical persuasion needs to be done through the analysis of Dickens's emotional expression. In the deaths of Paul and Jo he stays on the right side of the dangerous verge between sentiment and sentimentality.

Like Smike, Paul Dombey is marked for an early death from the start: Dickens's first fine stroke is to locate the boy's delicacy in the baby's double loss of good mother and of good mother-surrogate. This is a thoroughgoing explanation, so that we do not feel that there is any arbitrariness in the decision to kill the character, as we might about the deaths of Smike and Nell. Causality is tactfully and intelligently developed. In *Dombey and Son* Dickens expands his capacity for comic pathos. One of the funniest bits of internal narration, Mrs Wickham's cautionary tale about Betsey Jane, who is 'watched' by her dead mother, makes a link with Paul, through the themes of the watching mother, the 'old-fashioned child', and death. Death is treated amusingly in the joke about Betsey Jane's successful survival to marry a silver-chaser, in contrast to the high mortality amongst the people to whom she took fancies.

Paul is marked for death, but takes some time to die. What maternal and nursery deprivations begin is continued in the forcing-house of education. He dies in Chapter 16, 'What the Waves were always Saying', a short chapter which compresses a variety of psychological analysis and rhetorical activity. The elegiac presence of nature is again strong, but Dickens is economical with description, drawing on the matrix of sea and river imagery. These traditional religious and literary images were habituated and literalized through the sympathetic nature of the 'real' sea at Brighton, and its fascination for Paul has been fixed. In *Nicholas Nickleby* Dickens gave Smike one elegiac orchard scene, and then kept the autumn weather mild enough for death to take place at an open window. In *Dombey and Son* nature makes an entry indirectly, in Paul's London bedroom, through the sun's reflections on the wall, light patterns assimilated to waves by a clever visual and psychological stroke. In pictorial terms, the quivering reflections coming through the blinds (presumably venetian) justify the simile, 'like golden water', but the image is fortified by being located in the vividly creative fancy of Paul. His inventiveness is heightened by solitude, sickness, and a sharply reduced view. His impressions of nature are diminished, but 'When the sunbeams struck into his room . . . he knew that evening was coming on, and that the sky was red and beautiful.' The images of sun and sea are presented as benign, in contrast to the river image. This is blackened in the register of Paul's fancy by being identified with the polluted Thames:

> His fancy had a strange tendency to wander to the river, which he knew was flowing through the great city; and now he thought how black it was, and how deep it would look, reflecting the hosts of stars – and more than all, how steadily it rolled away to meet the sea.

Thereafter the pattern takes the form of a conflict between the two images, through which Dickens achieves his imaginative feat of internalizing the action of dying. Smike and Nell died gentle deaths; Paul's is a struggle. They felt no pain; he does. They had pleasant dreams; he has a difficult and frightening delirium:

> As it grew later in the night, and footsteps in the street became so rare that he could hear them coming, count them as they passed, and lose them in the hollow distance, he would lie and watch the many-coloured ring about the candle, and wait patiently for day. His only trouble was, the swift and rapid river. He felt forced, sometimes, to try to stop it – to stem it with his childish hands – or choke its way with sand – and when he saw it coming on, resistless, he cried out!

Smike and Nell are always smiling as they slowly die; Paul only smiles after he has told his bad dream to Florence. The pattern of conflicting images is repeated several times, always with the emphasis on the threat of the river, and the promise of the sea. The images are contrasted in colour, and also in motion: the dark river rushes and the golden water dances. After the pattern has been well established, it blurs into generalization:

> How many times the golden water danced upon the wall; how many nights the dark dark river rolled towards the sea in spite of him; Paul never counted, never sought to know.

The images take on moral and theological values which the author wishes to invoke, and are sensuous enough to register sufferings and struggle. Paul is felt to be ill in a way which Smike and Nell never are, because Dickens uses the imagery to convey a total response and breakdown, psychic and somatic, and at the same time to externalize the inner experience of the character, in a way wholly in character. The river is brought into the full affectivity of the medium, through its uncontrollable and quick flow, expressing Paul's feelings of being rushed, overwhelmed, and acted upon. A fine detail is his attempt to stop the river, 'to stem it with his childish hands – or choke its way with sand'. Rationality and irrationality are both registered.

The pattern of imagery is appropriately dynamic. It marks the process of dying in a way which is varied, heightened, and controlled, revealing the shortcoming in the monotonous and shapeless repetitions of Nell's death-scenes. In Paul's dying, the images conflict, then the conflict accelerates, in a way which appropriately blurs time. There is an end to the conflict of images when Paul wakes up, as Smike and Nell wake from their last dreams, but in a more startlingly particularized drama:

> 'Floy, is it to-morrow? Is she come?'
>
> Some one seemed to go in quest of her. Perhaps it was Susan. Paul thought he heard her telling him when he had closed his eyes again, that she would soon be back; but he did not open them to see. She kept her word – perhaps she had never been away – but the next thing that happened was a noise of footsteps on the stairs, and then Paul woke – woke mind and body – and sat upright in his bed. He saw them now about him. There was no grey mist before them, as there had been sometimes in the night. He knew them every one, and called them by their names.
>
> 'And who is this? Is this my old nurse?' said the child, regarding with a radiant smile, a figure coming in.

After this, the suffering and struggle vanish. The imagery of sea and river still record speed, but also release and relief:

> Sister and brother wound their arms around each other, and the golden light came streaming in, and fell upon them, locked together.
>
> 'How fast the river runs, between its green banks and the rushes, Floy! But it's very near the sea. I hear the waves! They always said so!'
>
> Presently he told her that the motion of the boat upon the stream was lulling him to rest. How green the banks were now, how bright the flowers

growing on them, and how tall the rushes! Now the boat was out at sea, but gliding smoothly on. And now there was a shore before him. Who stood on the bank! –

The light is picked up in the halo, then transformed (after an extra gap between paragraphs which marks an end and sets off the concluding generalization and commentary) into the 'golden ripple on the wall'. This time the image is exteriorized, Paul's fancy no longer at work, to establish the moment of death:

> The golden ripple on the wall came back again, and nothing else stirred in the room.

The process from resistance to tranquillity, consciousness to unconsciousness, action to inaction, is registered. The imagery of river and sea makes its last appearance (in this chapter) in the penultimate paragraph: 'when the swift river bears us to the ocean!' Throughout the scene Paul's point of view is dominant. In the earlier death-scenes there was a wavering from onlooker to sufferer, arbitrary and unemphatic. Here the detailed and dynamic record of Paul's interior experience not only registers that experience, but acts as a filter, sometimes half-blocked, sometimes clear, through which the exterior action of scene and characters is conveyed. All the comings and goings are done through Paul's sharp and shifting sensibility. Attentive to detail, as he was in his response to the rhythm of Dr Blimber's clock, he notices the difference in the sound of the doctors' watches. The detail recalls his birth-scene, when the speed and process of his mother's death were imaged in the racing, jostling and tripping watches of the two doctors.

Other characters are seen only through Paul's eyes. Dombey appears with unusual force in the vague and faltering vision of change and unreality:

> The people round him changed as unaccountably as on that first night at Doctor Blimber's - except Florence; Florence never changed - and what had been Sir Parker Peps, was now his father, sitting with his head upon his hand. Old Mrs Pipchin dozing in an easy chair, often changed to Miss Tox, or his aunt: and Paul was quite content to shut his eyes again, and see what happened next, without emotion. But this figure with its head upon its hand returned so often, and remained so long, and sat so still and solemn, never speaking, never being spoken to, and rarely lifting up its face, that Paul

began to wonder languidly, if it were real; and in the night-time saw it sitting there, with fear.

'Floy!' he said. 'What *is* that?'

'Where, dearest?'

'There! at the bottom of the bed.'

'There's nothing there, except Papa!'

The figure lifted up its head, and rose, and coming to the bedside, said: 'My own boy! Don't you know me?'

Paul's morbid emotion shows Dickens at last using simplicity and understatement in a highly economical way. The child's disintegrating consciousness articulates an external, but resonant, image of Dombey, movingly reduced to a shape of still and stooped grief.

Structure, particularity, economy, have replaced repetition, stereotype and exaggeration. Dickens is drawing on and combining the earlier sources of pathetic and compassionate appeal, even though his means are imaginative, ingenious and sophisticated. In the final two paragraphs of the scene, which necessarily shift from the point of view of Paul, who is now dead, to an authorial voice, we return to the paradisal imagery of Smike and Nell:

The old, old fashion! The fashion that came in with our first garments, and will last unchanged until our race has run its course, and the wide firmament is rolled up like a scroll. The old, old fashion – Death!

Oh thank GOD, all who see it, for that older fashion yet, of Immortality! And look upon us, angels of young children, with regards not quite estranged, when the swift river bears us to the ocean!

Dickens is economizing in his Christian appeal. There is a release from emotional particulars into a generalized imagery, though it is connected with the local imagery of river and ocean. There is nothing in the language which is simply vacant or abstract or generalized, as it often is in the death-scenes of Smike and Nell. The paradisal reference is subdued, and wittily relates the imagery of the old-fashioned child to the Fall, and Adam and Eve's shameful covering of nakedness with clothing. Imagery is transmuted and transformed through that metaphorical activity so marked in this novel. The other familiar Christian reference, to Immortality, is also given colour and continuity through the ironic image of 'fashion'. In spite of these qualities of motion, image, and structure, the final paragraph both over-reaches and diminishes feeling. Paul's excitements, pains, confusions and clarity, were so sharply and economically dramatized that there seems to be anti-climax and sermon where there should be augmentation and silence. We move into a cruder and thinner rhetoric in these last apostrophes and exclamations. The rhetoric of this death-scene has been complicated and animated in its capacity to render vision and sensation and outer life. The final reduction[2] to a simpler hortatory appeal is hard to take, though we must make allowance for the obstacles of our current taste for understatement and resistance to pious assumptions.

In *Bleak House*, Dickens at last finds a perfect voice for death. He integrates the points of view of 'character' and 'narrator', generalization and image, character and action. Jo's death-bed scene is so successful that it justifies the use of multiple affective appeal, which in *Nicholas Nickleby* and *The Old Curiosity Shop* had looked intrinsically ill-judged. Dickens is doing more than simply accumulating emotion, letting quantity stand for quality. If we look back from *Bleak House*, it seems that what he was attempting earlier, in the mythological invocation of the Fall, Heaven, angels, and Immortality – the central Christian symbols and doctrines – was not simply to set death elegiacally in the Christian context, but to achieve an act of imaginative enlargement. The individual experience is given a resonance and intensity, the reader's sympathy engaged through ritual or ritualistic appeal. In much affective writing, intensity is achieved not only through particularity, filling in the blank cheque presented by sentimentality, but also through a generalization which attaches the emotion dramatized inside the book to a broader emotional experience. Since Dickens's religious feelings were themselves unspecific and vague, the Christian myth was often a bad choice for him, but he hardly ever uses classical and other literary forms of deepening and broadening feeling. When Casaubon is facing death, for instance, death is imaged through the invocation of 'the dark river-bank' and 'the plash of the on-coming oar' (*Middlemarch*, Chapter 42). Casaubon's expectations of death are briefly set in relation to myth and poetry, given dignity and beauty. (Dickens's own use of the river and the sea is by comparison unspecific.) In *Bleak House*, however, Dickens made an imaginatively wise choice of an enlarging image, which happily replaced and made unnecessary his weak and inflated religious or religiose language. In *Bleak House* he invokes Christian faiths and consolations through the familiar and dignified language of the Lord's Prayer:

'Jo, can you say what I say?'
'I'll say anythink as you say, sir, fur I knows it's good.'
'OUR FATHER.'
'Our Father – yes, that's wery good, sir.'
'WHICH ART IN HEAVEN.'
'Art in Heaven – is the light a-comin, sir?'
'It is close at hand. HALLOWED BE THY NAME!'
'Hallowed be – thy –' (Chapter 47)

This ritual extension is assimilated, and made particular, through Jo's tersely rendered ignorance, and through his response to Woodcourt, who has guaranteed goodness in kindness. It may be significant that the words Jo responds to, 'Our Father', are those he can understand. (It is 'Mother' in Paul's vision.) Since it is men, Nemo, Snagsby, and Woodcourt, who have been good to him, Jo can be said to have experienced a kind of fatherliness. The repetition of 'Art in Heaven' is tactfully left without response, followed by doubt and question, and his repetition of 'Hallowed be thy name' broken, to register the end of speaking, but it is not the end of this passage of emotional expression, analysis, and manipulation.

Once more Dickens chooses an image as an objective correlative which registers the experience of the character. The image of the horse drawing the cart acts appropriately, complexly, and dynamically, like the device of the racing watches and the image of the river. Jo's image, like Paul's, is his own, drawn from the life of the streets and the experience of labour:

Allan Woodcourt lays his hand upon his pulse, and on his chest. 'Draw breath, Jo!' 'It draws,' says Jo, 'as heavy as a cart.' He might add, 'and rattles like it'; but he only mutters, 'I'm a-moving on, sir.'

Like the rushing river, the carthorse is an image for painful sensation, and joins with the old motif of 'moving on'. Its recurrences punctuate, emphasize, and mark a progress. When Jarndyce appears, Jo repeats his story, without significant variation: 'Only, that cart of his is heavier to draw, and draws with a hollower sound.' It recurs after he has asked Snagsby to write the letter to Woodcourt ('Jo's Will' is the title of the chapter):

For the cart so hard to draw, is near its journey's end, and drags over stony ground. All round the clock it labours up the broken steeps, shattered and worn. Not many times can the sun rise, and behold it still upon its weary road.

It appears again after Allan Woodcourt's return, 'The cart had nearly given up, but labours on a little more,' and again just before the prayer: 'The cart is shaken all to pieces, and the rugged road is very near its end.' Finally, it is subdued to the common image of the way, lending to it a local strength: 'the light is come upon the dark benighted way'.

The image is physically lucid. Like the river, it is well chosen for elaboration into a dynamic pattern, since it is an image of motion and journey. The inner life it registers is markedly different from the febrile brilliance of Paul's fancy, but it conveys the activity, effort, and pain of Jo, who may not be able to read or write but can make metaphors and symbols. The point of view which prevails in the chapter is that of the stern omniscient consciousness which takes over the image originated by Jo. Once more Dickens chooses an image which bridges outer and inner life, here first spoken by a dramatized character, then formalized and solemnized in the narrator's rhetoric.

The image of the cart and the horse registers the nature and passage of another hard dying, but is not the only means of imaging sensation and emotion. At one point Jo starts up, as he, like the earlier dying children, remembers the past. His associations with burials and graves are less quaint, calm, and pastoral than Smike's or Nell's, but he too is made to recollect love, and to associate it with the dead. Jo's wild look is not caused by fear of the 'berryin ground':

'It's time fur me to go down to that there berryin ground, sir, and ask to be put along with him. I wants to go there and be berried. He used fur to say to me, "I am as poor as you to-day, Jo," he ses. I wants to tell him that I am as poor as him now, and have come there to be laid along with him.'

It is a rich mixture, reminiscent of Smike's morbid amorousness. Here the grisly details are justified, by Jo's exposure to the disease and filth and bleakness which the novel images and narrates, but also by his love and gratitude. The hideous burying-ground is where his love is located, and in making us feel this, Dickens twists and startles our response. When Jo starts up with a wild look, it is the horror of the grave we briefly feel, but Dickens's irony insists that any place can be sanctified. Unlike the other children, Jo can have no dreams of Eden, and his dying imaginings are far from pastoral:

> 'P'raps they wouldn't do it if I were to go myself.'

and

> 'They'll have to get the key of the gate afore they can take me in, for it's allus locked. And there's a step there, as I used fur to clean with my broom.'

He cannot invoke Paradise, angels, or Heaven, but his dying is consoled by recollections and dreams.

When Jo's voice dies, the last two paragraphs release the narrator's solemn and formal appeal to the reader:

> The light is come upon the dark benighted way. Dead!
> Dead, your Majesty. Dead, my lords and gentlemen. Dead, Right Reverends and Wrong Reverends of every order. Dead, men and women, born with Heavenly compassion in your hearts. And dying thus around us every day.

Dickens does not end this death-scene with religious faith and joy, but with social anger. What religious reference there is, he places with precision and irony, as he emphasizes the natural but corruptible nature of compassion, with a characteristic assertion of his belief in original virtue, or innocence, and his knowledge of its corruptibility. The address is no longer excitedly exclamatory and pious, as in all three earlier instances, but implacable, formal and direct, like the address of a practised orator. It is the language no barrister, clergyman or politician in Dickens is allowed to speak, only the all-seeing narrator. Royalty, gentry, and clergy are appropriately picked out for special mention, but the ordinary men and women are responsible too; all estates are involved, as they are in the action of the novel. Last, the generalization is entirely successful, since it places Jo in his typicality, as a victim of social injustice. Instead of moving away, as I suggested we do after the death of Paul, we remain with Jo, since the compassion we have been made to feel for him – a mere figment in a fiction – is used to argue the commonness of his case, and the need for compassion in a real world. Out of the frame of language, we move into the larger frame of our own experience.

NOTES

1 'I never read printed words that gave me so much pain. I could not weep for some time. Sensation, sufferings have returned to me, that are terrible to awaken; it is real to me; I cannot criticise it.' *The Diaries of William Charles Macready 1833-1851*, William Toynbee (ed.) (London, 1912).

2 In the first edition, its reissues, and the cheap edition of 1858 the chapter ended with a particularized and thematic comment by Miss Tox: '"Dear me, dear me! To think," said Miss Tox, bursting out afresh that night, as if her heart were broken, "that Dombey and Son should be a daughter after all!"' Dickens's decision to drop this may be regretted but shows his anxiety about the structure and style of emotional appeal. The change was pointed out by Kathleen Tillotson, 'A Lost Sentence in *Dombey and Son*', *The Dickensian*, Vol. 47, 1951.

3

THACKERAY

Inconstant Passions

Thackeray's analysis of feeling is comic and profoundly serious. 'Pathos', he wrote, 'I hold should be very occasional indeed in humorous works and indicated rather than expressed or expressed very rarely. . . .' He goes on to give a paradigm of pathos from *Vanity Fair*, 'where Amelia is represented as trying to separate herself from the boy – She goes upstairs and leaves him with his aunt "as that poor Lady Jane Grey tried the axe that was to separate her slender life" I say that is a fine image whoever wrote it (& I came on it quite by surprise in a review the other day) that is greatly pathetic I think: it leaves you to make your own sad pictures – We shouldn't do much more than that I think in comic books – In a story written in the pathetic key it would be different & then the comedy perhaps should be occasional. Some day – but a truce to egotistical twaddle' (*The Letters and Private Papers of William Makepeace Thackeray*, Vol. 2, G.N. Ray (ed.), 1946).

Vanity Fair is a comic novel with many modulations to a pathetic key, but the earlier *Barry Lyndon*, written as an eighteenth-century pastiche, is the only work by one of the major Victorian novelists as totally comic as a novel by Fielding. Its medium is ironic, but it endows its comic hero with an emotional life, and is flexible enough to vary and complicate the record of Barry's feelings. The emotions of this autobiographical narrator are variously unreliable. Barry is a liar, a boaster, a self-flatterer and a sentimentalist, and his account makes an appeal which the reader recognizes as false, within a fiction of insincerity. Thackeray grants his hero and readers the luxury of sporadic insight into underlying emotional truths. As one of E.M. Forster's characters says in *Where Angels Fear to Tread*, 'wicked people are capable of love'. Even George Eliot, who would scarcely credit this since she saw wickedness as an incapacity for love, permits the villainous Dempster in 'Janet's Repentance', or Tito Melema in *Romola*, to participate in a kind of loving. Thackeray was much clearer about love as what Joyce calls 'the word known to all men', partly because he thought of himself and others, too, as bad – 'take the world by a certain standard . . . and who dares talk of having any virtue at all?' (*The Letters and Private Papers*, loc. cit.). His moral pattern is therefore more cross-hatched than George Eliot's. There is no virtue in Barry Lyndon, but he is endowed with some capacity for what we may call 'good' feeling. He is brilliantly shown as a master of almost all the forms of false feeling, but is allowed genuineness when he feels nostalgia, filial affection, paternal love, and hostility to war. These emotions are carefully oriented. Thackeray is intent on drawing a portrait of a villain through the subtle means of gauche confession. The autobiographer damns himself by high praise. Barry is the opposite of an artist and his emotional narration often imitates sentimental art, overreaching itself, for instance, with what Thackeray called 'mawkish' appeals to the reader. But most of the other characters are sentimentally contaminated too, finding fine words for false feeling. Barry's first love, Nora, and his rival, Quin, faintly echo the rhetorical aspirations of Richardson's Lovelace as they address each other in poetic diction learnt from novels. 'I vow before all the gods, my heart has never felt the soft flame!' Quin announces, and 'your passion is not equal to ours. We are like – like some plant I've read of – we bear but one flower and then we die!' stammers Nora (in Chapter 1). Thackeray enjoys displaying the rhetoric of predictable sentiment. Barry is allowed patches of candour, as when he admits that amorous nostalgia and remorse are sentiments beyond his experience.

Barry's first expression of intense feeling is fuelled by Thackeray's own anti-military anger and pity,[1] which is half-assimilated to character. The account of the battle of Minden begins with blunt and matter-of-fact detail, then makes a bid for pathos. Barry tells how he found in the pockets of the ensign he had killed a purse of gold and a silver *bon-bon* box, moving trifles twice repeated, and speaks of undignified recollections 'best passed over briefly'. Thackeray uses Barry's brusque callousness and sentimentality for effectively understated pathos, and follows it with Barry's outburst against war:

Such knaves and ruffians do men in war become! It is well for gentlemen to talk of the age of chivalry; but remember the starving brutes whom they lead - men nursed in poverty, entirely ignorant, made to take a pride in deeds of blood. . . . It is with these shocking instruments that your great warriors and kings have been doing their murderous work in the world; and while, for instance, we are at the present moment admiring the 'Great Frederick', as we call him, and his philosophy, and his liberality, and his military genius, I, who have served him, and been, as it were, behind the scenes of which that great spectacle is composed, can only look at it with horror. (Chapter 4)

Thackeray assimilates his own irony and compassion to the cynicism of Barry, but to do so is to make Barry momentarily a better man than he is: 'What a number of items of human crime, misery, slavery, go to form that sum-total of glory!' Thackeray ventriloquizes briefly, but at the end of this declamatory passage he returns us to the characterized stream of feeling; the experience described plausibly arouses distaste or remorse even in Barry Lyndon:

I can recollect a certain day, about three weeks after the battle of Minden, and a farmhouse in which some of us entered, and how the old woman and her daughters served us, trembling, to wine; and how we got drunk over the wine, and the house was in a flame, presently: and woe betide the wretched fellow afterwards who came home to look for his house and his children! (Chapter 4)

As Thackeray says about Amelia's rehearsal of grief, 'it leaves you to make your own . . . pictures'. Like Sterne, whom Thackeray detested but in some ways resembled, he knew the sentimental force of suggestiveness. Barry's hasty summary of rape and murder is perfectly in character, and perfectly serves the author's passionate sense of military waste and horror. This passion is scarcely central to Barry's character, but successfully accommodated to it. It perhaps does not quite fit Barry's report of his pleasure and profit in plunder, but he is made to write about various stages of recollected emotion. His character is destabilized by rôle-playing and dishonesty, and his contradictions and inconsistencies are used by Thackeray to express emotions discretely and discontinuously. But the assimilations are skilful. For instance, two chapters after the description of the battle of Minden, Barry speaks of having formed himself 'to the condition of the proper fighting beast: on a day of action I was savage and happy; out of the field I took all the pleasure I could get, and was by no means delicate as to its quality or the manner of procuring it'. Barry's discrimination of 'the proper fighting beast' is closer to Thackeray, in its irony, than to Barry, who is not usually 'delicate' even off the battlefield. We may try to make the passage 'realistic', by allowing for the protean attitudes of an unstable personality; or by seeing Barry's point of view as maturing in judgement. But there is an underlying difficulty in having Barry grow finer feelings with age, since in all other respects he appears to deteriorate in emotional scruple. He certainly gives us no clue (as Jane Eyre does) to his emotional 'development', and it seems that Thackeray, always peremptory in discounting order and convention, is cleverly creating a character of exceptional fragmentation, not to be judged by standards of realism.

Barry's erratic narrative is a vehicle Thackeray repeats from novel to novel, like the emotion of nostalgia. Some forms of nostalgia are in no way out of keeping with Barry's obtuse sensibility, and are entirely compatible with his facile and sentimental affections. Patriotism, filial love, and nostalgia are comically combined: 'I had not seen the dear soul's writing for five years,' he gushes over his mother's letter, which 'created in my mind a yearning after home, a melancholy which I cannot describe' (Chapter 7). He even gives up an engagement with Fraülein Lottchen, to pass 'a long night weeping and thinking about dear Ireland'. His tears are easily shed, and the combination of stimulants is irresistible: 'All the old days, and the fresh happy sunshine of the old green fields in Ireland, and her love, and my uncle . . . and everything that I had done and thought, came back to me.' Thackeray carefully places this sentimental outburst. The mother is replying to a diplomatic letter which Barry has designed to be read, to his own advantage, by his captain, and the night of weeping and thinking about 'dear Ireland' is followed by the next day's recovery: 'my spirits rose again, and I got a ten guinea bill cashed'.

On another occasion, Barry's sentimentality is not criticized by Thackeray, but used for the double purpose of expressing congenial feeling, while effectively enlarging character. Barry shows the emotions of nostalgia and parental love, for instance, like Dobbin and Henry Esmond, in whom they are sympathetic and benign feelings, though not untouched by Thackeray's caustic irony. Here is a delicate moment of inner experience, showing the gross and vicious anti-hero overwhelmed by involuntary memory. He is not a monster, but remembers, and anticipates remembering again, with affection, chagrin, and fear:

As for Castle Brady, the gates of the park were still there; but the old trees were cut down in the avenue, a black stump jutting out here and there, and casting long shadows as I passed in the moonlight over the worn, grass-grown old road. A few cows were at pasture there. The garden-gate was gone, and the place a tangled wilderness. I sat down on the old bench, where I had sat on the day when Nora jilted me; and I do believe my feelings were as strong then as they had been when I was a boy, eleven years before; and I caught myself almost crying again, to think that Nora Brady had deserted me. I believe a man forgets nothing. I've seen a flower, or heard some trivial word or two, which have awakened recollections that somehow had lain dormant for scores of years; and when I entered the house in Clarges Street, where I was born (it was used as a gambling-house when I first visited London), all of a sudden the memory of my childhood came back to me – of my actual infancy: I recollected my father in green and gold, holding me up to look at a gilt coach which stood at the door, and my mother in a flowered sack, with patches on her face. Some day, I wonder, will everything we have seen and thought and done come and flash across our minds in this way? I had rather not. I felt so as I sat upon the bench at Castle Brady, and thought of the bygone times. (Chapter 14)

Emotion is particularized in this charged descriptive set-piece, through the sacred objects and landscape of past youth. The moment is enlarged and dignified by generalization, in the observation about revived emotion, the suggestion that recurs in *Henry Esmond*, 'I believe a man forgets nothing', and the comment on involuntary memory. The passage repeats one of Barry's pet adjectives, 'old', later recalled by the attentive reader when Barry tells about his wanton and mercenary timber-felling. His sensitivity to place and nature is an easy encapsulation of nostalgia, making no demands. The significant details of the gambling-house, the finery, and the gilt coach, make their own terse contribution to an impression of Barry's nurture. The passage contains one of the deepest intimations of Barry's lower depths in that grim reserve about a final total recall he would 'rather not' experience. 'I had rather not' is Thackerayan in its wry candour, but assimilated to Barry's remorse, which flickers briefly as it dies. When Barry recounts the death of his son, in Chapter 19, the sorrow is not presented as excessive, feeble, or false. It is quietly but firmly marked by the characteristic pathetic adjectives 'poor', 'dear', and 'little' – 'My poor, dear little boy' and 'There he lay in his little boots and spurs'. 'I could only burst out into tears' is followed by a characteristic motion of the egocentric narration. He tells the moving, self-congratulatory story of the little drummer-boy he was 'fond of', to whom he ran to give water. As to remorse, he has boasted before of not feeling it. His son was killed because Barry bought him a dangerous horse and lay in a drunken sleep when the child went off to ride, hoping his 'fond father' would remit the threatened horse-whipping. The death-bed scene is brilliantly controlled. Barry's feelings are never complicated by the pangs of guilt, only by those of self-pity, 'Who cares for Barry Lyndon now?' and 'what soul is there alive that cares for Barry Lyndon?' (Chapter 14):

> During this time the dear angel's temper seemed quite to change: he asked his mother and me pardon for any act of disobedience he had been guilty of towards us; he said often he should like to see his brother Bullingdon. 'Bully was better than you, Papa,' he said; 'he used not to swear so, and he told and taught me many good things while you were away.' And, taking a hand of his mother and mine in each of his little clammy ones, he begged us not to quarrel so, but love each other, so that we might meet again in heaven, where Bully told him quarrelsome people never went. His mother was very much affected by these admonitions from the poor suffering angel's mouth; and I was so too. I wish she had enabled me to keep the counsel which the dying boy gave us.
>
> At last, after two days, he died. There he lay, the hope of my family, the pride of my manhood, the link which had kept me and my Lady Lyndon together. 'Oh, Redmond,' said she, kneeling by the sweet child's body, 'do, do let us listen to the truth out of his blessed mouth; and do you amend your life, and treat your poor, loving fond wife as her dying child bade you.' And I said I would: but there are promises which it is out of a man's power to keep; especially with such a woman as her. But we drew together after that sad event, and were for several months better friends. (Chapter 19)

The few traces of easy pity, 'dear angel' and 'poor suffering angel', pass almost without notice, as Barry's narration nearly rises to the occasion. (They are contaminated by many less discriminating uses.) The voice is solemn and restrained, but also egocentric and accusatory. Such episodes of feeling complete the picture of Barry's viciousness by adding to his falsities those of the sentimentalist, resilient, indulgent, more moved by past than present. Barry stands out amongst the emotional characters in Victorian fiction as a subtle study of weak and facile self-protection.

Thackeray is the Victorian novelist closest to Flaubert in being alive to the dangers of sentimentality. The cruelties and unrealities of the sentimentalist form a major theme in *Vanity Fair*. Amelia is introduced as the conventional heroine whose sweetness is dismissed as 'twaddle' by the imaginary reader Jones, and affectionately defended, for the moment, by the narrator, but her character is developed as a blend of idolatry and nostalgia. Amelia's love for George Osborne is unreal and inactive, composed of the response to a social stereotype of masculine charm:

> This young person (perhaps it was very imprudent in her parents to encourage her, and abet her in such idolatry and silly romantic ideas) loved, with all her heart, the young officer. . . . She had never seen a man so beautiful or so clever: such a figure on horseback: such a dancer: such a hero in general. (Chapter 12)

This is cleverly called 'Quite a Sentimental Chapter', the qualification clear in text as in title. The social typology at work in Amelia's feeling is composed of images of looks and motion, and underlined by comparisons with the Prince Regent and Beau Brummell. The only response which is not a physical one, 'so clever', is wrong, though understandable, given her education and knowledge. The judgement ('silly' and 'romantic') is endorsed by the banalities and raptures of the visions. Thackeray's preacher observes that such love 'is in the nature and instinct of some women', but this regrettably unironic remark is not supported by the particular case. Thackeray can express strong feelings as he sees through them. For instance, he uses comic hyperboles which are teasing and sympathetic:

> The fate of Europe was Lieutenant George Osborne to her. His dangers being over, she sang Te Deum. He was her Europe: her emperor: her allied monarchs and august prince regent. He was her sun and moon. . . . (Chapter 12)

The political scale of these comic grandiosities economically marks the limits of love and knowledge. Like Barry Lyndon, Amelia has no self-awareness. Like him, too, she finds it easier to feel for the past than the present.

After George's death, her feeling for him is replaced by an equally blind and selfish mother-love, sharply criticized for its self-indulgence. Amelia's strong feelings are contrasted with those of

Becky Sharp, whose pretensions to wifely devotion and mother-love are also criticized. The narrator of *Vanity Fair* criticizes everyone, including himself, for vain feeling. But Becky is compared, as well as contrasted, with Amelia, to expose the superficialities and selfishness of Amelia's affections. Thackeray shows very clearly that a self-congratulatory and sacrificial love can be cruel as it pampers the beloved and neglects the unloved. Amelia's parental doting has much in common with Barry Lyndon's. Her capacity for change is small but importantly present. One of the people used and discarded by her is Dobbin, whose decision to give up the patient suffering of romantic love comes as a relief and a release for character and reader. Thackeray exposes Amelia's lack of generosity and perceptiveness in a fine scene of love-reversal:

'Have I not learned in that time to read all your feelings, and look into your thoughts? I know what your heart is capable of: it can cling faithfully to a recollection, and cherish a fancy; but it can't feel such an attachment as mine deserves to mate with, and such as I would have won from a woman more generous than you. No, you are not worthy of the love which I have devoted to you. I knew all along that the prize I had set my life on was not worth the winning; that I was a fool, with fond fancies, too, bartering away my all of truth and ardour against your little feeble remnant of love. I will bargain no more: I withdraw. I find no fault with you. You are very good-natured, and have done your best; but you couldn't – you couldn't reach up to the height of the attachment which I bore you, and which a loftier soul than yours might have been proud to share. Good-bye, Amelia! I have watched your struggle. Let it end. We are both weary of it.'

Amelia stood scared and silent as William thus suddenly broke the chain by which she held him, and declared his independence and superiority. He had placed himself at her feet so long that the poor little woman had been accustomed to trample upon him. She didn't wish to marry him, but she wished to keep him. She wished to give him nothing, but that he should give her all. It is a bargain not unfrequently levied in love.

William's sally had quite broken and cast her down. *Her* assault was long since over and beaten back.

'Am I to understand then, – that you are going – away, – William?' she said.

He gave a sad laugh. 'I went once before,' he said, 'and came back after twelve years. We were young, then, Amelia. Good-bye. I have spent enough of my life at this play.' (Chapter 66)

Dobbin himself is criticized, in his turn, for his idolatries. He penetrates the nature of Amelia's illusions and indulgences, but turns from woman-worshipping to worshipping another idol, his child. All emotions are contaminated in *Vanity Fair*. The narrator's uncomfortable irony, not unrelieved by humour and sympathy, puts Amelia in her place.

> 'It was time you sent for me, dear Amelia,' he said.
> 'You will never go again, William?'
> 'No, never,' he answered: and pressed the dear little soul once more to his heart.
> As they issued out of the Custom-house precincts, Georgy broke out on them, with his telescope up to his eye, and a loud laugh of welcome; he danced round the couple, and performed many facetious antics as he led them up to the house. Jos wasn't up yet; Becky not visible (though she looked at them through the blinds). Georgy ran off to see about breakfast. Emmy, whose shawl and bonnet were off in the passage in the hands of Miss Payne, now went to undo the clasp of William's cloak, and - we will, if you please, go with George and look after breakfast for the Colonel. The vessel is in port. He has got the prize he has been trying for all his life. The bird has come in at last. There it is with its head on his shoulder, billing and cooing close up to his heart, with soft outstretched fluttering wings. This is what he has asked for every day and hour for eighteen years. This is what he pined after. Here it is - the summit, the end - the last page of the third volume. Goodbye, Colonel. God bless you, honest William! Farewell, dear Amelia. Grow green again, tender little parasite, round the rugged old oak to which you cling! (Chapter 67)

The feelings of the reader are also put in their place; they are first amused by the narrator's wit and irony, then implicated in unreality, as the ending of the lovers' story is cleverly assimilated to the ending of the novel, declaring fictionality and mocking expectation. What is deluded but tolerated in the sentiments of Amelia and Dobbin is matched by our indulged sense of a happy ending. Thackeray says we have got to the last page before we actually do, cunningly displacing even further our newest expectations; when we really get to the last page of the third volume, Dobbin is implicated in new unreal emotions. In a neat stroke Thackeray praises him for not loving Amelia too much, and for perceiving the limits of her feeling, and implicates him in a parental idolatry of his 'little Janey', of whom 'he is fonder than of anything in the world'. The refusal to make a tidy and moral ending compares the reality principle in the character with the reality principle in the novelist, and the reader. Thackeray distrusts closure and completion and likes to disconcert us when we expect solace. Here and in the teasingly reflexive ending of *The Newcomes* there is a final admission of fictionality. The characters in *Vanity Fair* are not only in love with vanities, but are mere puppets, as we expect in Vanity Fair. We have been criticizing idolatry, while caring about fictional images.

At the end of *The Newcomes*, Pendennis, Laura, Ethel and Clive 'fade away into fable-land'. The narrator observes of his characters: 'They were alive, and I heard their voices; but five minutes since was touched by their grief. And have we parted with them here on a sudden, and without as much as a shake of the hand?' Arthur Pendennis is dismissed before he can tell if Ethel has married, without answering the reader's 'sentimental question'. Thackeray raises at the ending the question of that oddity, the author's and reader's feeling for fictions. Though the tone is teasing, it is also melancholy, as the illusion of reality shrinks into the admission of art. It shrinks too in *Vanity Fair*, where there is a double sadness, that of the character diminished to puppet, and that of the reader, invited to share the realization of vanity:

> . . . Which of us is happy in this world? Which of us has his desire? or, having it, is satisfied? – Come children, let us shut up the box and the puppets, for our play is played out. (Chapter 67)

The awareness of the fiction plays its part within the emotional drama of the characters in *Pendennis*. Pen's amorous nights are marked by sound sleep, but the passions of Anxiety and Love are introduced, through the narrator's experience, in laconic and grave personifications:

> Even in later days and with a great deal of care and other thoughtful matter to keep him awake, a man from long practice or fatigue or resolution *begins* by going to sleep as usual, and gets a nap in advance of Anxiety. But she soon comes up with him and jogs his shoulder, and says, 'Come, my man, no more of this laziness, you must wake up and have a talk with me.' Then they fall to together in the midnight. Well, whatever might afterwards happen to him, poor little Pen was not come to this state yet; he tumbled into a sound sleep – did not wake until an early hour in the morning, when the rooks began to caw from the little wood beyond his bedroom windows; and – at that very instant and as his eyes started open, the beloved image was in his mind. 'My dear boy,' he heard her say, 'you were in a sound sleep, and I would not disturb you: but I have been close by your pillow all this while: and I don't intend that you shall leave me. I am Love! I bring with me fever

and passion: wild longing, maddening desire; restless craving and seeking.
Many a long day ere this I heard you calling out for me; and behold now I
am come.'
    Was Pen frightened at the summons? Not he. He did not know what was
coming: it was all wild pleasure and delight as yet. (Chapter 4)

Like the hyperbolic figures placing Amelia's passion, this is a fusion of
traditional intensification with irony. Pen's image of the beloved fuses
with the personification – 'many a long day ere this I heard you calling'
– to denote his love of Love as well as his delighted obsession. Irony is
explicit, 'There was no mistake about it now. He was as much in love as
the best hero in the best romance he ever read', which insists on the
flattery of our passions, and on their stereotypes, but the 'wild pleasure
and delight' are powerfully presented. Thackeray also uses scenes and
images as Dickens does, creating a symbolism for feeling to which the
characters are indifferent: 'The blue waters came rolling into the bay,
foaming and roaring hoarsely: Pen looked them in the face with blank
eyes, hardly regarding them. What a tide there was pouring into the
lad's own mind . . .' (Chapter 5). The comic medium is here also a
sympathetic one, as the narrator approaches his character, then turns
away a little to comment with the voice of worldly, but not cynical,
wisdom. Thackeray does not ridicule or pity his characters, but holds
ridicule and pity in a controlled suspension. Like the personification of
Love, the image of the tide is intense and relaxed; Thackeray reverses
Paul Dombey's appropriation of the metaphor of the waves, and shows
the oddity of a character passionately ignoring the symbol created to
express his passion. In the shift from the scene to the metaphor – 'What
a tide there was!' – there is both affectionate intimacy and the assertion
of fictional distance.
    In *Pendennis* Thackeray pursues the inquiry into passionate sincerity
which he began in *Barry Lyndon*. Pen and Blanche Amory (his second
love) play at loving, as their narrator observes. Pen, like a flimsier
Julien Sorel, acts himself into an approach to emotional reality, to be
rejected by Blanche. When Pen makes her an offer of marriage without
wealth, she gracefully simulates regret and self-pity. She puts on a
similar performance for the benefit of another lover, Foker, in which
her rounded periods, designed exclamations and falling cadences are
contrasted with Foker's broken sincerities. After this, she and Pen have
their last dialogue. She calmly takes him to task for having never cared
for her, and explains her own incapacity for genuine feeling, '*Et moi, c'est*

différent. I have been spoilt early. . . . If I cannot have emotions, I must have the world. You would offer me neither one nor the other'; when he comments on her *ennui*, she answers, '*Eh! Il me faut des émotions.*' (They both use French for elegant evasion and pose.) The narrator concludes:

> Pen had never seen her or known so much about her in all the years of their
> intimacy as he saw and knew now: though he saw more than existed in
> reality. For this young lady was not able to carry out any emotion to the full;
> but had a sham enthusiasm, a sham hatred, a sham love, a sham taste, a
> sham grief, each of which flared and shone very vehemently for an instant,
> but subsided and gave place to the next sham emotion. (Chapter 73)

Thackeray's problem is how to follow this, formally and psychologically, with Pen's final union with Laura. He begins with a preliminary understatement, just right as a contrast with false feeling and false speaking, in which the narrator shows Laura's pale face as Pen opens the door, asks, 'May we follow him?', and rises to a balanced and solemn generalization:

> The great moments of life are but moments like the others. Your doom is
> spoken in a word or two. A single look from the eyes; a mere pressure of the
> hand, may decide it; or of the lips, though they cannot speak. (Chapter 74)

There is an abrupt cut to a later moment, when narrator and reader are allowed to 'enter with her ladyship' to discover the lovers in a happy attitude; then the narrator swerves back to tell us what was omitted, to present, 'In a word', Pen's brief proposal, and Laura's speechless reply. It is an arch device, making and breaking a promise of restraint, tiptoeing round the almost inarticulate lovers. Later in the scene Thackeray refuses to simplify, showing Pen's implicit apology for the 'transaction' with Blanche, and reminding us of Laura's serious feeling for Warrington, her Bluebeard. Strong lines about Pen's awe 'in the contemplation of her sweet goodness and purity', are qualified, relieved, and particularized by the narrator's speculative, 'And she – very likely she was thinking, "How strange it is that I should ever have cared for another; I am vexed almost to think that I care for him so little, am so little sorry that he is gone away".' Laura's rapturous speech shows Thackeray's capacity for exaggerating sentiment without ironic comment:

I care about nothing but Arthur; my waking and sleeping thoughts are about him; he is never absent from me. And to think that he is to be mine, mine! and that I am to marry him, and not to be his servant as I expected to be only this morning; for I would have gone down on my knees to Blanche to beg her to let me live with him. And now – Oh, it is too much.

The language of feeling is placed, but not ridiculed.

Thackeray's greatest love story is *Henry Esmond*, a novel marked by the ruling passion of 'cut-throat melancholy' in which as in *Pendennis*, Thackeray unbosomed himself of his love for Jane Brookfield, but more passionately. His letters to Jane, after what seems to have been an admission of affection, express the irony, stoicism, restraint and affection which colour *Esmond*:

A change, a fine air, a wonderful sunshine and moonlight, and a great spectacle of happy people perpetually rolling by has done me all the good in the world and then one of the Miss Smiths told me a story which is the very thing for the beginning of Pendennis, which is actually begun and in progress – This is a comical beginning rather; the other, which I did not like, was sentimental; and will yet come in very well after the startling comical business has been played off. – See how beautifully I have put stops to the last sentence; and crossed the i's and dotted the t's! It was written 4 hours ago before dinner; before Jullien's concert, before a walk by the sea shore – I have been thinking what a number of ladies, and gentlemen too, live like you just now – in a smart papered room with rats gnawing behind the Wainscot. Be hanged to the rats! but they are a sort of company. You must have a poker ready, and if the rats come out, bang, beat them on the head. This is an allegory. Why, it would work up into a little moral poem, if you chose to write it. . . . I thought I would like to say good night to you. (*Letters and Private Papers*, op. cit., Vol. 2)

The first-person retrospect offered by the novel is a private memorial, a fantasy of unacted possibilities, and perhaps a melancholy message, like the letters. Nostalgia was one of Thackeray's favourite emotions, and the melancholy which is so strong in the remembrance of things past in *Henry Esmond* is not just a lament for Jane Brookfield. It marks a melancholy close to the sadness of those vanities in *Vanity Fair*, and here continues the theme of idolatry, dealing with it from the viewpoint of a latter-day Don Quixote, a man searching for name, title, legitimacy and identity. The use of the first-person pronoun is charged with emotional significance. The novel is melancholy but its passions are complex. It dramatizes and analyses a man's love for two women, with a remarkable imaginative coherence. The retrospective analysis of feeling in *Jane Eyre* and *David Copperfield* contrasts innocence with mature hindsight; in *Esmond* Thackeray deals with the complex experience of reviving past passion in memory. One of its dominant themes is the disturbed recollection of emotion, expressed in forms coloured by the narrator's experience, as dramatic utterance and knowledge.

Unlike *Vanity Fair*, *Esmond* no longer represents emotional constancy as sentimental, withdrawn, or unreal. Nostalgia is characterized through Esmond's retrospective narrations of love and grief. The introductory memoir by Esmond's daughter Rachel makes it clear that neither the physical deterioration of Beatrix Castlewood, referred to by her niece as 'our other relative, Bishop Tusher's lady', and presented through the compounded jealousies of daughter and mother, nor Esmond's love for his wife, have dispelled past feelings: 'papa said – "All women were alike; that there was never one so beautiful as that one; and that we could forgive her everything but her beauty".'

The narrative is appropriately fragmented in several ways. Emotions are variably expressed as they are recollected in variable moods. For instance, Esmond narrates the discovery of Beatrix's intrigue with the Pretender jealously and angrily. He reports the porter's story of the Prince's kisses, in the severity of third-person form:

> Esmond darkly thought, how Hamilton, Ashburnham, had before been masters of those roses that the young Prince's lips were now feeding on. He sickened at that notion. Her cheek was desecrated, her beauty tarnished; shame and honour stood between it and him. The love was dead within him. . . . (Book 3, Chapter 13)

The narration continues to show anger and jealousy, so contradicting the flat statement 'The love was dead'. It recalls Esmond's sense of her treachery and his wasted time, 'it was to win this that he had given a life's struggle and devotion', testifying to the animation of his feelings. These are not static, but fluctuate; his anger disappears as the Prince offers the reparation of crossing swords and puts honour before love, (rather belatedly) to touch Esmond 'by this immense mark of condescension and repentance'. A little later, when Beatrix glares at Esmond, looking 'quite old', and hisses, 'If I did not love you before,

cousin . . . think how I love you now', in words which would have
killed if they could, there is another assertion of the dead love:

> But her keen words gave no wound to Mr Esmond; his heart was too hard.
> As he looked at her, he wondered that he could ever have loved her. His love
> of ten years was over; it fell down dead on the spot. (Ibid.)

Esmond's repeated announcements of the death of love show love's
resilience. There is a shift from the third to the first person, two
sentences later, 'I have never seen her from that day', and soon
afterwards one more valediction, 'the drama of my own life was
ended'. Esmond moves into the oblique and reticent narration of his
second love and marriage:

> As I think of the immense happiness which was in store for me, and of the
> depth and intensity of that love which, for so many years, hath blessed me, I
> own to a transport of wonder and gratitude for such a boon.

The language is rapturous, pious, and exalted:

> In the name of my wife I write the completion of hope, and the summit of
> happiness. To have such a love is the one blessing, in comparison of which all
> earthly joy is of no value; and to think of her, is to praise God. (Ibid.)

This praises a love which is more than profane love, and not for the first
time. On earlier occasions he has clearly compared its sacred flame
with his passion for Beatrix. He tells Rachel, for instance, that his
fidelity to Beatrix 'is folly, perhaps' and that she herself 'is a thousand
times better: the fondest, the fairest, the dearest of women'. But he also
tells her, 'I cannot help myself. I love her.' Under the running title,
'Fidelity in Love', he meditates on the strangeness of fidelity, and the
irrelevance of the beloved's faults. When the narrator reports emotion,
he reports transience and momentariness. When he meditates on
recollection he insists, like Barry Lyndon, on the way memory keeps
faith, 'We forget nothing. The memory sleeps, but wakens again'
(Book 3, Chapter 7), and asserts:

> Years after this passion hath been dead and buried, along with a thousand
> other worldly cares and ambitions, he who felt it can recall it out of its grave,
> and admire, almost as fondly as he did in his youth, that lovely queenly

creature. I invoke that beautiful spirit from the shades and love her still; or
rather I should say such a past is always present to a man; such a passion
once felt forms a part of his whole being, and cannot be separated from it.
(Book 3, Chapter 6)

His love is imprinted, like the scar from his Blenheim wound, and
returns in celebrations and pains:

> It seemed to Esmond as if he lived years in that prison: and was changed and
> aged when he came out of it. At certain periods of life we live years of
> emotion in a few weeks – and look back on those times, as on great gaps
> between the old life and the new. You do not know how much you suffer in
> those critical maladies of the heart, until the disease is over and you look
> back on it afterwards. During the time, the suffering is at least sufferable.
> The day passes in more or less of pain, and the night wears away somehow.
> 'Tis only in after days that we see what the danger has been – as a man out a-
> hunting or riding for his life looks at a leap, and wonders how he should have
> survived the taking of it. O dark months of grief and rage! of wrong and
> cruel endurance! He is old now who recalls you. Long ago he has forgiven
> and blest the soft hand that wounded him: but the mark is there, and the
> wound is cicatrized only – no time, tears, caresses, or repentance can
> obliterate the scar. We are indocile to put up with grief, however. *Reficimus
> rates quassas*: we tempt the ocean again and again, and try upon new
> ventures. Esmond thought of his early time as a noviciate, and of this past
> trial as an initiation before entering into life – as our young Indians undergo
> tortures silently before they pass to the rank of warriors in the tribe. (Book 2,
> Chapter 1)

Though the novel coherently joins the two kinds of loving, profane
and sacred, the insistence on the inexorable recall of feeling, especially
in a story offered neither as a fiction nor a private history but a family
memoir, may seem strange. John Sutherland's analysis of deletions or
slips in the manuscript of the novel (*Thackeray at Work*, 1974) has made
it plain that Thackeray originally intended to make Esmond's 'boyish
adoration' for Rachel a 'harmless childish flame' which passes away,
and to replace it in proper sequence with the mature man's passion for
Beatrix (originally a Dantean 'Beatrice'). Revising and improvising as
he wrote, Thackeray found the name Rachel for her mother
(originally 'Dolly'), to 'keep alive the expectation of the ending by its
faint biblical allusion to the long deferred marriage of Jacob and
Rachel'. Sutherland shows how, 'by deliberate haziness, he manages
to imply that Esmond is deeply in love with both at once', in what 'is

not a case of oscillation so much as emotional ambiguity'. The novelist's creative disinclination to make radical revision produced an ambiguity which, according to Sutherland, 'enriched his novel with what he and most of his readers have felt to be his finest moments'.

These 'finest moments' create a tension between past and present passion, a refusal to simplify and separate acts of loving. Esmond has felt the goddess-like beauty of Rachel, his *dea certe*, from the beginning, and after her husband's death he proposes marriage, praising her as a boon and a blessing. His two loves continue for a while, their co-existence clarified and licensed by the distinction between sacred and profane. By refusing to be a story of emotional sequence, the novel breaks linear form to unfold the contradictions, tensions and fractures of emotion and emotional memory. Sutherland rightly singles out the scene in which Esmond sees Beatrix descending the great staircase:

> Esmond had left a child and found a woman, grown beyond the common height; and arrived at such a dazzling completeness of beauty, that his eyes might well show surprise and delight at beholding her. . . . As he thinks of her, he who writes feels young again, and remembers a paragon. (Book 2, Chapter 7)
>
> And so it is – a pair of bright eyes with a dozen glances suffice to subdue a man; to enslave him, and inflame him; to make him even forget; they dazzle him so that the past becomes straightway dim to him; and he so prizes them that he would give all his life to possess 'em. (Ibid.)

The ungainly third-person form, 'he who writes', comes into its own to make a precise and scrupulous admission of remembered and revived adoration. This time he remembers with delight, not pain. The recollection is clearly recognized as an act of loving praise. The narration of love's death was provisional, the product of a mood. There are no simple developments in *Esmond*, but a constant and complex return. This narrative evocation of past as present creates a new and sophisticated mode of representing memory; it breaks down the sense of a fixed actuality of action. The retrospect recalls the past differently in different moods, adopting for the purposes of narrative form what is a familiar experience outside fiction.

The representation of Esmond's feeling for Rachel is also productively equivocal in form:

His mistress, from whom he had been a year separated, was his dearest mistress again. The family from which he had been parted, and which he loved with the fondest devotion, was his family once more. If Beatrix's beauty shone upon him, it was with a friendly lustre, and he could regard it with much such a delight as he brought away after seeing the beautiful pictures of the smiling Madonnas in the convent at Cadiz, when he was despatched thither with a flag; and as for his mistress, 'twas difficult to say with what a feeling he regarded her. 'Twas happiness to have seen her; 'twas no great pang to part; a filial tenderness, a love that was at once respect and protection, filled his mind as he thought of her; and near her or far from her, and from that day until now, and from now till death is past, and beyond it, he prays that sacred flame may ever burn. (Book 2, Chapter 8)

The passionate adoration, desire, jealousy, anger, and regret which compose Esmond's love for Beatrix are narrated with passionate precision, but the feeling for Rachel is presented more obliquely, with cunning evasiveness. Here, for instance, is one of many ambiguous uses of 'mistress', and the topos of inexpressibility is convenient indeed, ''twas difficult to say'. The emotion is strong but tranquil – ''Twas happiness', ''twas no great pang'. It is called filial, but the filial feeling is placed in the past, 'as he thought of her'. The last sentence is true to the final feeling, with a suggestive but non-committal echo of the marriage vow, 'till death is past'. The reader is told a truth, to be fully discovered only on re-reading. The feelings in the past are recalled fluidly, and those imputed to the present shown vaguely, not to tell the whole truth, but still to tell a truth; past and present pivot on that semicolon in the last sentence. Thackeray's disordering of feeling is a brilliant, intuitive discovery, disturbing simplicities and sequences of psychological and artistic expectation.[2]

NOTES

1 Thackeray's essay, 'Meditations at Versailles', in his *Paris Sketch Book* (London, 1840), is one of his many explicit condemnations of war.

2 For a different judgement, see George Levine, *The Realistic Imagination: English Fiction from Frankenstein to Lady Chatterley* (Chicago and London, 1981). Levine rightly argues that Thackeray shows Pendennis as emotionally shallow, but is less convincing when he accuses him of evading emotional norms through retrospective narration and

multiple form. This is to ignore Thackeray's insistence that retrospect is affective, and to simplify the complex medium of irony and sympathy. Levine does not examine *Henry Esmond*, where the form is concentrated, and the analysis of affective memory prominent.

4

EMILY AND CHARLOTTE BRONTË

Morality and Passion

Emily Brontë's *Wuthering Heights* is often coupled with the novels of Charlotte Brontë, but though it resembles them in representing passionate conflict it is essentially different. Charlotte Brontë's novels analyse and moralize, like those of Dickens, Thackeray and George Eliot. Emily Brontë is a lyrical novelist, and *Wuthering Heights* as purely lyrical as a long novel can be, achieving an intensity and condensation of passion which is no mere outpouring but reflects subversively the restrictions of emotional behaviour and language.

Dickens exaggerates and generalizes; Emily Brontë focuses and substantiates the passions. His affective form is erratic, hers brings feeling close, yet holds it at a necessary distance. When we think of *Wuthering Heights*, we remember its moments of strong feeling: Catherine's declaration of her love for Heathcliff, 'I *am* Heathcliff', her distinction between her affection for Edgar Linton, like 'the foliage in the woods', and her feeling for Heathcliff, like 'the eternal rocks', her dream of misery in heaven and delighted reunion with earth. We remember the second Catherine's ideals of heaven and happiness, which echo her mother's harsher vitality, and show up Linton's relaxed visions. We remember Lockwood's panic and Heathcliff's possession by joy and compulsion by terror. We remember forebodings and fears at the end, succeeded but not cancelled by Lockwood's hopeful elegy.

Emily Brontë endows most of her characters, even the feeble frames of Linton and Lockwood, with strong feelings. Passion is no guarantee of moral strength, as it tends to be in Jane Austen and George Eliot. Emily Brontë anticipates Lawrence's break with the old, stable, moral ego he thought typical of nineteenth-century fiction. Her presentation of character does not depend on the moral taxonomy of other Victorian novelists of passion who work to a rational scheme which socializes, controls and limits lyrical intensities. The lyrical moments in *Wuthering Heights* have a curious and unusual relation to the novel's action: the flow of feeling is often separated from the flow of events and follows a separate course. Heathcliff, for instance, leaves Wuthering Heights when he overhears Catherine say, 'It would degrade me to marry Heathcliff, now', but though the declaration of her love is kept from him, he assumes its existence and quality on his return. The impact of passion on action has been weaker than we expected. Nor are the loves of Heathcliff and Catherine subject to change or development. Some of the strongest moments of passion are quite cut off from the action, like the heartbreak and joy of Catherine's dream told 'to explain' feeling, but going beyond the explanation of love to express a defiance of God and a joyous naturalism:

'I was only going to say that heaven did not seem to be my home; and I broke my heart with weeping to come back to earth; and the angels were so angry that they flung me out, into the middle of the heath on the top of Wuthering Heights; where I woke sobbing for joy. That will do to explain my secret, as well as the other. I've no more business to marry Edgar Linton than I have to be in heaven; and if the wicked man in there had not brought Heathcliff so low, I shouldn't have thought of it. It would degrade me to marry Heathcliff, now; so he shall never know how I love him; and that, not because he's handsome, Nelly, but because he's more myself than I am. Whatever our souls are made of, his and mine are the same, and Linton's is as different as a moonbeam from lightning, or frost from fire.' (Vol. 1, Chapter 9)

She tells this dream after Nelly Dean has refused to let her tell 'the other' dream which she says has changed and pervaded her 'like wine through water', and Nelly's refusal to listen turns the attempt into an alarming silence.

The gap in Heathcliff's history, like the mystery of his origin, encourages but checks speculation, opening cracks and crannies through which possibilities darkly glimmer. Critical attempts to read into the novel the very kind of rational background and explanation which the novelist leaves out offer explanations more obscure than the problems they try to solve - like Q.D. Leavis's proposal that Heathcliff is a bastard[1] - and show an insensitivity to the form and feeling of this lyrical novel. Unlike the copiously historicized plots of other Victorian novels, the action of *Wuthering Heights* depends on heightened and isolated moments, surrounded by silences and omissions.

The dreams of Catherine and Lockwood are not plot-devices in a thrilling story, but retarding images absorbing the reader in moments of contemplation. The passions of revenge, desperate love, and terror, are coloured and defined as individual experience, but not made morally illustrative. We see Earnshaw's 'wicked' revenge against Heathcliff, his jealous degradation of the foundling adopted by his father. Then we see Heathcliff's counter-revenge, as he takes Earnshaw's son, Hareton, and systematically deprives him of cultivation and education. We see the nature of desperate love, in Catherine and Heathcliff, who seem to Nelly to be 'of a different species', and which, as Charlotte Brontë insisted, is not a sympathetic emotion, but extreme in violence and ruthlessness. When Catherine makes the declaration of a love which annihilates identity, 'I *am* Heathcliff', she declares that his constant presence in her mind is not a source of pleasure, and later warns Isabella not to romanticize his cruelty. Affinity and need have seldom been so passionately but purely presented, without a bid for admiration. Expressive gesture or such situations as Heathcliff spending the night motionless as he waits for Catherine's death, or Catherine, Ophelia-like, plucking out the feathers from her pillow as she wills her death, are extreme images presented without explanation and analysis.

But as *Wuthering Heights* individualizes fantasy and passion, it makes some attempt to reflect on them. Catherine tries to describe honestly and empirically the nature of her feeling for two men. She is not wild, abandoned, and wilful, but rational. Her reason works vigorously, without education, though it is bewildered and defeated. Nelly Dean is an ordinary and conventional woman who is shocked by the imaginativeness and amorality of Catherine's attitudes to love and marriage. While we understand her dissent and disapproval, we see an unimaginative and moral person failing to comprehend an original and subversive one. As so often in this novel, we are made to feel the difficulties of judging and sympathizing. Nelly is forced to hear a candid and extraordinary account of loving:

'My great miseries in this world have been Heathcliff's miseries, and I watched and felt each from the beginning; my great thought in living is himself. If all else perished, and *he* remained, I should still continue to be; and, if all else remained, and he were annihilated, the Universe would turn to a mighty stranger. I should not seem a part of it. My love for Linton is like the foliage in the woods. Time will change it, I'm well aware, as winter changes the trees – my love for Heathcliff resembles the eternal rocks beneath – a source of little visible delight, but necessary. Nelly, I *am* Heathcliff – he's always, always in my mind – not as a pleasure, any more than I am always a pleasure to myself – but, as my own being – so don't talk of our separation again – it is impracticable; and –'

She paused, and hid her face in the folds of my gown; but I jerked it forcibly away. I was out of patience with her folly!

'If I can make any sense of your nonsense, Miss,' I said, 'it only goes to convince me that you are ignorant of the duties you undertake in marrying; or else, that you are a wicked, unprincipled girl.' (Vol. 1, Chapter 9)

Nelly's is the voice of common sense and conventional principle. Catherine has to use similes in order to re-define and re-name love, and in doing so exposes the inadequacy of conventions and language.

The terrors and mysteries of the novel are, similarly, also done from the inside. The ghosts move the reader, by terrifying or soliciting the characters in the novel. They are individualized ghosts, passionately reaching out to love, home, or earth. In his dread of the child who moans to be let in, Lockwood is moved to aggression, in a scene merging nightmare panic with primitive fear of supernatural intrusion, and quietly observing conditions and causes:

As it spoke, I discerned, obscurely, a child's face looking through the window – Terror made me cruel; and, finding it useless to attempt shaking the creature off, I pulled its wrist on to the broken pane, and rubbed it to and fro till the blood ran down and soaked the bed-clothes: still it wailed, 'Let me in!' and maintained its tenacious gripe, almost maddening me with fear. (Vol. 1, Chapter 3)

Heathcliff begs his dead love to come back, as she promised to do. Towards the end, obsessed with her presence and tormented by his survival, he is appalled by his sense of her spirit: 'By God! She's relentless. Oh, damn it! It's unutterably too much for flesh and blood to bear – even mine.'

The ghosts are not entirely internalized. Lockwood's dream is linked by a frightening coincidence to Cathy's delirious feeling that she was back in Wuthering Heights, and the child in the dream has the right name 'Linton'. At the end of the novel Lockwood, not insensitive but not passionate or active, makes a final comment on the violent passions he has witnessed. He responds to the benign sky, moths fluttering in the heath and harebells, and soft wind, with a refusal to believe that anyone could ever 'imagine unquiet slumbers for the sleepers in that quiet earth'. But unquiet slumbers are exactly what Emily Brontë has imagined. On the last pages of the novel a sinister ambiguity appears to suggest that the ghosts do haunt *Wuthering Heights*, an unrest readers will find it easy to envisage for the desperate lovers who have no right for an orthodox heaven and no desire for one. A little boy says he's been frightened by 'Heathcliff and a woman . . . under t'Nab', and though Nelly dismisses his story as the effect of nonsense heard from his parents she admits that she doesn't like being out in the dark 'now'. The attentive reader should observe that the boy realistically gives Heathcliff, whom he would have known, his name, but that Catherine, whom he could not have known, is simply 'a woman'. Emily Brontë provides fears and *frissons* for readers as well as characters.

Emily Brontë does not show her haunting through visible ghosts, but by creating visible states of desire, obsession and fear which terrify the watchers. Heathcliff's haunted dying is directly observed:

> Now, I perceived, he was not looking at the wall, for when I regarded him alone, it seemed, exactly, that he gazed at something within two yards distance. And whatever it was, it communicated, apparently, both pleasure and pain, in exquisite extremes: at least, the anguished, yet raptured expression of his countenance suggested that idea. (Vol. 2, Chapter 20)

His feelings emerge through Nelly Dean's story of what she sees, but cannot understand. Intensities are registered tersely, causalities are omitted.

> 'I cannot look down to this floor, but her features are shaped on the flags! In every cloud, in every tree - filling the air at night, and caught by glimpses in every object by day, I am surrounded with her image! The most ordinary faces of men and women - my own features - mock me with a resemblance. The entire world is a dreadful collection of memoranda that she did exist, and that I have lost her!
>
> 'Well, Hareton's aspect was the ghost of my immortal love, of my wild endeavours to hold my right, my degradation, my pride, my happiness, and my anguish -
>
> 'But it is frenzy to repeat these thoughts to you; only it will let you know why, with a reluctance to be always alone, his society is no benefit, rather an aggravation of the constant torment I suffer - and it partly contributes to render me regardless how he and his cousin go on together. I can give them no attention, any more.'

'But what do you mean by a *change*, Mr Heathcliff?' I said, alarmed at his manner, though he was neither in danger of losing his senses, nor dying; according to my judgment he was quite strong and healthy; and, as to his reason, from childhood he had a delight in dwelling on dark things, and entertaining odd fancies – he might have had a monomania on the subject of his departed idol; but on every other point his wits were as sound as mine. (Vol. 2, Chapter 19)

Emily Brontë's narrative device permits the feelings to be filtered through the observer, without complex psychological analysis. Like all observers, Nelly and Lockwood wonder, guess, and speculate, and the bluntedness and incompleteness of their interpretations help to register feeling which is especially intense and opaque because essentially beyond explanation and analysis.

Linton Heathcliff is interiorized by an isolated image which represents his affective energy. Though adversely contrasted with the second Catherine's vitality, his sensitivity is given a lyrical moment which animates an otherwise feeble character:

'He said the pleasantest manner of spending a hot July day was lying from morning till evening on a bank of heath in the middle of the moors, with the bees humming dreamily about among the bloom, and the larks singing high up over head, and the blue sky and bright sun shining steadily and cloudlessly. That was his most perfect idea of heaven's happiness – mine was rocking in a rustling green tree, with a west wind blowing, and bright, white clouds flitting rapidly above; and not only larks, but throstles, and blackbirds, and linnets, and cuckoos pouring out music on every side, and the moors seen at a distance, broken into cool dusky dells; but close by, great swells of long grass undulating in waves to the breeze; and woods and sounding water, and the whole world awake and wild with joy. He wanted all to lie in an ecstacy of peace; I wanted all to sparkle, and dance in a glorious jubilee.

'I said his heaven would be only half alive, and he said mine would be drunk; I said I should fall asleep in his, and he said he could not breathe in mine. . . .' (Vol. 2, Chapter 10)

It would be a mistake to speak of the novel as if it presented no more than a lyrical trajectory of feeling. Emily Brontë's intensities particularize concepts or commonplaces of romantic love: elective affinity, deathless passion, love's torment, overpowering force, constancy, and inaccessibility. The novelist discovers a form of narrative which eliminates traditional elements of fiction in order to shape and substantiate others.

Charlotte Brontë shared her sister's preoccupation with affinity, deathless attachment, pain, power, and constancy, but doubts if it is right to create characters like Heathcliff, and insists on the immaturity of Emily's art, even while she defends it:

> Had she but lived, her mind would of itself have grown like a strong tree, loftier, straighter, wider-spreading, and its matured fruits would have attained a mellower ripeness and sunnier bloom; but on that mind time and experience alone could work. . . . (Editor's Preface to the New Edition)

What she probably found most uncongenial in *Wuthering Heights* is its radical segregation of extremes of feeling and reason. Charlotte Brontë liked to place her imagined extremes in an acceptable moral scheme, which ultimately worked towards blame and approval. Emily Brontë placed her second generation of lovers between the poles of Heathcliff/Catherine and Nelly/Lockwood, but let passion articulate a superior and sometimes challenging energy. While Shakespeare can as easily create an Iago as an Othello, a Goneril as a Cordelia, his images of ruthless passion have no advantage over those of ruth and reason, and extremes are segregated in the ultimate interest of moral order and conclusion. Emily Brontë tames and socializes energy in Hareton and the second Catherine, but the particulars of romantic passion, in the first generation, challenge conventional limits, without glamour. Charlotte thrives on the polarities of violence and control, freedom and limit, passion and reason, but devises a moral structure which resolves conflict and makes extremes meet, in her strong, tormented, but morally civilized and triumphant characters, Jane Eyre, Robert Moore, and Lucy Snowe. These characters contain and are defined by the polarity of reason and passion. Jane Eyre and Lucy Snowe, even Robert Moore, Rochester and Paul Emanuel, pivot between the extremes represented by Nelly Dean and Heathcliff, but they are painfully controlled by a magnetic needle which veers towards judgement and control.

Although the narrative structure of *Wuthering Heights* separates hot feeling and cool reason, it is the reader who brings together the affective experiences juxtaposed in the novel. In the novels of Charlotte Brontë the extremes of experience are fused. The passion and the reason are presented and inspected within the same characters. Emily Brontë dehistoricizes and demoralizes the unreasonable affections of the heart, presenting them in isolation. Attempts at analysis like the self-justifications of the first Catherine, who hopes to live by two kinds of love, show up the social impossibility of the grand passion, honouring it while keeping it free of glamour. Thackeray spoke of Charlotte Brontë's 'passionate honour',[2] and it is ironic that the novels of both passionately honourable sisters should have created stereotypes for romantic fiction and have been frequently romanticized and vulgarized by critics and biographers. In their distinct ways, each novelist was attempting to appraise passion. Charlotte Brontë's effort to inspect its ravages and defects is done through a delicately psychologized analysis, which is placed in character, and is itself made the subject of meditation and mediation. Her favourite method is that of allegorical fragmentation. Like Richardson's Clarissa, her characters inspect their emotions, to utter feeling and judgement at the same time. Like Sophia Western in *Tom Jones*, the characters are analysed in terms of a faculty psychology, an inner drama in which parts of the whole are set in conflict. In her first novel, *The Professor*, written in 1843-6, and published posthumously in 1857, she was deliberately saying farewell to romantic fantasy – 'the burning climes' of Angria – and taking the foreseen risk of disappointing publishers who 'would have liked something more imaginative and poetical – something more consonant with highly-wrought fancy, with a taste for pathos, with sentiments more tender, elevated, unworldly'. The novel is a restrained novel of feeling, its hero, William Crimsworth, the first of Charlotte Brontë's restrained and passionate protagonists.

The congenial emotions found in all four novels are passionate attachment and affinity, jealousy, deprivation, stoicism, loneliness, and depression. The congenial emotional situation which forms contrast and tension in *Jane Eyre* and *Villette* is that of struggle and control. In *The Professor* some of the congenial emotions are present but not organized into a clear dynamic pattern. Where the struggle and control are shown, the drama is unmotivated or not kept up. The novelist seems to need to express the feelings, but has not yet found a satisfactory form for development and analysis.

Like *Jane Eyre* and *Villette*, *The Professor* is a first-person narration, meditative and introspective. The allegory of Reason and the Passions has similar functions in all three novels. It represents the strong passions and scrupulous intelligence of William Crimsworth, Jane Eyre, Lucy Snowe and the more reckless intelligence of Rochester. It brings out conflict and an effort to question, suppress, support, or attack strong feelings which may not be freed or indulged. It shows the separations of a faculty psychology in ways which refuse and resist simplifications and barriers: Reason is impassioned, the Passions intelligent and clever. It creates an image of the mind and passions of a divided self, endowing strong feelings or passions like desire, love, pride, jealousy, depression, self-justification, and creativity with argumentative and evaluative powers. Affective allegory is the appropriate register for Charlotte Brontë's brave, imaginative, violent, tormented, and reasonable characters.

The Professor lacks the continuity of conflict sustained in *Jane Eyre* and *Villette*, but it is a first experiment in allegorical method. There are stretches of narrative, particularly at the beginning and end, where no conflict occurs, and though conflict is not necessary for emotional continuity, Charlotte Brontë is not good at showing absences or flatnesses of feeling.[3] Her characters need to tick over in intense nervous experience in order to keep going. In *The Professor* there are times when the novelist seems to be working up unconvincing situations of emotional conflict, as in the account of Crimsworth's relations with Madamoiselle Reuter, which is improbable, if we think in terms of realism, and superficial, if we think in terms of psychological inquiry.

Crimsworth's boyhood, his relations with his family, and his ambitions, are shadowy, thinly narrated compared with the stories of Jane Eyre and Lucy Snowe. When he is brought into antagonistic relation with his brother there is an abrupt whipping-up of tension. Edward's hostility to his younger brother is interestingly worked out in terms of stereotyped capitalist oppression, and also in terms of moral envy. The emotions and their conjunction are promising, but Charlotte Brontë rushes over this early episode, as she does not do in the two tiers of preliminary action in *Villette*, and character and feeling are given summary treatment.

Crimsworth is one of her impassioned, rational, and analytic people, as his first metaphorical self-definition reveals:

> I had an instinctive feeling that it would be folly to let one's temper effervesce often with such a man as Edward. I said to myself, 'I will place my cup under this continual dropping; it shall stand there still and steady; when full, it will run over of itself - meantime patience.' (Chapter 2)

This image is characteristically composed, in both senses of the word. It ironically uses and refuses the traditionally joyful biblical associations of cups running over, indicating capacity, tension, limit, self-control, and perception, 'it would be folly to let one's temper effervesce'. It marks a decreed limit for patience, 'it will run over of itself'. It is a good early example of the interplay of intelligence and feeling; a moment of release is calmly and rationally anticipated. This emotional episode is characteristic of Charlotte Brontë's characters, who suffer and order their suffering. They are capable of abandonment and patience, and have the imaginative ability to understand their range of experience and its implications.

The cup overflows, as it was expected and designed to do; we sympathize as Crimsworth loses control and shows his anger. In the episode showing Crimsworth's antipathy for his brother, the novelist makes her first use of allegory for the notation of passion:

> I am not of an impatient nature, and influenced by the double desire of getting my living and justifying to myself and others the resolution I had taken to become a tradesman, I should have endured in silence the rust and cramp of my best faculties; I should not have whispered, even inwardly, that I longed for liberty; I should have pent in every sigh by which my heart might have ventured to intimate its distress under the closeness, smoke, monotony and joyless tumult of Bigben Close, and its panting desire for freer and fresher scenes; I should have set up the image of Duty, the fetish of Perseverance, in my small bed-room at Mrs King's lodgings, and they two should have been my household gods, from which my darling, my cherished-in-secret, Imagination, the tender and the mighty, should never, either by softness or strength, have severed me. But this was not all; the antipathy which had sprung up between myself and my employer striking deeper root and spreading denser shade daily, excluded me from every glimpse of the sunshine of life; and I began to feel like a plant growing in humid darkness out of the slimy walls of a well.
>
> Antipathy is the only word which can express the feeling Edward Crimsworth had for me – a feeling, in a great measure, involuntary, and which was liable to be excited by every, the most trifling movement, look, or word of mine. (Chapter 4)

As Wordsworth says, the very use of personification marks intensity. This rhetoric is also an appropriate medium for analysis. Crimsworth observes that his brother's antipathy is 'a feeling, in great measure, involuntary, and which was liable to be excited by every, the most trifling movement, look, or word of mine':

> If he could have once placed me in a ridiculous or mortifying position, he would have forgiven me much, but I was guarded by three faculties –

Caution, Tact, Observation; and prowling and prying as was Edward's malignity, it could never baffle the lynx-eyes of these, my natural sentinels. Day by day did his malice watch my tact, hoping it would sleep, and prepared to steal snake-like on its slumber, but tact, if it be genuine, never sleeps. (Ibid.)

As so often in Charlotte Brontë, control is marked by a certain grim humour, inseparable from the caution, tact, and observation amusingly animating the neat play, 'did his malice watch my tact'. At this stage Charlotte Brontë needs such external aids as Yorke Hunsden (who whips up Crimsworth's feelings). She shifts from the inner record of feeling to an external account of gesture and behaviour. Crimsworth's physical response is dramatized and analysed: it is described and distinguished from inner feeling:

I had got a good way on my return to my lodgings before I found out that I was walking very fast, and breathing very hard, and that my nails were almost stuck into the palms of my clenched hands, and that my teeth were set fast; on making this discovery, I relaxed both my pace, fists, and jaws, but I could not so soon cause the regrets rushing rapidly through my mind to slacken their tide. (Ibid.)

The last sentence returns to a straightforward statement of inner and outer response, neatly modulating into the key of social oppression:

I got no sleep; my head burned, my feet froze; at last the factory bells rang, and I sprang from my bed with other slaves.

More inner debate is introduced by direct comment, 'Self-dissatisfaction troubled exceedingly the current of my mediations', to move into a colloquy between the self, addressed as 'William Crimsworth', and 'my conscience, or whatever it is that within ourselves takes ourselves to task'. Conscience, or whatever it is, takes over Hunsden's goading, contemptuous of premature ideas of solution, sardonic about failing resolution, ironically rubbing in the facts of fatiguing routine and solitude, unflatteringly mocking notions of friendship, 'never hope, then, to gather the honey of friendship out of that thorn-guarded plant', and discouragingly introducing the imagery of love:

'Hollo, Crimsworth! where are your thoughts tending? You leave the recollection of Hunsden as a bee would a rock, as a bird a desert; and your aspirations spread eager wings towards a land of visions where, now in advancing daylight, - in X—— daylight - you dare to dream of congeniality, repose, union. Those three you will never meet in this world; they are angels. The souls of just men made perfect may encounter them in heaven, but your soul will never be made perfect.' (Chapter 5)

Reasonable goadings generate less reasonable ones, until self-pity is provoked to combine with self-control and temporarily resolve the conflict:

'Work, work!' reiterated the inward voice. 'I may work, it will do no good,' I growled; but nevertheless I drew out a packet of letters and commenced my task - task thankless and bitter as that of the Israelite crawling over the sun-baked fields of Egypt in search of straw and stubble wherewith to accomplish his tale of bricks. (Ibid.)

Here again powerful imagery combines with dramatized introspection. The debate itself refuses to simplify: conscience is impassioned and irrational, while resentment is sensible and obedient. As so often in Charlotte Brontë, the emotional episode has an unexpected shape, here moving rather abruptly out of inner debate into the quarrel between the brothers. In the scene of Edward's fury and physical threats, the language becomes crude, 'His fury boiled up, and when he had sworn half-a-dozen vulgar, impious oaths', but such banality lessens as the narration becomes introspective, 'A warm excited thrill ran through my veins, my blood seemed to give a bound, and then raced fast and hot along its channels'. The candour of 'seemed' and the exactness of physiological details like 'raced', 'bound' and 'channels' individualize the feelings.

The inner and outer episodes come together at the end of the chapter, in a record of action and reaction which combines imagery with analysis:

I only thought of walking, that the action of my muscles might harmonize with the action of my nerves; and walk I did, fast and far. How could I do otherwise? A load was lifted off my heart; I felt light and liberated. I had got away from Bigben Close without a breach of resolution; without injury to my self-respect. I had not forced circumstances, circumstances had freed me. Life was again open to me; no longer was its horizon limited by the high black wall surrounding Crimsworth's mill. Two hours had elapsed before my sensations had so far subsided as to leave me calm enough to remark for what wider and clearer boundaries I had exchanged that sooty girdle. . . . There was a great stillness near and far; the time of the day favoured tranquillity, as the people were all employed within doors, the hour of evening release from the factories not being yet arrived; a sound of full-flowing water alone pervaded the air, for the river was deep and abundant, swelled by the melting of a late snow. I stood awhile, leaning over a wall; and looking down at the current, I watched the rapid rush of its waves. I desired memory to take a clear and permanent impression of the scene, and treasure it for future years. Grovetown Church clock struck four; looking up, I beheld the last of that day's sun, glinting red through the leafless boughs of some very old oak trees surrounding the church – its light coloured and characterized the picture as I wished. I paused yet a moment, till the sweet, slow sound of the bell had quite died out of the air; then ear, eye and feeling satisfied, I quitted the wall, and once more turned my face towards X——. (Ibid.)

Images of stillness, solitude and the flowing river emphasize pleasure, relief, and release. The natural scene is easily evoked, with sympathetic rather than symbolic emphasis, and the sense of emotional crisis and decision registered quickly in the willed formation of image, 'I desired memory to take a clear and permanent impression'. The novelist observes the imagistic impact of emotional crisis, as George Eliot does in the famous scene in *Middlemarch* where Dorothea's feelings of depression take the permanent imprint of the red hangings of St Peter's. In this instance Charlotte Brontë places the psychological observation in character; Crimsworth's decision reflects intelligence, perception, and will.

In *Jane Eyre* the allegorical mode is fully developed as a mode of presenting tension and conflict. The analytic concept of moral and psychic division is now thoroughly imagined and dramatized in Jane, Rochester and St John Rivers. The treatment of the two male characters is foreshortened, and their inner lives only occasionally percolate through the narrating consciousness of Jane. In the case of Rochester, the conflict of feeling appears prominently in two scenes. The first is the fortune-telling, where Rochester, the false gypsy, characteristically teases and tests Jane, 'I wonder with what feelings you came to me tonight'. The words refer superficially to the actual situation where Jane's thoughts are 'busy' in her heart while the 'fine people' flit before her 'like shapes in a magic lantern', but also frame a key question for Rochester, and for the moral pattern of the novel. The clairvoyance he has been assuming with the other women gives way to a scrutiny of physiognomy. The brooding and incantatory style is as appropriate to Rochester as to the fortune-teller:

> 'The flame flickers in the eye; the eye shines like dew; it looks soft and full of feeling; it smiles at my jargon: it is susceptible; impression follows impression through its clear sphere; when it ceases to smile, it is sad; an unconscious lassitude weighs on the lid: that signifies melancholy resulting from loneliness. It turns from me; it will not suffer farther scrutiny; it seems to deny, by a mocking glance, the truth of the discoveries I have already made, – to disown the charge both of sensibility and chagrin; its pride and reserve only confirm me in my opinion. The eye is favourable.
>
> 'As to the mouth, it delights at times in laughter; it is disposed to impart all that the brain conceives; though I dare say it would be silent on much the heart experiences. Mobile and flexible, it was never intended to be compressed in the eternal silence of solitude: it is a mouth which should speak much and smile often, and have human affection for its interlocutor. That feature, too, is propitious.
>
> 'I see no enemy to a fortunate issue but in the brow; and that brow professes to say, – "I can live alone, if self-respect and circumstances require me so to do. I need not sell my soul to buy bliss. I have an inward treasure, born with me, which can keep me alive if all extraneous delights should be withheld; or offered only at a price I cannot afford to give". The forehead declares, "Reason sits firm and holds the reins, and she will not let the feelings burst away and hurry her to wild chasms. The passions may rage furiously, like true heathens, as they are; and the desires may imagine all sorts of vain things: but judgment shall still have the last word in every argument, and the casting vote in every decision. Strong wind, earthquake-shock, and fire may pass by: but I shall follow the guiding of that still small voice which interprets the dictates of conscience."' (Vol. 2, Chapter 4)

He reads Jane's qualities and anticipates her later conflict, commenting on his own play of feeling, 'I have formed my plans – right plans I deem them – and in them I have attended to the claim of conscience, the counsels of reason.' His interpretation is sounder than his scenario, which turns out to be unplayable. Conflict and character are personified again in his song 'The truest love', which contains the characters Hate, Right, Might and Love set in an allegorical landscape and journey. In Rochester's final narration, after the reunion, he speaks straightforwardly about emotions and emotional change. Charlotte Brontë reserves emblematic and allegorical language for his evasions and sleights of feeling.

The inner life of St John Rivers occupies one scene of emotional conflict, though there is no doubt about its resolution. After Jane forces him to admit his self-despised love for Rosamund Oliver, there is a curious episode in which he characteristically times the licensed moments as he, temporarily and histrionically, submits to the fantasy of love. Putting his watch on the table, he indulges the dream, handing over the imaginative responsibility for the scenario to Jane, who has initiated the subject. It is humorously and sharply performed, modulating from the cool tone of 'It is very pleasant to hear this . . . very: go on for another quarter of an hour', through the transitional, 'Fancy me yielding', and finally generating the full freedom of fancy, 'She is mine – I am hers – this present life and passing world suffice to me' (Vol. 3, Chapter 6). Then he picks up the watch, puts down Rosamund's portrait to leave 'that little space . . . given to delirium and delusion'. St John's personifications are appropriately distinct from those in Rochester's inner drama. He uses images which fuse indulgence and judgement: 'human love rising like a freshly opened fountain in my mind, and overflowing with sweet inundation all the field I have so carefully . . . prepared', a 'nectarous flood', 'delicious poison' and later, after the fantasy moves from present to past, 'I rested my temples on the breast of temptation', 'there is an asp in the garland' and 'The pillow was burning'. The elaborate drama he composes does not separate reason and passion; it is a controlled exhibition, not a conflict. The rhetorical mode is apt; St John is not divided, like Jane and Rochester. Their dividedness is essentially that of average sensual human beings, with Christian conscience and reason, while he is an absolutist, for whom human love holds only imaginary temptations.

Jane's conflicts are intuitive and reasoned struggles with passion. After Bertha's attempt to burn Rochester in his bed, he makes loving overtures of speech and touch, from which she retires to a night of ambiguous arousal, presented in sea-images: 'I was tossed on a buoyant but unquiet sea, where billows of trouble rolled under surges of joy' (Vol. 1, Chapter 15). The mixture is like that of St John's images, but unlike them in the absence of moral definition. There are moral undertones: 'now and then a freshening gale, wakened by hope, bore my spirit triumphantly towards the bourne: but I could not reach it, even in fancy, – a counteracting breeze blew off land, and continually drove me back. Sense would resist delirium: judgment would warn passion.'

The conflict becomes clear in the light of day, after Rochester's departure, and Mrs Fairfax's gossip about Blanche Ingram, as Jane conducts a characteristically sharp self-scrutiny, social and moral, in which self is judge and defendant. The allegorical drama complicates and confuses the action of intelligence and feeling:

> Arraigned at my own bar, Memory having given her evidence of the hopes, wishes, sentiments I had been cherishing since last night . . . Reason having come forward and told, in her own quiet way, a plain, unvarnished tale, showing how I had rejected the real and rabidly devoured the ideal; – I pronounced judgment. . . . (Vol. 2, Chapter 1)

Self then addresses self, using the imagery of surfeiting 'on sweet lies' and swallowing poison 'as if it were nectar', which links Jane with St John. With this difference: his conflict is imaged once, within that self-imposed restraint of clocktime, but Jane's goes on for the length of the book, until the natural miracle reunites her with Rochester. Throughout this section she wills a rational act of occupational therapy, crayoning her own portrait and painting the ivory miniature 'of an imaginary Blanche Ingram', forcing herself to recognize contrast, and exercise a self-control which 'kept my head and hands employed, and had given force and fixedness to the new impressions I wished to stamp indelibly on my heart'. The response is controlled, matter-of-fact, and active in mode: Jane's moral conflicts terminate in action. But neither conflict nor action has long-lasting effects. She hears that Rochester may not return. She feels 'a strange chill and failing at the heart', and struggle starts again:

> I was actually permitting myself to experience a sickening sense of disappointment: but rallying my wits, and recollecting my principles, I at once called my sensations to order; and it was wonderful how I got over the temporary blunder. . . . Not that I humbled myself by a slavish notion of inferiority: on the contrary, I just said: –
> 'You have nothing to do with the master of Thornfield, further than to receive the salary he gives you for teaching. . . .' (Vol. 2, Chapter 2)

The allegorical drama is perfectly in character: terse, prim, proud, and with a touch of wry humour. Its victory is temporary; after Rochester returns, to tease and provoke love through jealousy, Jane unsays her interpretation and advice, 'Did I say, a few days since, that I had nothing to do with him . . .? Every good, true, vigorous feeling I have, gathers impulsively round him' (Ibid.). The often-repeated rhythm is one of conflict ending in resolution, resolution undone, and renewed conflict. The allegory is moral, but the detail particularized to blur the outlines and cross the provisional gaps and distinctions between reason and feeling.

Such conflicts are those of a woman's sequestered inner experience, but there are others which align the inner voices with the supernatural structure argued and animated by the novel. Jane externalizes her uncertainties and fluidities, but the voices that articulate her divisions of feeling and reasoning often connect the inner life with an external force. The voices come both from her own mind and from the invisible world postulated and dramatized by the novel, traditional in origin and particularized in psychic action. After telling Rochester of her decision to leave him, she asks characteristically, 'What am I to do?' and is answered characteristically, 'Leave Thornfield'. The answer is spoken in direct speech by her 'mind', her emotional response is made auditory:

> But the answer my mind gave - 'Leave Thornfield at once' - was so prompt, so dread, that I stopped my ears. . . . (Vol. 3, Chapter 1)

Such physical concreteness is part of Charlotte Brontë's method. The inner voice is given substance by the physical act of hearing. It figures the strength and range of the conflict, breaking down divisions of interior and exterior, idea and act. The substantiality of gesture in that stopping of the ears is abstracted in the large-scale allegory that follows, where 'the voice within' is located as resolution. A traditional scene of inner battle takes place, and its physicality, though traditionally biblical, and puritan, is extended and sensational:

> I wrestled with my own resolution: I wanted to be weak that I might avoid the awful passage of further suffering I saw laid out for me; and conscience, turned tyrant, held passion by the throat, told her, tauntingly, she had yet but dipped her dainty foot in the slough, and swore that with that arm of iron, he would thrust her down to unsounded depths of agony.
> 'Let me be torn away, then!' I cried. 'Let another help me!'
> 'No; you shall tear yourself away; none shall help you: you shall, yourself, pluck out your right eye: yourself cut off your right hand: your heart shall be the victim; and you, the priest, to transfix it.' (Vol. 3, Chapter 1)

Conscience is masculine, and passion feminine, Charlotte Brontë exploiting even the allegory of masculine tyranny, violence and war.

Then the divided action stops, and the traditional imagery of eye and hand insists on the organic, unitary nature of the conflict, refusing to go on with the artificial solace of personified aspects of self. The passage is punctuated with reflection and self-awareness. After the voice declares that it must all be done by self, to self, and within self, there is a return to the ordinary mind, located in the everyday world:

> I rose up suddenly, terror-struck at the solitude which so ruthless a judge haunted, - at the silence which so awful a voice filled. My head swam as I stood erect: I perceived that I was sickening from excitement and inanition; neither meat nor drink had passed my lips that day, for I had taken no breakfast. (Ibid.)

We pass from the awful voice to the lack of breakfast.

Jane's inner conflict is observed and interpreted by Rochester. In his confessional narrative after the interrupted wedding, he pauses to observe her response, sees that she looks 'almost sick' and asks if he should stop, to be told that what she feels is pity, 'I pity you - I do earnestly pity you.' Though his reply is characteristically tender and judicial, his allegorical invention is facile and convenient:

> 'Pity, Jane, from some people, is a noxious and insulting sort of tribute, which one is justified in hurling back in the teeth of those who offer it; but that is the sort of pity native to callous, selfish hearts: it is a hybrid, egotistical pain at hearing of woes, crossed with ignorant contempt for those who have endured them. But that is not your pity, Jane; it is not the feeling of which your whole face is full at this moment - with which your eyes are now almost overflowing - with which your heart is heaving - with which your hand is trembling in mine. Your pity, my darling, is the suffering mother of love: its anguish is the very natal pang of the divine passion. I accept it, Jane: let the daughter have free advent - my arms wait to receive her.' (Ibid.)

Not for the first time, his impassioned analysis is inaccurate. The 'true Wisdom' of his song was false intelligence which did not show the right path, and though he sees and appraises Jane's pity correctly, his imagery hopefully simplifies her emotional conflict. Jane's pity may be the suffering mother of love, but the daughter cannot have the 'free advent' of the ingenious allegory. Maternal anguish does not guarantee a live birth; the masculine argument mishandles metaphor.

The allegory of feeling takes unexpected turns, even in Jane's

personal record. When Rochester accuses her of driving him to despair
for the transgression of 'a mere human law', she suffers the worst attack
of self-division. Allegory of feeling once more splinters the self but
shows a residual self co-existing with the fragmented parts and
answering their persuasions:

> and while he spoke my very Conscience and Reason turned traitors against
> me, and charged me with crime in resisting him. They spoke almost as loud
> as Feeling: and that clamoured wildly. 'Oh, comply!' it said. 'Think of his
> misery; think of his danger – look at his state when left alone: remember his
> headlong nature; consider the recklessness following on despair – soothe
> him; save him; love him: tell him you love him and will be his. Who in the
> world cares for *you*? or who will be injured by what you do?' (Ibid.)

There follows the assertion of self. The voices that uttered bad faith
split away, to leave the genuineness and stability of the core:

> '*I* care for myself. The more solitary, the more friendless, the more
> unsustained I am, the more I will respect myself. I will keep the law given by
> God; sanctioned by man. I will hold to the principles received by me when I
> was sane, and not mad – as I am now.' (Ibid.)

In this last colloquy with Rochester Jane wins both the argument,
insisting that she is directed by 'no mere human law', and the battle, in
which self fights self. Rochester is made to see the outcome as her eye,
described as 'an interpreter' of the soul, meets his eye, in the
unanswered assurance of self-possession, 'I still possessed my soul'. The
fragmentation of allegory renders exactly the apparent dissolution and
the real establishment of Jane's identity. The analytic allegory of the
inner life then comes to an end. Jane's trouble and decision are figured
by the dream image of the presiding and protective spirit-world.
Rochester's image of the mother giving birth to love is revised by the
woman's figure in the dream sky, which 'spoke to my spirit . . . My
daughter, flee temptation!' to elicit the reply, 'Mother, I will.' As so
often in this Providence novel, inner experience finds an external
endorsement.

The allegorical mode frequently gives way to the imagistic. After the
broken marriage ceremony Jane's cold solitude is figured in metaphor
and personification. The images are locally striking and drawn from the
matrices of Bewick, Jane's paintings, her nightmares, and traditional
nature archetypes:

Jane Eyre, who had been an ardent, expectant woman – almost a bride – was a cold, solitary girl again: her life was pale; her prospects were desolate. A Christmas frost had come at midsummer: a white December storm had whirled over June; ice glazed the ripe apples, drifts crushed the blowing roses; on hay-field and corn-field lay a frozen shroud: lanes which last night blushed full of flowers, to-day were pathless with untrodden snow; and the woods, which twelve hours since waved leafy and fragrant as groves between the tropics, now spread waste, wild and white as pine-forests in wintry Norway. My hopes were all dead – struck with a subtle doom, such as, in one night, fell on all the first-born in the land of Egypt. I looked on my cherished wishes, yesterday so blooming and glowing; they lay stark, chill, livid – corpses that could never revive. I looked at my love: that feeling which was my master's – which he had created; it shivered in my heart, like a suffering child in a cold cradle; sickness and anguish had seized it: it could not seek Mr Rochester's arms – it could not derive warmth from his breast. (Vol. 2, Chapter 11)

The startling, inventive imagery emerges suddenly from the dead metaphors of 'ardent', 'cold', 'pale', and 'desolate'. And at the end of the novel, when there is no dividedness to be expressed in the allegory of division, imagery works by itself, in a way both precise and thrilling:

The one candle was dying out: the room was full of moonlight. My heart beat fast and thick: I heard its throb. Suddenly it stood still to an inexpressible feeling that thrilled it through, and passed at once to my head and extremities. The feeling was not like an electric shock; but it was quite as sharp, as strange, as startling: it acted on my senses as if their utmost activity hitherto had been but torpor; from which they were now summoned, and forced to wake. They rose expectant: eye and ear waited, while the flesh quivered on my bones. (Vol. 3, Chapter 9)

Here Charlotte Brontë makes one of her rare uses of the topos of inexpressibility; it is given definiteness by the physiological details, 'beat thick and fast', 'throb', 'thrilled it through', by the exactness of analogical search and scrupulousness, 'not like an electric shock', and the simplicity of 'flesh quivered on my bones'. The image of electricity, which Lawrence uses so lavishly in descriptions of feeling and sensation, makes an early appearance in English fiction, for the purposes of emotional definition. The words 'thrilled' and 'quivered', which are to become clichés, are used with clarity and purpose, preparing and justifying Jane's judgement, 'it is the work of nature'.

The allegory of feeling makes its occasional presence felt in *Shirley*, but as that novel scarcely deals at all with emotional conflict and dilemma, the language of feeling has fewer functions to fulfil. Its allegorical method is largely restricted to descriptions of character and characteristic feeling which show how phrenology extended and encouraged types of emotional notation.[4] In *Villette* there is a continuation of *Jane Eyre's* preoccupation with the divided self, and its collisions of Reason with Passion. The interaction of metaphorical and literal narration becomes even more elaborate than in *Jane Eyre*.

A perception about acting, in *Villette*, illuminates Charlotte Brontë's own presentation of passion. Lucy Snowe describes the passionate experience of seeing a great actress perform with this insight: 'To her, what hurts becomes immediately embodied: she looks on it as a thing that can be attacked, worried down, torn in shreds. Scarcely a substance herself, she grapples to conflict with abstractions' (Chapter 23). Charlotte Brontë's experience has ripened intuition into awareness. In this last novel she embodies tragic passions and grapplings with abstraction. Crimsworth and Jane Eyre grappled, in crises, conflict, collision, uncertainty and control, but the narratives were always preparing reconciliation and a happy ending. For Lucy there is a tragic rhythm, a falling cadence, a movement from victory to defeat. *Villette* is as much a Providence novel as *Jane Eyre*, but the Providential pattern is shown, and seen by the heroine, to lead towards loss. The angel of the plot is Azrael.

In *Villette* we find the continuation of that physical embodiment of passion illustrated by the snake in the waistcoat and Jane's return to the world of breakfasts, with a prominent use of transformations of tropes into allegory.

The first of many prominent miniature dramas occurs in Chapter 5, where there is a half-humorous debate between self and one faculty, common-sense:

> Into the hands of common-sense I confided the matter. Common-sense, however, was as chilled and bewildered as all my other faculties, and it was only under the spur of an inexorable necessity that she spasmodically executed her trust. Thus urged, she paid the porter: considering the crisis, I did not blame her too much that she was hugely cheated; she asked the waiter for a room; she timorously called for the chambermaid. . . . (Chapter 5)

The personification is not performing in the inner drama alone, but is identified as an actor in the actual scene and event. There is a direct

line from the private to the public world, and the embodied
abstraction moves along it. The passage bridges the gap between the
puzzled self's fear and the composed self's 'quiet manner'. To
common-sense are delegated common-sense functions, the practical
acts which the total self feels must be done through an instrument, but
the personified faculty behaves like the self, possessing inner feeling and
outer conduct. Lucy's dislocations of feeling are amusingly demonstrated,
as common-sense is uncommonsensically chilled, bewildered, and
disconcerted. The humour is Charlotte Brontë's, but placed in
character, for Lucy's stoicism, like Jane's governess-like self-regulation,
is dramatized and narrated in the medium of a sustaining humour.
The allegory of self is more physical and more subtle than it has been
before; the lack of clarity is functional, showing a tension and
wholeness of feeling. This is a drama of faculties which shows the
limitations of faculty psychology, an allegory which shows the divided
self with divisions overwhelmed. Though the episode of common-sense
in the hotel is a small and comic drama, it begins a mode of analysis
which increases in tension and complexity. Personifications are
becoming as animated as persons.

In *Jane Eyre*, the bestiary is used to describe a jealousy imagined
rather than experienced: 'Had Miss Ingram been a good and noble
woman, endowed with force, fervour, kindness, sense, I should have
had one vital struggle with two tigers – jealousy and despair.' In *Villette*
the same animal images a different passion: anxiety is compared to 'a
tiger crouched in a jungle'. The simile aptly images a hidden threat;
Lucy tells us she possesses something 'of the artist's faculty of making
the most of present pleasure', but anxiety lies in wait. The image of the
tiger moves from simile to allegory:

> my fancy budded fresh and my heart basked in sunshine. These feelings,
> however, were well kept in check by the secret but ceaseless consciousness of
> anxiety lying in wait on enjoyment, like a tiger crouched in a jungle. The
> breathing of that beast of prey was in my ear always; his fierce heart panted
> close against mine; he never stirred in his lair but I felt him: I knew he
> waited only for sun-down to bound ravenous from his ambush. (Chapter 7)

The enlargement of image takes us from pleasure to terror. Charlotte
Brontë is like Shakespeare in *Hamlet* in revealing a tragic character's
capacity for ordinary untragic existence, but the image of the tiger
emerges to remind us that this is tragedy. The enlargement of the

simile shapes that falling cadence to which Lucy is always ironically attuned.

Jane Eyre showed a consciousness of the need for psychic rehearsals but Lucy scarcely needs to learn and practise. She appears at the beginning of the novel habituated to suffering, loss, and the subduing of self, though she already shows the urge to break out of control, often in unspecified and undirected passionate energy. The central image of storm[5] makes many appearances in the novel, as prolepsis and omen, as an 'actual' somatic influence, and at the end as the tragic instrument of loss. On one occasion it is presented as a powerful stimulant, which Lucy dreads. She remembers the past, 'Oh, my childhood! I had feelings: passive as I lived, little as I spoke, cold as I looked, when I thought of past days, I *could* feel . . . in catalepsy and a dead trance, I studiously held the quick of my nature' (Chapter 12). Accidents of the weather occur, and set up cravings of impulse: she longs to stay 'with the wild hour' of the storm 'black and full of thunder . . . pierced by white and blinding bolts'. This capacity for threat and wildness is both sexual and more than sexual; she has no outlet for energy. The imagery of rational control is as violent as the storm imagery which figures that energy:

> I did long, achingly, then and for four and twenty hours afterwards, for something to fetch me out of my present existence, and lead me upwards and onwards. This longing, and all of a similar kind, it was necessary to knock on the head; which I did, figuratively, after the manner of Jael to Sisera, driving a nail through their temples. Unlike Sisera, they did not die: they were but transiently stunned, and at intervals would turn on the nail with a rebellious wrench: then did the temples bleed, and the brain thrill to its core. (Chapter 12)

Once more there is the embodiment of hurt in a persistently physical image. Once more; there is a transference of the forces of reason and passion, a refusal to attribute coolness and restraint to self-control. The self is divided,[6] but the implications are those of a suffering integrity.

This image of energy and control is elaborated as we move from the violence of the restraining and restrained passions into a passage of calm. The structure of narration in this chapter swerves out of sequence. Lucy begins to describe a tranquil moonlit night, to recall childhood, passion, and the experience of storm. When she returns from turbulent retrospect to inner and outer quiet, the continued allegory of Jael and Sisera returns us to calm, with appropriate revision:

> To-night, I was not so mutinous, nor so miserable. My Sisera lay quiet in the tent, slumbering; and if his pain ached through his slumbers, something like an angel – the ideal – knelt near, dropping balm on the soothed temples, holding before the sealed eyes a magic glass, of which the sweet, solemn visions were repeated in dreams, and shedding a reflex from her moonlight wings and robe over the transfixed sleeper, over the tent threshold, over all the landscape lying without. Jael, the stern woman, sat apart, relenting somewhat over her captive; but more prone to dwell on the faithful expectation of Heber coming home. By which words I mean that the cool peace and dewy sweetness of the night filled me with a mood of hope. . . .
> (Ibid.)

The sense of wholeness is stressed, in a new version of the identity of control and object: the victim Sisera lulled and the murderess Jael relenting. Charlotte Brontë imbues this narrative with a sense of conscious art, in that concluding sentence which translates the image and the allegory, but marks only a misleading and temporary lull, like the imaged dreaming. In a further movement of self-conscious reflection, the narrator observes, 'Presently the rude Real burst coarsely in – all evil, grovelling and repellent as she too often is.' This embodiment of an abstraction announces Lucy's distaste for vulgarity and deception, and completes the falling rhythm. These emotional allegories mark the tragic decline.

These are the first links in a long chain of extended allegories, with full development in scene and character. In Chapter 13, 'A Sneeze out of Season', Lucy's amusement at Madame Beck's baseless suspicions about Dr John is immediately followed by 'a kind of wrath', 'bitterness' and 'hot tears'. Mixed emotions are personified, 'soreness and laughter, and fire, and grief, shared my heart between them'; and extended by the image 'the rock struck, and Meribah's waters gushing out', in a terse representation of six lines.

In Chapter 15, 'The Long Vacation', there is a long and elaborate representation of 'hypochondria' (depression or melancholy). The central image is that of climate. The heat of an Indian summer and the equinoctial storms combine as influences and symbols. Personification marks a dislocated time-sense, 'for nine dark and wet days, of which the Hours rushed on all turbulent, deaf, dishevelled', and registers illness and insomnia, 'Sleep went quite away. I used to rise in the night, look round for her, beseech her earnestly to return.' The drama of abstractions takes place in the solidly realized places, times and climate of Villette. The separateness of symbols and physical actualities is dissolved in delirium, the white beds of the dormitory becoming spectres, the bedheads turning into deathheads. Lucy feels 'the conviction that Fate was of stone, and Hope a false idol – blind, bloodness, and of granite core'.

After the episode of the visit to the confessional, the urge towards release comes back in 'wild longing to breathe this October wind on the little hill far without the city walls'. This longing changes; ceasing to be an imperative impulse, it softens into a wish which Reason can handle. But the downward turn comes, and after Lucy gets lost (as on other occasions) the longed-for meeting with storm takes a painful shape, abstract and physical:

> Strong and horizontal thundered the current of the wind from north-west to south-east; it brought rain like spray, and sometimes, a sharp hail like shot; it was cold and pierced me to the vitals. I bent my head to meet it, but it beat me back. My heart did not fail at all in this conflict; I only wished that I had wings and could ascend the gale, spread and repose my pinions on its strength, career in its course, sweep where it swept. While wishing this, I suddenly felt colder where before I was cold, and more powerless where before I was weak. I tried to reach the porch of a great building near, but the mass of frontage and the giant-spire turned black and vanished from my eyes. Instead of sinking on the steps as I intended, I seemed to pitch headlong down an abyss. (Chapter 15)

The abyss stays open between the last chapter of Volume One and the first of Volume Two: 'Where my soul went during that swoon I cannot tell.' Personification and allegory dramatize the return of consciousness, after a space which has registered its absence:

> The divorced mates, Spirit and Substance, were hard to re-unite: they greeted each other, not in an embrace, but a racking sort of struggle. The returning sense of sight came upon me, red, as if it swam in blood; suspended hearing rushed back loud, like thunder; consciousness revived in fear. (Chapter 16)

The images and the relationship between images are violent, but also ironically and appropriately amorous. Once more, abstraction and physicality are joined.

The three volumes of *Villette* deal with three large conflicts of feeling. The first tells Lucy's story of isolation and inhibited energy. The second tells the story of Lucy's relationship with John Graham Bretton, developing a companionship and affection which the heroine refuses to call love, followed by withdrawal and loss. The conflict of the first section is continued, for Lucy's struggles are still those of the inner life; like Jane Eyre, she speaks of the benefit of 'struggles with the natural character, the strong native bent of the heart', but she is uncertain about the outcome:

> They tend, however slightly, to give the actions, the conduct, that turn which Reason approves, and which Feeling, perhaps, too often opposes: they certainly make a difference in the general tenor of a life, and enable it to be better regulated, more equable, quieter on the surface; and it is on the surface only the common gaze will fall. As to what lies below, leave that with God. (Chapter 17)

The confession is full and frank, exposing what lies below the public surface. Lucy does not benefit from her struggles with the natural character as clearly as Jane Eyre does from her exercises in self-control, but suffers new assaults. Lucy is handicapped by the lack of reciprocity and relationship in the social world, which offers her only auxiliary roles and limited relationships. The renewed friendship with the Brettons gives her the rest and refreshment of a brief holiday, but she has been tutored by solitude, alerted to the dangers of ideals and Imagination. The holiday episode of calm and pleasure opens with the ironic invocation of a spirit stirring the waters of Bethseba ('perhaps not the shape you dreamed') and with the anticipation of Azrael, angel of death. As new life begins for her, she thinks of herself as a creature doomed to storm, and of Louisa Bretton, handily abstracted by a metaphor of the boat, the 'Louisa Bretton', as a protected life, safe in harbour.

Lucy uses imagination to prepare for the worst and to avert the temptation to hope for the best. She is happy, sleeps soundly, enjoys the social pleasures of the gallery, the concert, and the theatre, but is never allowed to see 'the radiant present' undarkened by 'the shadow of the future'. When she goes back to the Pensionnat after the 'comforts and modest hope' of friendship, another period of grappling begins. Lucy fights with Reason, imaged as a stepmother, and a withered old woman 'frostily touching my ear with the chill blue lips of eld':

Long ago I should have died of her ill-usage: her stint, her chill, her barren board, her icy bed, her savage, ceaseless blows; but for that kinder Power who holds my secret and sworn allegiance. Often has Reason turned me out by night, in mid-winter, on cold snow, flinging for sustenance the gnawed bone dogs had forsaken: sternly has she vowed her stores held nothing more for me - harshly denied my right to ask better things. . . . (Chapter 21)

Reason relieves 'the guard' after Imagination's 'watch', and her pains blend with the physical pangs of waking, which 'snatched me out of bed like a hand with a giant's gripe', to the realities of raw dawn and ice-cold water. The inner conflict is externalized by slight personifi-cations, like that of waking, or the wind's 'peevish cry', and the story modulates from image to object. Lucy argues formally with herself, 'on life and its chances, on destiny and her decrees', prohibits retrospect, enjoins 'reliance on faith' and hushes 'the impulse to fond idolatry'. Reason is a complex and changing personification here, first appearing in Lucy's monologue about Graham's letter, where she is located in a real place, moving stealthily 'through the twilight of that long, dim chamber', first almost humorous, whispering sedately, then transformed by monstrous images of cruelty and harshness. She returns when Graham's letter comes, in the moment of 'happy feeling' as Lucy holds in her hand 'a morsel of real solid joy'. The sensuously specified description of the letter merges with metaphors of nourishment, and leads to the luxuriously savoured reading, violently interrupted by the nun in the attic. Reason and Feeling play out their roles as Lucy meditates:

Does the reader, remembering what was said some pages back, care to ask how I answered these letters: whether under the dry, stinting check of Reason, or according to the full, liberal impulse of Feeling?

To speak truth, I compromised matters; I served two masters: I bowed down in the house of Rimmon, and lifted the heart at another shrine. I wrote to these letters two answers - one for my own relief, the other for Graham's perusal.

To begin with: Feeling and I turned Reason out of doors, drew against her bar and bolt, then we sat down, spread our paper, dipped in the ink an eager pen, and, with deep enjoyment, poured out our sincere heart. When we had done - when two sheets were covered with the language of a strongly-adherent affection, a rooted and active gratitude - (once, for all, in this parenthesis, I disclaim, with the utmost scorn, every sneaking suspicion of what are called 'warmer feelings': women do not entertain these 'warmer feelings' where, from the commencement, through the whole progress of an acquaintance, they have never once been cheated of the conviction that to do so would be to commit a mortal absurdity: nobody ever launches into Love unless he has seen or dreamed the rising of Hope's star over Love's troubled waters) – when, then, I had given expression to a closely clinging and deeply-honouring attachment – an attachment that wanted to attract to itself and take to its own lot all that was painful in the destiny of its object; that would, if it could, have absorbed and conducted away all storms and lightnings from an existence viewed with a passion of solicitude – then, just at that moment, the doors of my heart would shake, bolt and bar would yield, Reason would leap in vigorous and revengeful, snatch the full sheets, read, sneer, erase, tear up, re-write, fold, seal, direct, and send a terse, curt missive of a page. She did right. (Chapter 23)

. Feeling is articulated and discriminated in the careful refusal to name love, and the insistence on affection and gratitude is part of an intelligently impassioned discrimination of feeling. The personifications cross and change places: Reason is as impassioned as Feeling, and the last sentence describes and enacts the feelings in its asyndeton, accumulation and verbs of action. The self is central, first companioned by Feeling, finally accepting and approving Reason. The physical drama is precise, the theatre marked by the barred door and the break-in, images close to the novel's physical space, closure, and intrusion.

After the return of Paulina, Lucy's solitude closes in once more, as she is transformed into a painfully controlled spectator. Just as Graham Bretton made his first appearances in the first volume before becoming central in the second, so Paul Emanuel starts to emerge in the second volume. He reinforces Lucy's passionate conflict in his image of sweet poison, and his wrath and jealousy become active, though necessarily backgrounded, in Lucy's first love-story. He moves into the position abdicated by Graham in the third volume, after the valedictory blend of symbolic and real action with which Lucy buries her dead Hope, 'following an agony so lingering, death ought to be welcome' (Chapter 26), and the packet of Graham's letters. With her usual discrimination of feeling, Lucy says she is stoical but not 'quite a stoic', and sheds 'one sultry shower, heavy and brief' (Ibid.).

The image of burial is picked up later, when Paul Emanuel tells Lucy of his buried passion, and asks why she starts at the word: 'Because I said passion? Well, I say it again. There is such a word, and there is such a thing' (Chapter 29). In the story of this last passion, new personifications appear. As Lucy grapples with the compulsions of

Creative Impulse, which is imaged as masculine, master, deity and demon, she feels a characteristic mixture of pain and pleasure. Another new figure appears in Lucy's *devoir*, written as the allegory of 'Human Justice' ('a red, random beldame', a bad mistress, a bad mother, bestowing sugar-plums only on the 'strong, lively, and violent') devised in a contemptuous display of her talent, and her teacher's integrity, for the menacing fops, Boissec and Rochemorte, who had pursued Lucy on her arrival in Villette. Charlotte Brontë develops new passions of submission and aggression for her heroine.

Amongst the new abstractions is one embodied quietly, in a transient recognition of happiness, which is guardedly deprived of the usual capital letter: 'to see unhoped-for happiness take form, find place, and grow more real as the seconds sped, was indeed a new experience' (Chapter 35). The old antagonists, Reason and Imagination, recur in the curt account of the solicitations of Catholicism:

> Many people – men and women – no doubt far my superiors in a thousand ways, have felt this display impressive, have declared that though their Reason protested, their Imagination was subjugated. I cannot say the same. (Chapter 36)

After the theological difference is settled, peace follows, but not as 'the cold daughter of divorce'. The subdued allegory of emerging love is scrupulously related, to bring out the sense of process, increase, and dangerous security:

> The jar was over; the mutual understanding was settling and fixing; feelings of union and hope made themselves profoundly felt in the heart; affection and deep esteem and dawning truth had each fastened its bond. (Chapter 38)

After Lucy is given the opiate, which acts as stimulant instead of sedative, she goes out to find Villette alive and festive in the light of a full moon:

> Instead of stupor, came excitement. I became alive to new thought – to reverie peculiar in colouring. A gathering call ran among the faculties, their bugles sang, their trumpets rang an untimely summons. Imagination was roused from her rest, and she came forth impetuous and venturous. With scorn she looked on Matter, her mate –
> 'Rise!' she said. 'Sluggard! this night I will have *my* will; nor shalt thou prevail.'

'Look forth and view the night!' was her cry; and when I lifted the heavy
blind from the casement close at hand – with her own royal gesture, she
showed me a moon supreme, in an element deep and splendid.

To my gasping senses she made the glimmering gloom, the narrow limits,
the oppressive heat of the dormitory, intolerable. She lured me to leave this
den and follow her forth into dew, coolness, and glory. (Ibid.)

We move into another grappling with jealousy, and a new definition of
love. Lucy is placed in a state of unnamed emotion. Having 'shaken
hands' with 'Happiness or Hope' but scorning 'Despair', she has the
feverish urge to look at the moon in the stone-basin's 'circular mirror of
crystal'. Seeking coolness, she finds heat. The Gothic legend of the nun
was re-substantiated in the story of Paul Emanuel's lost love, Justine
Marie, and returns with the appearance of the new Justine Marie.
Lucy's old desire to penetrate 'to the real truth' and seek the goddess in
her temple, 'daring the dread glance', blends her pursuit of the real
and her delight in extremity. The personifications of Rumour,
Presentiment, Fact, Truth, Lie, and Falsehood, enact her drugged and
febrile consciousness and keep up the cool, even playful, allegory of
feeling. The image of Conviction echoes past emblems of violence and
battle:

> No. I hastened to accept the whole plan. I extended my grasp and took it
> all in. I gathered it to me with a sort of rage of haste, and folded it round me,
> as the soldier struck on the field folds his colours about his breast. I invoked
> Conviction to nail upon me the certainty, abhorred while embraced, to fix it
> with the strongest spikes her strongest strokes could drive; and when the iron
> had entered well my soul, I stood up, as I thought renovated.
>
> In my infatuation, I said, 'Truth, you are a good mistress to your faithful
> servants! While a Lie pressed me, how I suffered! Even when the Falsehood
> was still sweet, still flattering to the fancy, and warm to the feelings, it
> wasted me with hourly torment. The persuasion that affection was won could
> not be divorced from the dread that, by another turn of the wheel, it might
> be lost. Truth stripped away Falsehood, and Flattery, and Expectancy, and
> here I stand – free!' (Chapter 39)

She tries not to look at the scene, whose characters and drama she
misinterprets; theatrical images register illusion and distance, then
give way:

> Nothing remained now but to take my freedom to my chamber, to carry
> it with me to my bed and see what I could make of it. The play was not yet

indeed quite played out. I might have waited and watched longer that love scene under the trees, that sylvan courtship. Had there been nothing of love in the demonstration, my Fancy in this hour was so generous, so creative, she could have modelled for it the most salient lineaments, and given it the deepest life and highest colour of passion. But I *would* not look; I had fixed my resolve, but I would not violate my nature. And then – something tore me so cruelly under my shawl, something so dug into my side, a vulture so strong in beak and talon, I must be alone to grapple with it. I think I never felt jealousy till now. (Ibid.)

Reason breaks down: the traditional emblem of a vulture is brought monstrously close to bite under the shawl. The grappling is a new one, Lucy's jealousy more violent and impulsive than the rationally controlled jealousy of Jane and Rochester. Intensified by her drugged state of mind, it is also a discovery of love:

This was not like enduring the endearments of Dr John and Paulina, against which while I sealed my eyes and ears, while I withdrew thence my thoughts, my sense of harmony still acknowledged in it a charm. This was an outrage. (Ibid.)

This jealousy is justified by a rational and enamoured recognition:

The love, born of beauty was not mine; I had nothing in common with it: I could not dare to meddle with it, but another love, venturing diffidently into life after long acquaintance, furnace-tried by pain, stamped by constancy, consolidated by affection's pure and durable alloy, submitted by intellect to intellect's own tests, and finally wrought up, by his own process, to his own unflawed completeness, this Love that laughed at Passion, his fast frenzies and his hot and hurried extinction, in *this* Love I had a vested interest; and whatever tended either to its culture or its destruction, I could not view impassively. (Ibid.)

In Chapter 41 Lucy thinks she is saying a last goodbye to Paul Emanuel, and is prepared to 'smite' out of her 'path even Jealousy herself', but Paul Emanuel reads her eyes: 'there is no denying that signature: Constancy wrote it; her pen is of iron. Was the record painful?' This marks a climax and declaration, through a personification offered in the intense and playful language of character and narrator. But the novel takes another downward turn.

The conclusion marks the frustration of hope and love: stormy nights and red mornings 'shame Victory in her pride'. Storm and allegory are completed as 'the destroying angel of tempest' does his work, but the novel ends with an appearance of ambiguity:

> Trouble no quiet, kind heart; leave sunny imaginations hope. Let it be theirs to conceive the delight of joy born again fresh out of great terror, the rapture of rescue from peril, the wondrous reprieve from dread, the fruition of return. (Chapter 43)

The abstractions are ironic in their play and provisionality. The novel of passion ends with a grim invitation to the participating reader, a last offering of the humour which has been a mark of Lucy's rational control. There is a refusal to name the emotions of grief and horror, except through their opposites; the ending mocks the pain of closure by pretending to openness, but the falling cadences of image and feeling, like the virginal retention of Lucy Snowe's name, make it clear that tragic loss is all we are finally invited to contemplate.

There is one deviant form of impassioned outburst in *Jane Eyre* and *Shirley*, remarkable for its detachment from the main current of action and feeling. It resembles the authorial address to the reader characteristic of Thackeray and George Eliot, but it appears abruptly, seeming to break the bounds set by the narration. In each novel the impassioned apostrophe has the same subject, that of a woman's feelings, and the exceptional occurrence brings with it a licensed outrage, breaking out of personal into generalized appeal and attack. In *Shirley* it emerges suddenly in the middle of the representation of Caroline Helstone's experience of check and rebuff in her love for Robert Moore:

> A lover masculine so disappointed can speak and urge explanation; a lover feminine can say nothing: if she did, the result would be shame and anguish, inward remorse for self-treachery. (Chapter 7)

There follows a bitter and violent physical image, 'You expected bread, and you have got a stone', which moves from biblical quotation to a strongly substantial extension, imagining and enacting the metaphor of disappointed appetite: 'break your teeth on it, and don't shriek because the nerves are martyrized: do not doubt that your mental stomach - if you have such a thing - is strong as an ostrich's - the stone will digest.' This continues in the variation of 'You held out your hand for an egg, and fate put into it a scorpion', which is in the vein of playful and intense stoicism found in the personifications of Jane Eyre and Lucy Snowe. But it appears as a polemical digression, in some ways intensely personal, in some ways highly political. It protrudes, a feminist declaration, fracturing the form, then stopping as abruptly as it began: 'But what has been said in the last page or two is not germane to Caroline Helstone's feelings'.

In *Jane Eyre* there is a more delicate modulation, within the first-person narrative, as Jane conveys her feelings of stagnation and restlessness, and moves from her special case to generalize about women's feelings:

> It is in vain to say human beings ought to be satisfied with tranquillity: they must have action; and they will make it if they cannot find it. Millions are condemned to a stiller doom than mine, and millions are in silent revolt against their lot. Nobody knows how many rebellions besides political rebellions ferment in the masses of life which people earth. Women are supposed to be very calm generally: but women feel just as men feel; they need exercise for their faculties, and a field for their efforts as much as their brothers do; they suffer from too rigid a restraint, too absolute a stagnation, precisely as men would suffer; and it is narrow-minded in their more privileged fellow-creatures to say that they ought to confine themselves to making puddings and knitting stockings, to playing on the piano and embroidering bags. (Vol. 1, Chapter 12)

These two passages stand apart from the primary form of narration, using the impassioned and reasonable language of the narrators, but making a direct discursive address in a manner never appearing elsewhere in the novels. There is of course a link with the occasional authorial address, as in 'Reader, I married him', but these political appeals move into a generalization, as well as a recognition of the reader's existence and interest. They differ from the discursive utterances of Dickens, Thackeray, and George Eliot in being formal exceptions, rather than regularized and assimilated conventions. The novelist whose authorial commentary most resembles them is, ironically, Jane Austen, whose ignorance of the 'stormy sisterhood' of the Passions, as Charlotte Brontë mistakenly judged it, seemed to the later novelist to mark a gap between them. Certainly, Jane Austen's occasional long discursive address, on the subject of sibling-love in *Mansfield Park*, or of the seriousness of fiction, in *Northanger Abbey*, is elegant and humorous, while Charlotte Brontë's two outbursts have the appearance of a spontaneous overflow of feelings too strong to remain within the form of fiction. Too rare to be considered as generalized devices of art, they are powerful reminders of the novelist's feelings, baring the rough stone which is carved into particulars of character and action. They may be seen as feminist deviations from a structural norm.

NOTES

1   Q.D. Leavis, 'A Fresh Approach to *Wuthering Heights*' in F.R. and Q.D. Leavis, *Lectures in America* (London, 1969), p. 89.

2   In 'The Last Sketch', his introduction to Charlotte Brontë's fragment *Emma*, Thackeray refers to her 'burning love of truth, the bravery, the simplicity, the indignation at wrong, the eager sympathy, the pious love and reverence, the passionate honour, so to speak, of the woman' (*Cornhill*, Vol. 1, No. 486, April 1860).

3   This is why she omits eight years from the irregular autobiography of *Jane Eyre*, as she explains in Chapter 10.

4   For instance: 'Mr Yorke, in the first place, was without the organ of Veneration – a great want, and which throws a man wrong on every point where veneration is required. Secondly, he was without the organ of Comparison . . . and, thirdly, he had too little of the organs of Benevolence and Ideality' (*Shirley*, Chapter 14).

5   This traditional image appears in Charlotte Brontë's letters but the most elaborate anticipation of its use in *Villette* occurs in a letter written by her father, Patrick Branwell, on the death of his wife:

>   When I first came to this place, though the angry winds which had been previously excited were hushed, the troubled sea was still agitated, and the vessel required a cautious and steady hand at the helm. I have generally succeeded pretty well in seasons of difficulty; but all the prudence and skill I could exercise would have availed me nothing had it not been for help *from above*. I looked to the *Lord* and He controuled the storm and levelled the waves and brought my vessel safe into the harbour. But no sooner was I there than another storm arose, more terrible than the former – one that shook every part of the mortal frame and often threatened it with dissolution. (*The Brontës: Their Lives, Friendships and Correspondence*, T.J. Wise and J.A. Symington (eds.), Vol. 1 (Oxford, 1933), p. 58.)

6   For a very different interpretation of the debates and divisions in Charlotte Brontë's allegory, see Mary Jacobus, 'The Buried Letter: Feminism and Romanticism in *Villette*', in *Women Writing and Writing about Women* (London, 1979).

5

GEORGE ELIOT

1 Allegory and Analysis

Like Charlotte Brontë, George Eliot makes full use of the figure of
personification for the representation of feeling. She sometimes
generates it to make explicit comments about affective experience.
'Our passions', she writes in *Middlemarch*, 'do not live apart in locked
chambers, but, dressed in their small wardrobe of notions, bring their
provisions to a common table and mess together, feeding out of the
common store according to their appetite' (Chapter 16). This is an
ironic use of a figure which schematizes and simplifies to delineate the
interfusion of 'the passions', anticipating Lawrence's uses of personification to attack classification. An early use of the figure for the same
purpose of definition comes in 'Amos Barton':

> For love is frightened at the intervals of insensibility and callousness that
> encroach by little and little on the dominion of grief, and it makes efforts to
> recall the keenness of the first anguish. (Chapter 10)

But in the action of *Scenes of Clerical Life* the feelings are rendered by
simple devices of scene and imagery, and the use of emotional allegory
does not appear. Even in *The Mill on the Floss*, where the use of images
and episodes from *A Pilgrim's Progress* is structurally central and
conspicuous, the allegorical method is not used, and it is associated
with a late and self-conscious analytic tendency.

In the novels before *Middlemarch* the representation of feeling is not
simply local; imagery which marks emotionally strong and crucial
episodes is frequently drawn from matrices in the novel. In 'Mr Gilfil's
Love-Story' the uncontrolled passions of Caterina are frequently
expressed in the dominant imagery of flowers, animals, and climate, in

'Janet's Repentance' in the imagery of desert and spring, in *The Mill on the Floss* in imagery of flood and storm, inner 'voices', music, battle, and pilgrimage.

Like Dickens, George Eliot relates crises of passion to the novel as a whole. Moments of local intensification are brought into the dominant pattern. In *Middlemarch* and *Daniel Deronda* allegory plays a prominent part, working together with the symbolic scene and image, but recurring with sufficient frequency to make it a structuring, as well as an intensifying, device. Its use is often provisional and ironic. The analysis is psychological, like Charlotte Brontë's, but places a moral emphasis on undesirable fragmentation.

In *Middlemarch* there is a recurring personification of feeling, more various than that in *Villette*. Bulstrode's passions are appropriately allegorized, reminding us of the Puritan inheritance which he has corrupted, and figuring his evasions and impersonations:

> It was only the common trick of desire – which avails itself of any irrelevant scepticism, finding larger room for itself in all uncertainty about effects, in every obscurity that looks like the absence of law. (Chapter 70)

> Strange, piteous conflict in the soul of this unhappy man, who had longed for years to be better than he was – who had taken his selfish passions into discipline and clad them in severe robes, so that he had walked with them as a devout quire, till now that a terror had risen among them, and they could chant no longer, but threw out their common cries for safety. (Ibid.)

> His conscience was soothed by the enfolding wing of secrecy, which seemed just then like an angel sent down for his relief. (Ibid.)

These passages come from Bulstrode's crisis of conscience over Raffles, lying sick and vulnerable. Their rhetoric draws attention to a disintegration which marks and judges secret habits of mind and feeling. Bulstrode has taken over the Christian theological abstractions, to invent and perform the false drama of the hypocrite, and also to play tricks on himself: he is not candid and whole in his inner life. George Eliot's is no common study of hypocrisy, since she does not show a break between the private and public lives, but a break and deception within the consciousness. Bulstrode's desire is segregated from conscience, his passions deceptively imitate a holy choir, his conscience is protected by secrecy, which is no angel. The habit of impersonation is perfectly figured through the act of abstraction. Christian allegory is perverted. The appropriate and ironic rhetoric is not static, but adapts itself to changed circumstances. After he has been found out and forgiven by his anguished wife, whose actions of disrobing and dressing show the progress and process of finding a decorous costume of redress, his internal play continues, unconverted. In Chapter 85, where he makes a last appearance, George Eliot uses the trial of Faithful, from *A Pilgrim's Progress*, as epigraph, to present Bulstrode as Faithful's opposite, the hypocrite who has broken faith, with religion, self, and community, as the man who is justly stoned, and who cannot take easy refuge in depersonalizing the opposition:

> The pitiable lot is that of the man who could not call himself a martyr even though he were to persuade himself that the men who stoned him were but ugly passions incarnate. . . .

'The man' makes a bridge from Bunyan's picture of the persecuting passions to the analysis of Bulstrode withering under this consciousness, and allegory formulates an act of convenient imaginative abstraction. Personification continues Bunyan's court-scene, in an image whose abstraction represents a reality which Bulstrode has not invented and so dreads:

> The duteous merciful constancy of his wife had delivered him from one dread, but it could not hinder her presence from being still a tribunal before which he shrank from confession and desired advocacy.

This earthly tribunal repeats an earlier image of a divine tribunal, made for his own moral convenience. Here its aspect changes: it demands restitution, not the self-prostration he has formulated. Even the imagined acceptance of restitution is illusory; he is ignoring George Eliot's dogma, translatable into Christian terms, that our deeds determine us, so total restitution is impossible. The impersonations of passion and conscience are related in an ironical process of accretion and comparison. The form of Bulstrode's fragmenting imagination is said to be a convenient deception. After the brilliant flashback (in Chapter 61) which relates Bulstrode's history to the reader at the moment when he can no longer generalize but must relive the past in painful particularity, the narrator discriminates between the sequentiality and continuity of the form in which the story has been told to the reader, and the discontinuity of Bulstrode's memorial reconstruction: 'But for himself at that distant time, and even now in burning memory, the fact was broken into little sequences, each justified as it came by reasonings which seemed to prove it righteous.'

Charlotte Brontë uses the allegorical method in much the same way, to represent the passions of Crimworth, Jane, Lucy, Rochester, and St John Rivers. George Eliot uses it, as she used lexis and syntax, in a discrimination of character, a means of separating and defining individual modes of thinking, feeling, and acting. At first sight it may seem astonishing that the candid and single-minded Dorothea shares the allegorical habit with Bulstrode. Once more there is a religious aptness, since Dorothea is the other Evangelical in the novel, though her Evangelicism fades quietly away. Her emotional crises are analysed in a form much like Bulstrode's. After the rejection of her compassion, Casaubon goes to his library and she goes to her boudoir, each to an appropriately furnished private theatre. Dorothea's crisis is located in the room where she has suffered and struggled on earlier occasions, a room of sacred objects, a room with a view of the outside world. On this occasion the concentration on inner drama is intense and the physical scene is positively and negatively symbolic. Its history makes it emblematic for the reader, but, like Lear, Dorothea feels that the body's delicate only when the mind's free. She throws herself down, indifferent to the discomfort, serenity, glory, and scope offered by the environment:

The open bow-window let in the serene glory of the afternoon lying in the avenue, where the lime-trees cast long shadows. But Dorothea knew nothing of the scene. She threw herself on a chair, not heeding that she was in the dazzling sun-rays: if there were discomfort in that, how could she tell that it was not part of her inward misery?

She was in the reaction of a rebellious anger stronger than any she had felt since her marriage. Instead of tears there came words: –

'What have I done – what am I – that he should treat me so? He never knows what is in my mind – he never cares. What is the use of anything I do? He wishes he had never married me.'

She began to hear herself, and was checked into stillness. Like one who has lost his way and is weary, she sat and saw as in one glance all the paths of her young hope which she should never find again. And just as clearly in the miserable light she saw her own and her husband's solitude – how they walked apart so that she was obliged to survey him. If he had drawn her towards him, she would never have surveyed him – never have said, 'Is he worth living for?' but would have felt him simply a part of her own life. Now she said bitterly, 'It is his fault, not mine.' In the jar of her whole being, Pity was overthrown. Was it her fault that she had believed in him - had believed in his worthiness? - And what, exactly, was he? - She was able enough to estimate him - she who waited on his glances with trembling, and shut her best soul in prison, paying it only hidden visits, that she might be petty enough to please him. In such a crisis as this, some women begin to hate.

The sun was low when Dorothea was thinking that she would not go down again, but would send a message to her husband saying that she was not well and preferred remaining up-stairs. She had never deliberately allowed her resentment to govern her in this way before, but she believed now that she could not see him again without telling him the truth about her feeling, and she must wait till she could do it without interruption. He might wonder and be hurt at her message. It was good that he should wonder and be hurt. Her anger said, as anger is apt to say, that God was with her - that all heaven, though it were crowded with spirits watching them, must be on her side. (Chapter 42)

Dorothea sat almost motionless in her meditative struggle, while the evening slowly deepened into night. But the struggle changed continually, as that of a man who begins with a movement towards striking and ends with conquering his desire to strike. The energy that would animate a crime is not more than is wanted to inspire a resolved submission, when the noble habit of the soul reasserts itself. That thought with which Dorothea had gone out to meet her husband - her conviction that he had been asking about the possible arrest of all his work, and that the answer must have wrung his heart, could not be long without rising beside the image of him, like a shadowy monitor looking at her anger with sad remonstrance. It cost her a litany of pictured sorrows and of silent cries that she might be the mercy for those sorrows - but the resolved submission did come. . . . (Ibid.)

George Eliot is characteristically giving social and physical solidity to the emotional crisis and merging the outer life with inner feeling. Dorothea's response to the outside world registers inner inclination. There is a typical movement out of emotional description, 'in the grip of a rebellious anger', to inner dialogue. The description uses common metaphors, 'grip' and 'rebellious', to prepare for the movement into an abstract play of personified passions. Before we come to them, we are told how Dorothea listens to her own words, exercising a first effort of control, to be 'checked into stillness'. Imagery taken from the novel's pattern of metaphor, 'the paths', initiates an extended action of feeling. 'The paths' develop into the place where 'young hope' has been lost, and the familiar metaphor gives place to a newer, stronger one, with no antecedent in the novel: 'shut her best soul in prison'. At this point, the allegory reveals its local theme: it represents a sense of dislocation and alienation, hope lost, and soul sequestered. When we move to Dorothea's vision of an anger that tells her 'God was with her' we are close to the action of Bulstrode's self-deceptive and convenient dissociations. The inserted generalization, 'as anger is apt to say', places allegory as a feverishly unjust act of imagination, and the 'shadowy monitor' makes a necessary adjustment, in the allegorical mode, but marking the return to her spontaneity and integrity, 'rising beside the image of him'. Both anger and pity are raised into personification by the creative stimulus of love and anger, local and placed in character.

In the scene of emotional crisis in Chapter 80, after Dorothea has controlled her feelings with a strong repressive force which breaks down, her emotional state is named as anguish, but the simple name is qualified by animated epithet and metaphor: 'she had sunk back helpless within the clutch of inescapable anguish'. We move from metaphor to event, as Dorothea dismisses her maid and casts herself on the bare floor to 'let the night grow cold around her'. As in the earlier boudoir scene, she responds significantly to the environment: she 'besought hardness and coldness and aching weariness to bring her relief from the mysterious incorporeal might of her anguish'. George Eliot is not above soliciting sympathy for her characters, and in the words, 'grand woman's frame' and 'she repeated what the merciful eyes of solitude have looked on for ages in the spiritual struggles of man', there is overt appeal. There is also internal justification: anguish is called strong ('might'), and more than physical ('incorporeal'), and beyond reach of understanding ('mysterious'). Even the epithet 'grand' does not just appeal for extra compassion, but emphasizes the incongruous sobs like those of a 'despairing child'. Here there is no sense of division in the experience, it is represented as one clutch, one might, one anguish. What is shown through a divided structure is her image of Will, 'the bright creature' and 'a detected illusion'. Her dismay makes division, into 'two living forms that tore her heart in two'. This sustained image-drama is a revision of the judgement of Solomon, in which the simile presents the rescued child of the story as cut in half, and severance is repeated in the real mother's heart. Dorothea's emotional state is not static; she moves from 'anguish' through 'agony' to 'despair', and 'discovered her passion to herself' in what is called 'the unshrinking utterance of despair'. The movement records a feeling only for 'the bright creature', half of the image. The 'changed belief exhausted of hope', and the 'detected illusion' produce 'scorn and indignation and jealous offended pride' and 'fitful returns of spurning reproach'. The anger, which we have met before, is shown in sobs and questions, until she cries herself to sleep. She wakes to follow her previous movement from anger into pity. Once more she applies controls, deliberately recalling the previous day and examining her feelings. 'In her first outleap of jealous indignation and disgust, when quitting the hateful room, she had flung away all the mercy with which she had undertaken that visit', but once more the 'dominant spirit of justice' makes her look at things freshly, to master feelings which had seemed overpowering:

> vivid sympathetic experience returned to her as a power: it asserted itself as acquired knowledge asserts itself. . . . She said to her own irremediable grief, that it should make her more helpful, instead of driving her back from effort.

Control is imaged as the attempt to 'clutch' her 'own pain and compel it to silence'. Personification shows a desirable division within the self: the repetition of that active 'clutch', which had earlier been attached to anguish, shifts her from passivity to activity. Such movements of language make an imaginative and dynamic representation of what we vaguely call self-control, in a particularization of the nuance and energy of compounded experiences of feeling. The use, then disuse, of personification enacts the loss and recovery of control. George Eliot has recorded the experiences of Dorothea's slow emergence from delusive self-command and temporary loss of control to the significant turn towards the world outside the window, where the bending sky, light, and 'wakings of men to labour and endurance' associate her with 'that involuntary palpitating life' which she cannot just observe or escape. George Eliot's presentation of emotional experience is marked by continuity and exceptional flexibility of form.

Another *Middlemarch* character represented through an individualized allegory is Will Ladislaw. In his case, the dissociating force is idealistic and romantic, as he imaginatively makes a throne for Dorothea, dangerously simplifying love. In Chapter 47, George Eliot gives him full space for imagining, and shows the process of simplification at work within his reverie, paradigmatically emerging in a hymn-like poem, whose beginning and end chime, refrain-like, to personify love's needs and spare satisfactions:

O me, O me, what frugal cheer
My love doth feed upon!

The allegorical mode, only glancingly treated in the poem, appears
more comically and less lyrically in Will's anticipations and conflicts,
as he decides to see Dorothea, in a movement of what George Eliot calls
the tender 'contradictoriness and rebellion' he sometimes feels towards
his generosity and passion. His reverie has a tendency to convert
experience into heroic myths and images, and here he thinks of staying
near Dorothea, 'whatever fire-breathing dragons might hiss around
her'. Ladislaw's Sunday-morning walk to Lowick is determined by a
vexed sense of failure, 'He had often got irritated, as he was on this
particular night, by some outside demonstration that his public
exertions with Mr Brooke as a chief could not seem as heroic as he
would like them to be', and a feeling that the 'sacrifice of dignity for
Dorothea's sake' is foolish:

> suddenly reflecting that the morrow would be Sunday, he determined to go
> to Lowick Church and see her. He slept upon that idea, but when he was
> dressing in the rational morning light, Objection said –
> 'That will be a virtual defiance of Mr Casaubon's prohibition to visit
> Lowick, and Dorothea will be displeased.'
> 'Nonsense!' argued Inclination, 'it would be too monstrous for him to
> hinder me from going out to a pretty country church on a spring morning.
> And Dorothea will be glad.'

What George Eliot originally calls 'the inward debate' begins as an
integrated stream of feeling and reflection, hardens into this colloquy
between Objection and Inclination (in which Objection is 'silenced by
force of unreason') and at last rises into lyric. When Will arrives at
church, things are not what impassioned abstraction and anticipation
foretold, and he realizes the limits of what he simplified: 'Why had he
not imagined this beforehand?' Debate and lyric were not imaginative
enough, and Will is forced to contrast the schematic humour of
Objection and Inclination with the intransigent complexities of 'real'
time, place, and people, the sweet deprivations of fantasy with 'real'
loss and isolation. This is a briefer piece of impassioned abstraction
than the sustained and recurring analyses of Bulstrode and Dorothea,
but the same process is economically and suggestively at work. As the
narrator observes in this chapter, 'there is no human being who having
both passions and thoughts does not think in consequence of his

passions – does not find images rising in his mind which soothe the passion with hope or sting it with dread'. The generalization itself heralds the local personifications, constructed 'in consequence of . . . passions'. George Eliot uses the figure of allegory to analyse a state of simplification, like that of Bulstrode's theological drama. In Will's case, the analysis takes the appropriate form of flippant colloquy and reverential lyric, both carefully placed, neither giving a sufficient account of passion or reason, but emerging clearly from wish-fulfilment to knowledge.

In *Daniel Deronda* the figure presents the passions and dissociations of Gwendolen Harleth. Daniel Deronda prescribes psychic therapy, in which she should recognize her prevailing fear, and 'turn it into a safeguard'. The proposal depends on his recognition that fear is only one force in the psyche, and can be dealt with by a residual self, rather like the ego. Gwendolen takes his advice, and achieves a form of transient control:

'Turn your fear into a safeguard. Keep your dread fixed on the idea of increasing that remorse which is so bitter to you. Fixed meditation may do a great deal towards defining our longing or dread. We are not always in a state of strong emotion, and when we are calm we can use our memories and gradually change the bias of our fear, as we do our tastes. Take your fear as a safeguard. It is like quickness of hearing. It may make consequences passionately present to you. Try to take hold of your sensibility, and use it as if it were a faculty, like vision.' (Chapter 36)

her vision of what she had to dread took more decidedly than ever the form of some fiercely impulsive deed, committed as in a dream that she would instantly wake from to find the effects real though the images had been false: to find death under her hands, but instead of darkness, daylight; instead of satisfied hatred, the dismay of guilt; instead of freedom, the palsy of a new terror – a white dead face from which she was for ever trying to flee and for ever held back. She remembered Deronda's words: they were continually recurring in her thought –

'Turn your fear into a safeguard. Keep your dread fixed on the idea of increasing your remorse. . . . Take your fear as a safeguard. It is like quickness of hearing. It may make consequences passionately present to you.'

And so it was. In Gwendolen's consciousness Temptation and Dread met and stared like two pale phantoms, each seeing itself in the other – each obstructed by its own image; and all the while her fuller self beheld the apparitions and sobbed for deliverance from them.

Inarticulate prayers, no more definite than a cry, often swept out from her into the vast silence, unbroken except by her husband's breathing or the plash of the wave or the creaking of the masts; but if ever she thought of definite help, it took the form of Deronda's presence and words, of the sympathy he might have for her, of the direction he might give her. It was sometimes after a white-lipped, fierce-eyed temptation with murdering fingers had made its demon-visit that these best moments of inward crying and clinging for rescue would come to her, and she would lie with wide-open eyes in which the rising tears seemed a blessing, and the thought, 'I will not mind if I can keep from getting wicked,' seemed an answer to the indefinite prayer. (Chapter 54)

The personification gains special intensity from repetition, as her memory recalls the very words which drew attention to remorse as well as fear. It wears the image of the dead face in the Spanish painting, which startled Gwendolen out of statuesque acting into feeling. George Eliot does not simply recapitulate this key image, or Daniel's personifications, but revives them, remade by the activity of the passionate antagonists Temptation and Dread, who have replaced Fear and Remorse in Gwendolen's inner theatre. Daniel's advice has been taken, so remorse has transformed mere fear into Dread, with its capital letter and its enlargement into something stronger and more awful than fear. As imagination is imagined, the self is larger than the play of its passions: 'Her fuller self beheld the apparitions'. Analysis takes the form of a haunting, continuing imagery of spiritual powers drawn from the novel's epigraph, 'Let thy chief terror be of thine own soul'. The allegory is dynamic: after the image of deadlocked struggle in which Temptation and Dread are exactly matched, 'each seeing itself in the other – each obstructed by its own image', emotionally strong as an image of conflict and physically precise as an image of balanced powers, there later appears the demonic image of 'white-lipped fierce-eyed temptation, with murdering fingers', threatening the fuller self, as the shift to the personal makes plain: 'She would lie with wide-open eyes'. There is also a shift from inner allegory to the physical 'reality' of the bed where she lies beside her breathing husband, which insists on the substantiality of passion.

She tells Daniel about the development of tumult after Grandcourt's death. This time the allegorical probing shows a division, like that dismissed by Mordecai when he tells Mirah she is influenced by writers 'showing the human passions as indwelling demons, unmixed with the relenting and devout elements of the soul' (Chapter 61). Gwendolen uses simple language, calling the passions by their conventional names, and not personifying them, 'I was full of rage at being obliged to go – full of rage', 'I had cruel wishes':

> And what had been with me so much, came to me just then – what you once said – about dreading to increase my wrong-doing and my remorse – I should hope for nothing then. It was all like a writing of fire within me. Getting wicked was misery – being shut out for ever from knowing what you – what better lives were. (Chapter 56)

As in *Middlemarch* the contrasts in analytic modes make distinctions between characters. Gwendolen translates the sophisticated analytic terms of Daniel's therapy into a cruder style, though she is allocated an eloquent metaphor for conscience, 'a writing of fire'. What she conceives in her untutored style is a divided self, half active and half passive: 'it came back to me then – but yet with a despair – a feeling that it was no use – evil wishes were too strong. . . . I only know that I saw my wish outside me' (Ibid.).

The simple naming of feeling is in keeping with broken syntax and informal punctuation as Gwendolen takes the allegory of passion to the extremity where the fuller self has lost control, and the guilty wish has power. When later on she tells her uncertain story of Grandcourt's death, there is a different movement: 'I was leaping away from myself – I would have saved him then. I was leaping away from my crime. . . .' Indeterminacy is stressed in her narration and in Daniel's subsequent reflections, but it is not part of the (relatively) open ending. Daniel is not sure of the relationship between feeling and acting, and his sense of uncertainty is the fine point of his speculative analysis:

> Gwendolen's confession, for the very reason that her conscience made her dwell on the determining power of her evil thoughts, convinced him the more that there had been throughout a counterbalancing struggle of her better will. It seemed almost certain that her murderous thought had had no outward effect – that, quite apart from it, the death was inevitable. Still, a question as to the outward effectiveness of a criminal desire dominant enough to impel even a momentary act, cannot alter our judgment of the desire; and Deronda shrank from putting that question forward in the first instance. He held it likely that Gwendolen's remorse aggravated her inward guilt, and that she gave the character of decisive action to what had been an inappreciably instantaneous glance of desire. But her remorse was the precious sign of a recoverable nature. . . . (Ibid.)

George Eliot makes him register the probable errors of self-analysis, as he sees the difference between 'the inappreciable instantaneous glance of desire', 'decisive action', and the unreliability of 'remorse which may have aggravated . . . guilt'. His illuminating insights are part of the novelist's self-referential insistence on the inaccessibility of emotional life, and the inevitable difficulty of understanding it. Implicit also, I think, is the suggestion that analysis, however doomed to tentativeness, is an inevitable response. If Daniel gave up analysis, depairing of its inaccuracy, he would retreat from sympathy. He may be a mentor, but he exemplifies a scepticism about analytic procedures which the novel itself employs. His imagined uncertainty is entirely in character, but erodes the solidity of fictional form. As it analyses, it questions analysis.

Such openness in *Daniel Deronda* is appropriate to the speculative nature of its arguments and to its convolutions and fractures of narrative. George Eliot's personifications and allegories are extensions of a traditional mode, but one which is explicitly permuted, tested, and judged.

2 *Narrators, Actors, and Readers*

George Eliot's notebook, which she called *Quarry for Middlemarch*, contains a series of overlapping plans and outlines of situations, events and 'Relations to be developed', which refer in detail to feelings and passions. The first set of chapter plans mostly consist of summaries, such as 'The two suitors persevere' and 'Bulstrode with Lydgate & Vincy', which show concern for structure and scene, and occasionally include emotional details, as if even a briefly sketched situation carried with it the imagined mood; so 'Dorothea in tears', 'Lydgate & Rosamond in flirtation'. Later sections elaborate the theme, noting: 'Dorothea in tears', 'Family consternation', 'Embarrassment of Lydgate', 'Fred Vincy becomes jealous', 'Lydgate's first anguish', 'Mrs Bulstrode learns her sorrow' and 'Dorothea in her anguish'. The question of emotional detail becomes even more prominent in the section headed 'Elements', which notes Lydgate getting 'more embarrassed' and moody in consequence, and forecasts a scene (not part of the novel) in which Will and Dorothea meet after the discovery-scene (Chapter 77), which is formulated exclusively in terms of the passions of 'anger, jealousy and reproach, ending in Dorothea's passionate avowal', followed by further details of reproach, alarm, jealousy and pity. The section headed 'Scenes' plans even more frequently and consistently in emotional terms, repeating Lydgate's embarrassment and moodiness, and adding his anger, Rosamond's discontent, Bulstrode's constraint 'by fear & conscience', and Dorothea's discovery of Will and Rosamond, 'in emotion – together'. There is another slightly more limited plan for the unincluded scene 'of anger & jealousy between Will and Dorothea, ending in her avowal of love & resolve not to marry him', followed by details of Dorothea 'wrought on by compassion' and 'terror of Bulstrode'. In the 'Sketches' which overlap with the 'Scenes' we find 'indifference' in both Will and Rosamond, Will's impatience, Rosamond's pining and outpouring of 'feeling' joy, Lydgate's high spirits and Rosamond's 'repulsion', Will and Rosamond in 'confusion', Dorothea 'repressing her anguish' and carrying out 'her intended admonitions', Rosamond 'shivering', Bulstrode's terrors, Lydgate's misery, Lydgate's outpouring of misery to Dorothea, her comfort, another version of the Will and Rosamond discovery, with 'their emotion', and another version of Dorothea's response, this time omitting the projected scene with Will, 'Her emotions of jealousy', which make her 'more distinctly aware of her love', and 'her struggle to overcome her selfish feeling'. There follow 'Lydgate's first anguish', Mrs Bulstrode's 'sorrow', Will's 'outburst of bitterness against Rosamond' and 'Dorothea's anguish and struggles'. Detail and repetition emphasize George Eliot's plans for the represen- tation of emotion. Her art needed such plans and forecasts, but they set out the feelings very simply, with the single exception of the formulation, 'in emotion', used of Will and Rosamond in the discovery-scene, which avoids conventional naming.

When George Eliot came to carve stone into sculpture, her representation of feeling was complex and dynamic. There is one marked omission from the plans and preparations for the emotion in the novel. They make no mention of the emotions of the narrator. George Eliot plans scenes, relationships, and development in terms of emotion, and she creates an effective continuity. The narrator's emotions, implicit and explicit, fill in the spaces between the feelings of the characters. The novelist devises a rhetoric for the development and differentiation of these characters, and invariably supplements the drama of her characters' emotional life by the fluent ironies and sympathies of the omniscient but reticent narrative voice. This narration ensures emotional continuity, marks development and openly manipulates the reader's response. In some ways it resembles Dicken's narrative voice, but it is more sustained and complex. While the emotions and passions of love, jealousy, embarrassment, anguish, and consolation are represented through dialogue, description, imagery, and allegory, they are at the same time placed in the context of an authoritative action of judgement and explication, itself coloured by a variety of moods and emotions.

Like Charlotte Brontë, George Eliot locates passion and a knowledge of passion within character, but she has a more Shakespearian capacity to explore varieties of emotional experience. At times she sets up a contrast between the representative narrator's wisdom and the limited power of an Amos Barton, a Hetty Sorrel, or a Silas Marner. At times she creates intelligent, imaginative, and even learned characters, like Daniel Deronda or Will Ladislaw, who have a capacity to analyse feeling and passion. She moves between these poles, but most often works with characters who are gifted and limited. Her preference is for a contrast of historical viewpoint, rather than intelligence. She is centrally concerned with power and limits, as in Adam Bede, Maggie Tulliver, Dorothea Brooke, and Gwendolen Harleth. Maggie's moral imagination insists on locating the needs of self by referring to the needs of others, but she has been brought up in a social and psychological ignorance, 'unhappily quite without that knowledge of the irreversible laws within and without her . . .' (Chapter 32). Dorothea Brooke is an exact contemporary of Maggie's who is endowed with a keener historical consciousness, asking what she 'can do' 'now – in England', but at the end of the story, 'becoming assimilated to the life of another', and placed by the narrator's ironic insistence that 'nobody could ever say what else she could have done'. Gwendolen Harleth is less visionary and altruistic than her heroic predecessors, but slowly develops a sense of self in relation to the world; she is left without the conventional properties of husband, children, and mentor, though the 'grand and vague' conclusion is furnished with the images of social likelihood, such as family, home, and an eligible suitor. George Eliot tells the stories of these women from a double viewpoint, insisting that their emotions, relationships, and actions are determined by historical conditions, while at the same time showing her melancholy knowledge of time and space beyond their destinies.

There is always a double point of view, marking the imaginary life of constricted feeling, and a larger sympathy and knowledge. But the character is shown in developmental terms, for better or for worse. The characteristic pattern is moral and emotional. George Eliot creates characters who commit themselves to dealing with the larger world egocentrically, damaging themselves and others, or, altruistically, creating something for themselves and others. She plans and constructs continuities of feeling, but her affective form is always illustrative, and has a parable-like pattern, after the model of Bunyan, of progress or deterioration.

In the early stories, *Scenes of Clerical Life*, we can see the emergence of this form. In 'The Sad Fortunes of the Reverend Amos Barton' and 'Mr Gilfil's Love-Story' there is continuity; we see links between character and emotion, in a narrative infused with feeling. There are emotional links between events and scenes, but there is no marked progression or deterioration. The lives are too short and simple. The structural pattern most marked is the contrast between the limits of the characters (Amos, Gilfil, Caterina) and the melancholy, nostalgic, ironic, and compassionate feelings of the story-teller. The third story, 'Janet's Repentance', contains George Eliot's first developmental representation of morality and feeling, in Janet's struggles and conversion. George Eliot endows a heroine constricted by a woman's dependence with a capacity for self-knowledge, control and independence. The end of the story leaves her, like Gwendolen, morally settled, and deprived of the traditional ties and relationships of woman's life. The Christian impress on the pattern of growth, change, and salvation may veil the final isolation, but that isolation is significantly present.

There also appears for the first time George Eliot's creation of a character's finely impassioned intelligence. The action is located within the mind, and within the feelings. Thinking and feeling are dealt with together, as the author finely adjusts language to its task of dramatized analysis. The characters are dealt with physiologically as well as psychologically; George Eliot pioneers the observation, in fiction, of the cyclical nature of a woman's emotional life. Her narrator speaks of Janet's depression from a knowledge of all the conditions: a fit of depression is particularized in terms of tears, loss of appetite, and lack of concentration, then enlarged and generalized: 'It is such vague undefinable states of susceptibility as this – states of excitement or depression, half mental, half physical – that determine many a tragedy in women's lives' (Chapter 25). This act of generalization shows

George Eliot's constant movement away from mimesis. Character is particularized, but assimilated to a larger category. The narrative points towards the fictitious case, but then moves from drama to taxonomy. This is a simple instance, yet it not only combines the fictitious and taxonomic, but insists on the uncertainty of knowledge, as it describes the emotion as 'vague' and 'undefinable'. Where the emotional state is less vague, though still inaccessible to naming or classifying, the formal shift between narrator and character may be less clear. We begin to find the brilliant use of the free indirect style, merging the dramatized character with the narrating authorial presence. Character becomes more intelligently reflective:

> Her ideas had a new vividness, which made her feel as if she had only seen life through a dim haze before; her thoughts, instead of springing from the action of her own mind, were external existences, that thrust themselves imperiously upon her like haunting visions. The future took shape after shape of misery before her, always ending in her being dragged back again to her old life of terror, and stupor, and fevered despair. Her husband had so long overshadowed her life that her imagination could not keep hold of a condition in which that great dread was absent; and even his absence – what was it? only a dreary vacant flat, where there was nothing to strive after, nothing to long for.
>
> The daylight changes the aspect of misery to us, as of everything else. In the night it presses on our imagination – the forms it takes are false, fitful, exaggerated; in broad day it sickens our sense with the dreary persistence of definite measurable reality. The man who looks with ghastly horror on all his property aflame in the dead of night, has not half the sense of destitution he will have in the morning, when he walks over the ruins lying blackened in the pitiless sunshine. That moment of intensest depression was come to Janet, when the daylight which showed her the walls, and chairs, and tables, and all the commonplace reality that surrounded her, seemed to lay bare the future too. . . .
>
> Everywhere the same sadness! Her life was a sun-dried, barren tract, where there was no shadow, and where all the waters were bitter.
> No! she suddenly thought – and the thought was like an electric shock – there was one spot in her memory which seemed to promise her an untried spring, where the waters might be sweet. (Chapter 16)

These passages alternate with dialogue and the narration of external events. George Eliot places descriptions of feeling in the physical contexts of the outside world of ordinary living, in which Janet is warmed, relaxed, and mentally stimulated by drinking tea, talking to her friend, and in which she gets up, dresses, and decides to see Tryan. Internal and external events blend into each other, not simply as part of recorded existence, but as cause and effect. The tea-drinking stimulates energies already heightened by distress, as the imagery of desolation evokes an opposite figure of sweet spring-water. Such interaction was present in Dickens and Charlotte Brontë, as the London light playing on the walls of Paul Dombey's room was assimilated to the river imagery, and as the inner chill of Lucy Snowe's fantasy met a cold dawn. George Eliot adds the element of narrative reflection, and this too is merged with the representation of the character's emotions. Two modes of analysis combine: the narrator's 'as if' in the first passage describes what the character feels, 'as if she had only seen life through a dim haze before', and then makes way for the more sophisticated analytic language, 'her thoughts, instead of springing from the action of her own mind'. But Janet is shown as aware of that action: there are two sources of reflection, two actions of consciousness. Narrator and character collaborate in commentary, and there are points where they are hard to separate. 'The future took shape' is formulated by the generalizing narrator, with a concern for form, but the shape-taking happens within Janet's imagination and memory, as she is 'dragged back again to her old life of terror'. The narrator formulates the faculty, 'her imagination could not keep hold', but the question and answer dramatizes Janet's act of imaging absence through the interrogation, 'what was it?' and the answering image, 'only a dreary vacant flat', locates the tropes in her imagination.

In the second passage the narrator's presence is more detached from the rendering of inner life, as the imagery of day and night, and the ruined property, make their generalization distinct, before explicitly moving back to the particular and fictitious, 'That moment . . . was come to Janet', where we are located within the disenchanted reality of 'walls, and chairs, and tables'. The simple linking by the accumulated copulas dramatizes the inner motion. And in the last section the metaphor is shared by narrator and character, as the 'No!' of direct speech and dramatic exclamation transports Janet from the imagery of the desert to that of spring, as if the extremity of image suggested a solution through language. The analysis is located within and outside the character; character and category are set side by side. The narrator is using the power of apt and traditional biblical imagery and the surface of the story to blend the mind that describes with the mind being described. There is a clash of imagery, in the movement from the blackened ruins of the example to the 'real' house in the story, and in the interruption of the simile, 'like an electric shock', which shocks by its shift of register. Janet is given a fullness of attention, in characterization and story, which we do not ordinarily associate with illustrativeness, and generalized analysis is given an imagistic and narrative vitality. Discourse is dramatized to blend with the drama.

This early example shows George Eliot's ability to represent in order to analyse, and to analyse in order to represent. The duality of motion guards against dangers of confusing discursive and dramatic modes. Fiction is broken, generalization made lively. This is far from being the only way in which the novelist presents affective events. There are many moments in these stories where the gap between character and narrator is a large one, where commentary on feeling is solicitous, but didactic, and unparticularized. George Eliot's commentary, like Dickens's, is often made in the interests of exhortation. On one occasion, observing the rarity of emotional communication stripped of disguise and free from social restriction, the narrator is direct and peremptory. As Janet tells Tryan the story of her temptation, speaking artlessly, in hesitant and broken phrases or urgent questions, stage-direction becomes generalized, as if the narrator is moved as well as the characters:

'Have you ever known any one like me that got peace of mind and power to do right? Can you give me any comfort – any hope?'

While Janet was speaking, she had forgotten everything but her misery and her yearning for comfort. Her voice had risen from the low tone of timid distress to an intense pitch of imploring anguish. She clasped her hands tightly, and looked at Mr Tryan with eager questioning eyes, with parted, trembling lips, with the deep horizontal lines of overmastering pain on her brow. In this artificial life of ours, it is not often we see a human face with all a heart's agony in it, uncontrolled by self.consciousness; when we do see it, it startles us as if we had suddenly waked into the real world of which this everyday one is but a puppet-show copy. For some moments Mr Tryan was too deeply moved to speak.

'Yes, dear Mrs Dempster', he said at last, 'there *is* comfort, there *is* hope for you.' (Chapter 18)

Representation and analysis are subtly combined in the account of Dorothea's response to Rosamond and Will 'in emotion' together, in Chapter 77 of *Middlemarch*. Dorothea's response is first represented behaviouristically, through speech, gesture, and act. When she sees Rosamond, 'flushed and fearful', and Will clasping her hand, she is confused, moves back, finds some piece of furniture in the way; until her emotion is seen through Will, who finds in her eyes 'a new lightning'. She speaks firmly, delivers her letter, includes Rosamond and Will 'in one distant glance and bow', and walks to her carriage 'with her most elastic step':

> 'Drive on to Freshitt Hall,' she said to the coachman, and any one looking at her might have thought that though she was paler than usual she was never animated by a more self-possessed energy. And that was really her experience. It was as if she had drunk a great draught of scorn that stimulated her beyond the susceptibility to other feelings. She had seen something so far below her belief, that her emotions rushed back from it and made an excited throng without an object. She needed something active to turn her excitement out upon. She felt power to walk and work for a day, without meat or drink. And she would carry out the purpose with which she had started in the morning, of going to Freshitt and Tipton to tell Sir James and her uncle all that she wished them to know about Lydgate, whose married loneliness under his trial now presented itself to her with new significance, and made her more ardent in readiness to be his champion. She had never felt anything like this triumphant power of indignation in the struggle of her married life, in which there had always been a quickly subduing pang; and she took it as a sign of new strength. (Chapter 77)

The free indirect style moves us into the inner action of Dorothea's feelings and reflections on feelings. She feels a 'more self-possessed energy' and physical power, anticipates her movements, compares this emotional experience with others and attempts interpretation. A comment which seems to belong to the narrator's awareness is the brilliantly figurative and analytic comparison of her feeling to a stimulating draught, a simile followed by a precise and generalized metaphor, 'her emotions rushed back from it and made an excited throng without an object'. (This assessment anticipates, conceptually, T.S. Eliot's complaint that Hamlet lacks an objective correlative for affective response.) These comparisons and comments are profound; they also make the causal link, of which the character is not aware, between excitement and reaction. The lack of awareness is crucial; she is in a state of shock, and misjudges composure and power. The next chapter takes her into uncontrollable grief and jealousy. There is a step-by-step record of thinking and feeling, a counting of the atoms as they fall on heart and mind. The record consists of particularized reflections, characteristic of Dorothea, combined with terse and exact narrative comment, which marks the subjectivity of her judgements and resolutions. The narration is analytically informative and dramatically introspective, following and furthering the particulars of character. Like the crisis of Janet's depression, this episode of feeling is part of the moral programme of the novel. Dorothea overestimates her resilience, prematurely celebrates and justifies her scorn, and congratulates herself on her self-command. In the scene which follows, she succumbs to the passions of jealous reproach, and is then restored to her habitual tendency of caring. The emotional episodes play their part in a moral pattern, where two structural principles are at work, the illustrative and the dramatic.

Chapter 42 is a fine example of this same combination. It cunningly and imaginatively manipulates the reader's response:

> Lydgate, certain that his patient wished to be alone, soon left him; and the black figure with hands behind and head bent forward continued to pace the walk where the dark yew-trees gave him a mute companionship in melancholy, and the little shadows of bird or leaf that fleeted across the isles of sunlight, stole along in silence as in the presence of a sorrow. Here was a man who now for the first time found himself looking into the eyes of death – who was passing through one of those rare moments of experience when we feel the truth of a commonplace, which is as different from what we call knowing it, as the vision of waters upon the earth is different from the delirious vision of the water which cannot be had to cool the burning tongue. When the commonplace 'We must all die' transforms itself suddenly into the acute consciousness 'I must die – and soon', then death grapples us, and his fingers are cruel; afterwards, he may come to fold us in his arms as our mother did, and our last moment of dim earthly discerning may be like the first. To Mr Casaubon now, it was as if he suddenly found himself on the dark river-brink and heard the plash of the oncoming oar, not discerning the forms, but expecting the summons. In such an hour the mind does not change its life-long bias, but carries it onward in imagination to the other side of death, gazing backward – perhaps with the divine calm of beneficence, perhaps with the petty anxieties of self-assertion. What was Mr Casaubon's bias his acts will give us a clue to. He held himself to be, with some private scholarly reservations, a believing Christian, as to estimates of the present and hopes of the future. But what we strive to gratify, though we may call it a distant hope, is an immediate desire: the future estate for which men drudge up city alleys exists already in their imagination and love. And Mr Casaubon's immediate desire was not for divine communion and light

divested of earthly conditions; his passionate longings, poor man, clung low and mist-like in very shady places. (Chapter 42)

George Eliot is here combining two movements. She exalts awe and fear in the character, and sympathy in the reader, through scene, image, and mythological enlargement, then also deflates and denies sympathy, and refuses to valorize Casaubon's passions. Sympathy is invited through traditional imagery, 'the dark yew-trees gave him a mute companionship in melancholy', with resonant music thrown in for extra measure, 'the little shadows of bird or leaf that fleeted across the isles of sunlight, stole along in silence as in the presence of a sorrow'. Pathetic fallacy plays its part, together with incantatory and sensuously pleasing language. We are lulled into sympathy. George Eliot makes an almost Dickensian use of the pastoral background and the solemnizing paraphernalia of death. Ritual and generalization invite us to imagine on our own behalf the imminence of death. The personifications of grappling death's cruel fingers and comforting death's maternal embrace are arousing and persuasive. Finally, the sonorously invoked tradition takes us into ritual and myth, to the 'dark river-brink', hearing the oars and 'expecting the summons'. But the resemblance to the structures and language of Dickens's death-scenes soon disappears.

George Eliot makes the narrator deceive us, though the deceit itself is only superficial, always eroded by qualification and speculation. The first images work without qualification, the mute melancholy and sorrow can be imputed even to Casaubon, but the imagery of a sympathetic phenomenal world is, on close inspection, presented tentatively. An 'as' disclaims fiction and admits mere resemblance: 'as in the presence of a sorrow'. The yews are traditionally morbid trees, but the birds simply part of the superficial appearance of tact and solicitous silence. The word 'mute' is of course accurate (trees don't talk) and suitably funereal. But the powerful personifications belong to narrative generalization, are not committed to Casaubon's particular experience, though they are not uncommitted either. They tell us that the announcement of death is cruel and inexorable, that death itself may be comforting. The imagery of Styx and Charon, while appropriate in an account of the mortal illness of a classical scholar (he was misled by the classical poets' account of amorous passion), is not imputed to the character's imagination. It is also distanced by another candid 'as': 'To Mr Casaubon now, it was as if he suddenly found himself on the dark river-brink', but the resonance of style and myth is lulling, dignifying, and associative, generalization persuading us to sympathy by the Aristotelian means of self-reference. Thinking solemnly of death will help us to think solemnly of this death, as self-pity moves into compassion.

But not entirely: 'the mind does not change its lifelong bias', and we move from traditional and poetic rites of passage to the scrupulous imagining of imagination. We are being asked to sympathize, but also to appraise, and not to sentimentalize. We are shifted from dignity and solemnity to pettiness. The narrator does not let us down abruptly, but moves tactfully along rhythmical alternations of the general and the particular, in and out of fiction. 'Perhaps' is crucial: 'perhaps with the divine calm, perhaps with the petty anxieties'. The narrator plays fair, in a cunning way, through revisions and provisionality. We are told of the alternatives, then reminded of the likelihood, which we have learnt and are expected to remember: 'What was Mr Casaubon's bias his acts will give us a clue to.' There follows the withdrawal of dignifying conjecture, generalization, and poetry, in a sentence which recalls the imagery and bias of his passions, which 'poor man, clung low and mist-like in very shady places'. The tone of 'poor man' is compassionate, regretful, and belittling.

We are invited to sympathize, so that sympathy may be educated, elucidated, refined. The rhetoric is self-analytic, inviting and relying on a careful reading of words and structures. George Eliot both uses and appraises the conventional rhetoric of feeling, in ways which deepen the particularity of character and assert its fictitiousness. The affective medium uses the facile response of the reader, intent on fiction and poetry, and forces it to inspect itself. We are not asked to give up pity, but to give a pity which is scrupulously particularized and analysed.

On another occasion the reader's response is teased, and teased out, less quietly and gently. In Chapter 20, Dorothea's feelings are ill-defined, and the character's incapacity is related to the narrator's generalization: 'Dorothea was crying, and if she had been required to state the cause, she could only have done so in some such general words as I have already used: to have been driven to be more particular would have been like trying to give a history of the lights and shadows.' This refusal to be particular is delivered in a way which shows a full awareness of the dual language being used, the language used by characters and used about characters. The narration avoids particulars and accretes massive sentences, appropriate not only to the delineation of emotional vagueness, but to the vast and elusive presence of Rome. Like the culture and the city, Dorothea's grievance is not single or distinctly 'shapen'; Rome presents a stupendous 'fragmentariness', and Dorothea feels confused and strange. Rome is more than an objective correlative, blending cause and symbol, locale and metonymy. Once more there is analysis of feeling, in explicit and metaphorical terms:

> all this vast wreck of ambitious ideals, sensuous and spiritual, mixed confusedly with the signs of breathing forgetfulness and degradation, at first jarred her as with an electric shock, and then urged themselves on her with that ache belonging to a glut of confused ideas which check the flow of emotion. Forms both pale and glowing took possession of her young sense, and fixed themselves in her memory even when she was not thinking of them, preparing strange associations which remained through her after-years. (Chapter 20)

The narration works through the accumulation of similar images and the friction of opposing ones. The image of the electric shock clashes with the classical and monumental imagery, and aptly renders the 'jarring'. There follows a passage which is entirely directed outward, towards the reader, in an apostrophe which takes us from sympathy and exaltation to an attack on the literary response, comparable to Dickens's address to the readers on the occasion of Jo's death:

> Not that this inward amazement of Dorothea's was anything very exceptional; many souls in their young nudity are tumbled out among incongruities and left to 'find their feet' among them, while their elders go about their business. Nor can I suppose that when Mrs Casaubon is discovered in a fit of weeping six weeks after her wedding, the situation will be regarded as tragic. Some discouragement, some faintness of heart, at the new real future which replaces the imaginary, is not unusual, and we do not expect people to be deeply moved by what is not unusual. That element of tragedy which lies in the very fact of frequency, has not yet wrought itself into the coarse emotion of mankind; and perhaps our frames could hardly bear much of it. If we had a keen vision and feeling of all ordinary human life, it would be like hearing the grass grow and the squirrel's heart beat, and we should die of that roar which lies on the other side of silence. As it is, the quickest of us walk about well wadded with stupidity.

Feeling is imputed to character, narrator, and reader. The feelings of the character are represented, in the convention of psychological realism, but the fiction of Dorothea's character is dealt with 'as if' real. The narrator is engaged in addressing the reader, and describing the character. The representation is character-centred, but also reader-centred, uttered in expressed awareness of art and of an affective response to that art. The modes are joined, to merge. The narrator's discursive and emotional address is generalized, as it discusses sympathy and sensibility, and also particularized. The bridge passages tend to present character as illustrative, 'Not that this inward amazement of Dorothea's was anything very exceptional', moving easily into the category and out of the individual case, 'many souls in their young nudity'. They present generalization to explicate: 'However, Dorothea was crying', immediately follows the generalized address to the reader, 'the quickest of us walk about well wadded with stupidity'.

The next turns towards, and away from, the reader; the form has discontinuity and continuity: change of gear, but the engine has gone on running. The presentation of Dorothea's 'states of dull forlornness' and 'fit of weeping' may expect sympathy, but dryly disclaims such expectation, in a form of *occupatio*. The narrator does not expect the situation to be 'regarded as tragic', even while asserting the view that it is tragic, 'the element of tragedy which lies in the very fact of frequency'. The reader is expected to be unsympathetic but to learn to be appropriately sympathetic. Implicit in the narrator's argument is a knowledge of conventional expectations derived from the element of tragedy which lies in the fact of exceptionality.

The fluent narrative moves us from one feeling to another, and is ironically aware of the reader, likely to respond facilely to local rhetorical pressures. The language of appeal becomes heightened, resonant, lyrical, imagistic, as it suggests that we associate ourselves not with coarse emotion but with finer feelings, and invites us to adopt the 'keen vision and feeling' for all ordinary life. The images propose to slow down the normal time-flow, and to create a new space-relation, formulating the possibility of 'hearing the grass grow and the squirrel's heart beat', though at the expense of being deafened by 'that roar which lies on the other side of silence'. When we have been sufficiently flattered by the shifts in pace and perspective and the fictitious chance to feel finely and die nobly, we are as violently switched back to normal conditions as we were transported from them into hyper-sensitive close-up. Having ascended the heights to which literature can sublimate response, we are bluntly accused of comfortable obtuseness: 'As it is, the quickest of us walk about well wadded with stupidity.' It is an adroit, analytic reminder of the strength of literary language and the susceptibility of literary response. 'The quickest of us' is self-referential, allowing for no exceptions as the text opens out vertiginously and rebukingly to the world where sympathy is hard to get and give.

We have moved a long way from the intense, high-toned appeals on behalf of Amos Barton, Caterina Sarti, and Seth Bede. In the earlier novels, George Eliot's narrator may imagine a reader below the reasonable level of expectation, flattering the sympathetic response by singling out an exemplary unexemplary reader in the manner of Sterne and Thackeray, but in *Middlemarch* there is a refusal to praise the average sympathetic reader. The emotional processes of reading are teased and criticized, revealing some impatience with the solicitations of text as well as the facile readiness of response. George Eliot is capable of refusing to privilege the novel. Such refusal is entirely in keeping with the (relative) openness of the conclusions to *Middlemarch* and *Daniel Deronda*.

The openness of *Daniel Deronda* is a familiar subject of critical inquiry, but the end of *Middlemarch* is often judged as a conventional closure. George Eliot's representation and reflexive analysis of emotional appeal and response is at work in its 'Finale', making a conspicuous admission of literary conditions, as well as providing a conventionally sublime peroration:

> Certainly those determining acts of her life were not ideally beautiful. They were the mixed result of young and noble impulse struggling amidst the conditions of an imperfect social state, in which great feelings will often take the aspect of error, and great faith the aspect of illusion. For there is no creature whose inward being is so strong that it is not greatly determined by what lies outside it. A new Theresa will hardly have the opportunity of reforming a conventual life, any more than a new Antigone will spend her heroic piety in daring all for the sake of a brother's burial: the medium in which their ardent deeds took shape is for ever gone. But we insignificant people with our daily words and acts are preparing the lives of many Dorotheas, some of which may present a far sadder sacrifice than that of the Dorothea whose story we know.
>
> Her finely-touched spirit had still its fine issues, though they were not widely visible. Her full nature, like that river of which Cyrus broke the

strength, spent itself in channels which had no great name on the earth. But the effect of her being on those around her was incalculably diffusive: for the growing good of the world is partly dependent on unhistoric acts; and that things are not so ill with you and me as they might have been, is half owing to the number who lived faithfully a hidden life, and rest in unvisited tombs.

Dorothea is exalted by heroic comparison, 'a new Theresa', and praise, 'finely-touched spirit'. The narrator appeals on her behalf for pity: 'sadder sacrifice', and for admiration: 'her effect of her being on those around her'. But she is also represented as an illustration. Her centrality and her particularity are disturbed by the plural, 'many Dorotheas', and by the implications of typology, 'a new Theresa' and 'a new Antigone'. The appeal at the conclusion is clamant and melancholy, not ironic, but irony is directed towards the fictions of Dorothea's own determining acts, 'not ideally beautiful', and of the generalized views of Middlemarch. The last sentence of the novel is discursive, turned away from the particularities of story and character, while completing the address of the fictitious narrator, intent on that world outside Middlemarch and *Middlemarch*, which has been represented by the metonymy of the novel as a whole. Reminding us of a world beyond fiction, the last words make an emotional appeal. The narrative voice moves beyond the praise and pity of Dorothea to speak in pity, melancholy, hope, and celebration, on behalf of those 'who lived faithfully a hidden life, and rest in unvisited tombs'. The rhythm comes to a funereal halt.

It is not surprising that George Eliot's last book, *Theophrastus Such*, which abdicates the role of the novelist, returns to that thinly fictionalized discursive mode of her first essays, and clearly questions the position of the novelist. Her first narrator, MacCarthy,[1] a failed writer whose unpublished work is collected by an editor, was inhibited by a sensibility to the corruption, disorder and ugliness of 'outward existence' too painful for artistic transformation. Theophrastus who is the spokesperson within a discourse which is not a work of art, articulates the artist's difficulty:

> The illusion to which it is liable is not that of habitually taking duck-ponds for lilied pools, but of being more or less transiently and in varying degrees so absorbed in ideal vision as to lose the consciousness of surrounding objects or occurrences; and when that rapt condition is past, the sane genius discriminates clearly between what has been given in this

parenthetic state of excitement, and what he has known, and may count on, in the ordinary world of experience. (*Impressions of Theophrastus Such*, 'How we come to give ourselves false testimonials, and believe in them')

The awareness of the simplifications and selections of passion punctuates and permeates the novels, and its implications are plain in this last questioning of the temptations of artistic vision and communication.

NOTE

1 'Poetry and Prose, From the Notebook of an Eccentric', 1846–7, reprinted in *Essays of George Eliot*, T. Pinney (ed.) (London, 1963).

6

THOMAS HARDY

1 *Passion in Context*

Hardy's lyrics show his restraint in emotional representation. His eloquence is muted, pure, stark, and intense, startling us by quiet means, letting feeling well up in the spaces between utterances, or resound after silence. In 'Overlooking the River Stour', he spends almost the whole poem on brilliantly incised visual images – swallows, moorhens, kingcups – of a world of non-human nature outside his window. Then he shocks us by uttering a feeling for what was not seen, or regarded, inside the room, revealing regret and remorse, while refusing to relate. The reticence of 'the more' is strong and delicate:

> And never I turned my head, alack,
>   While these things met my gaze
>   Through the pane's drop-drenched glaze,
> To see the more behind my back. . . .
> O never I turned, but let, alack,
>   These less things hold my gaze!

In a similarly reserved poem, 'After a Romantic Day', Hardy once more lets feeling's pressure stir through ellipsis, curtness, understatement, and implication:

> The railway bore him through
> An earthen cutting out from a city:
>   There was no scope for view,
> Though the frail light shed by a slim young moon
>   Fell like a friendly tune.
>   Fell like a liquid ditty,

158

And the blank lack of any charm
   Of landscape did no harm.
The bald steep cutting, rigid, rough,
   And moon-lit, was enough
For poetry of place: its weathered face
Formed a convenient sheet whereon
The visions of his mind were drawn.

Here he is able not only to represent feeling, but also, within the purity
of lyric, to meditate on that feeling, to show and to marvel at a fullness
of feeling which needs no objective correlatives, in life or art, though
that blank and bald cutting acts as a functional negation of the objective
correlative. Hardy's caressing touch passes over those untold visions of
his mind, the experience reverberating for the man who has just passed
through it, and into whose silence it enters, creatively. Emotion fills the
imagination, to the brim. What rings for him, without symbol or
name, speaks silently to us. Hardy's lyric poetry, like all great lyric
poetry, depends on a refusal to give, in complete or elaborate form,
characters and histories. It respects the intimacy and mystery of what
John Stuart Mill called the 'deeper and more secret workings of
human emotion'.

   In the novels the conditions are different. The means are narrative
and dramatic. Lyricism is present in the service of narrative and
dramatic forms, dwelling intensely on emotional experiences which
are fully placed in character, history, and environment. T. S. Eliot,
who discussed Hardy's art (in *After Strange Gods*) entirely in terms of its
emotional expression, found it lacking in affective differentiation,
accusing Hardy of being concerned not with minds but with passions,
and of handling them as states of 'emotional paroxysm' in which, Eliot
proposes, human beings are all alike. Hardy is a novelist of violent
feeling; in his Preface to the first edition of *Jude the Obscure*, his most
tragic, dogmatic, and illustrative novel, he speaks of showing 'the
strongest passion known to humanity', and of telling 'without a
mincing of words, of a deadly war waged between flesh and spirit'. The
epigraph to Part First, 'At Marygreen', is a quotation from Esdras
about men running 'out of their wits' for women, but the implied
violence and extremity do not prepare us for the analytic nature of the
novel. Its characters are represented through the continuity, variety
and rhythm of their emotional lives. Those lives move in and out of
crisis with a full sense, on the part of their author, of the individual
creature and the external conditions. Like George Eliot, Hardy

disagrees with Novalis in order to emphasize a belief that tragedy is created from within and from without. Jude is frustrated by birth and class but also by the motions of his sexual appetites. It is important to see that Hardy does not mark him out as singular in sexual vitality but as a common and natural example, not differentiated by a special flaw. What is special is his intelligence and personality, not his desires. Like *Jane Eyre* and *Villette*, the novel offers its version of the conflict and communion of reason with passion. Hardy finds powerful images for Jude's passionate pull away from the rational course, from self-improvement, from study, from the world of his candle's light on the book:

> It had been no vestal who chose *that* missile for opening her attack on him. He saw this with his intellectual eye, just for a short fleeting while, as by the light of a falling lamp one might momentarily see an inscription on a wall before being enshrouded in darkness. And then this passing discriminative power was withdrawn, and Jude was lost to all conditions of things in the advent of a fresh and wild pleasure. . . . (Part 1, Chapter 6)

> In short, as if materially, a compelling arm of extraordinary muscular power seized hold of him – something which had nothing in common with the spirits and influence that had moved him hitherto. This seemed to care little for his reason and his will, nothing for his so-called elevated intentions, and moved him along, as a violent schoolmaster a schoolboy he has seized by the collar, in a direction which tended towards the embrace of a woman for whom he had no respect, and whose life had nothing in common with his own except locality. (Part 1, Chapter 7)

The analysis is conducted by narrator and character. The character is allowed to understand the conditions of his passion, while the narrator remarks the irrelevance of insight. This is not a conflict between mind and appetite, though the divided self is shown in that image of brief illumination, 'the light of a falling lamp'. Sexual desire is shown through a refusal to personify rather than through personification, signified in a passive voice, 'this passing discriminative power was withdrawn'. The images which follow are partial personifications, organs and not wholes, held at arm's length by a scrupulous assertion of comparison, 'In short, as if materially'. The personified power seems the more active for being peculiarly specialized, nothing but arm, convincingly called 'compelling' and 'extraordinary'. When one image is changed for another, there is the bizarre juxtaposition of the isolated arm and the 'violent schoolmaster', and the schoolmaster simile then interacts grotesquely with the literal, unfigurative acts and characters, 'in a direction which tended towards the embrace of a woman for whom he had no respect'. This rhetoric has a particular reference: the images of the schoolmaster and the inscription on the wall derive from Jude's love of learning, while their implications of force make plain the natural power he is up against. When Hardy presents emotional crisis it is not, like Charlotte Brontë and George Eliot, to emphasize moral debate and division, but in order to show the overwhelming power of passion, even when working in and on high intelligence. Charlotte Brontë's Reason would be irrelevant here, not because Hardy is showing a weak man, but because he is showing an overwhelming force. Within the fully delineated social circumstance, the force defeats Jude's passionate aspirations. But Eliot is wrong: passion is placed and differentiated by character.

Hardy does not write allegories of passion in which the forces are evenly matched, and tends to avoid decisive crises of passion. He shows few moments of high affective drama, where a moment's decision can influence the whole life. Far from showing character in states of emotional paroxysm, he prefers to show the combination and accretion of many impassioned occasions. Where the crisis of passion occurs, it is often offstage, narrated rather than dramatized in present-tense intensity. Sometimes the expected passion is displaced, as in *Tess of the d'Urbervilles*. The celebrated seduction is neither shown nor related, and the murder of Alex d'Urberville is narrated indirectly and curiously, first through the bloodspot on the ceiling, then in Tess's singular confession. The expected passions are guilt, fear, or remorse, but what Angel (and the reader) hear is innocent and expectant love:

> 'I have done it – I don't know how. . . . Still, I owed it to you, and to myself, Angel. I feared long ago, when I struck him on the mouth with my glove, that I might do it some day for the trap he set me in my simple youth, and his wrong to you through me. He has come between us and ruined us, and now he can never do it any more. I never loved him at all, Angel, as I loved you. . . . only, Angel, will you forgive me my sin against you, now that I have killed him? I thought as I ran along that you would be sure to forgive me now I have done that. It came to me as a shining thing that I should get you back that way.' (Chapter 57)

Angel interprets this simplicity and candour as delirium, comes to judge it as sanity. She asks forgiveness, not for murder, but for unchastity. Hardy brilliantly endows her with perverse feelings whose perversity is comprehensible. The naive words and form of the narration are both pure and grotesque. Angel first thinks she is speaking metaphorically, then that she is exaggerating:

> By degrees he was inclined to believe that she had faintly attempted, at least, what she said she had done; and his horror at her impulse was mixed with amazement at the strength of her affection for himself, and at the strangeness of its quality. (Ibid.)

The 'phase' in which this chapter appears is ironically called 'Fulfilment'. Tess's insistence on the fulfilment of love overrides our expectations of a fulfilment of revenge or justice. Angel's feelings perfectly match hers, at last: like her he is confused, excited and unable to reason. Her assurance puts refusal out of the question: love utters an imperative. Her language infects his: the free indirect style which registers his response takes on her matter-of-factness and simplicity:

> It was very terrible if true; if a temporary hallucination, sad. But, anyhow, here was this deserted wife of his, this passionately-fond woman, clinging to him without a suspicion that he would be anything to her but a protector. He saw that for him to be otherwise was not, in her mind, within the region of the possible. Tenderness was dominant in Clare at last. (Ibid.)

The penultimate chapter of the novel, the last in which Tess appears, continues this guilt-free imperative and unjudging response. The simple assumptions of love, on which Tess had once acted and expected Angel to act, overcome reason and morality. The passionate faith first assumes and then creates a responsive tenderness. The novel has shown feelings and relationships conditioned and constricted by social laws, and now insulates feelings from convention for a brief space. The completeness of the tacit asking and giving makes any suggestion of sexuality irrelevant; this is one of those rare occasions in fiction when the lover's closeness may or may not be sexual. What is stressed is the unconditional, the relaxed freedom of an enclosed but private time and place, out of time and place:

> 'I am not going to think outside of now. Why should we! Who knows what to-morrow has in store?' (Chapter 58)

Her command of the present almost casts a charm over time, 'But it apparently had no sorrow'. There follows a passage of time-lapse which is tenderly appropriate to this time-haunted novel, for these time-haunted lovers:

> They were indisposed to stir abroad, and the day passed, and the night following, and the next, and next; till, almost without their being aware, five days had slipped by in absolute seclusion, not a sight or sound of a human being disturbing their peacefulness, such as it was. The changes of the weather were their only events, the birds of the New Forest their only company. By tacit consent they hardly once spoke of any incident of the past subsequent to their wedding-day. The gloomy intervening time seemed to sink into chaos, over which the present and prior times closed as if it never had been. Whenever he suggested that they should leave their shelter, and go forwards towards Southampton or London, she showed a strange unwillingness to move.
>
> 'Why should we put an end to all that's sweet and lovely!' she deprecated. 'What must come will come.' And, looking through the shutter-chink: 'All is trouble outside there; inside here content.'
>
> He peeped out also. It was quite true; within was affection, union, error forgiven: outside was the inexorable. (Ibid.)

There is a double current of feeling, as the reader's expectation and tension move across the enclosure and stasis of the characters. The naive style is used in Tess's mild and surprised observation of her past gentleness, 'Yet formerly I could never bear to hurt a fly'. It is used also in the lovers' literal-minded acceptance of 'content' within and 'trouble' outside, as she looks through the shutters and he then peeps out to see and accept what her simple vision sees, 'It was quite true'. The naively registered emotional state can be seen as that of abnormal shock, for both, but it is also structural, presented as a form of the defiant, rational, and tranquil rejection of social circumstance which the novel has been pleading for since Tess's seasonal recuperation. Hardy presents a two-faced situation. It is disturbed and abnormal, if we judge by the conventional standards the novel has been subverting, but understandable and admirable, if we can imagine the severance of the individual from the larger world. Hardy is no fantasist, and sets a limit to this episode of rational madness. The feelings of loving union and harmony are rendered mildly, in an understatement entirely fitted to the narrative rhythm, establishing a lull before the expected storm. It is right that the suspension of law and convention should be initiated by Tess, who has always been capable of pure, unconventional feeling, not only in her recuperation, but in her later empirical expectations of Angel's love and sympathy. The replacement of guilt by love is in keeping with her rejections of history, both naive and intelligent. She refused Angel's characteristically improving offer of history lessons on the grounds that all she will learn is her descent from a line of identical victims, 'there is set down in some old book somebody just like me' (Chapter 19), and her fear of tomorrows 'all in a line, the first of them the biggest and clearest, the others getting smaller . . . very fierce and cruel' (Ibid.) is equally eloquent of her sense of what is threatening to the individual in the inescapable environment. Angel diagnoses her sense of historical melancholy as the 'ache of modernism', ironically placed, in a character with a fine sense of instinctive and untutored feelings, able, like Angel's music, to 'drive such fancies away': it is these natural feelings which help her, the pure, or natural woman, to revive and rally, to defeat or resist the larger environment, in brief but significant episodes. In this final episode of love and death, Hardy assimilates the individual drama through cadences of expectation, tension, fulfilment, and shock, to his larger structure of natural motion, change, loss, and renewal. This is the cyclical form with which he rejects George Eliot's ethical relish at the determination of deeds. Hardy shows that the deeds of Tess and Angel have determined events, but he knows, and also shows, and makes them come to know, that deeds don't necessarily determine emotions. Here, where there might be guilt and horror, there is love.

Tess is simple but ruminative. At the beginning of the novel, when she compares earth to a blighted fruit, she reflects on experience, and at the end she reflects both on the relaxation and the tension, the freedom and the limits, of love's five days of borrowed time and space. Angel's loving becomes purified, in Hardy's sense of the word. It is eased and simplified as he gives not only what she asks but more, what she asked on their marriage: 'I do love you, Tess – oh, I do – it is all come back!' The future is held at bay, and there is a return, an undoing of the past. They feel nothing 'subsequent to their wedding-day'. Angel's earlier sophistry about loving someone who wasn't there is finally revised and dismissed. Tess's outside was her inside too, a natural integrity. Their discovery of each other, and Angel's self-discovery, are not projected in any imaginable social paradigm, but in this repose and interval between the discovery of murder, 'Drip, drip, drip', and the final arrest, both inexorable social acts of cause and effect. Tess is allowed a final rebellious questioning, this time not of society but of Heaven which turns out to be emptier than earth, 'I wanted so much to see you again . . . What – not even you and I, Angel who love each other so well?' The following image of the landscape's massive refusal to answer is sensuously and symbolically exact: 'the whole enormous landscape bore that impress of reserve, taciturnity, and hesitation which is usual just before day.' The humanizing of nature is gently done, in a transference of feeling which just stops short of personification. Nature seems sympathetic, but like humanity, cannot console. Hardy sets the individual feelings, as Lawrence saw, against the natural landscape, and he shows the frail connection between the human and the non-human phenomenal world. His assertion of the connection and the separation, at this point of crisis and conclusion, defines the loneliness of the human pair, as the environment closes around them after an interval which lets them love.

What Hardy does is not at all what Eliot accuses him of doing. Far from showing paroxysms of passion in which character and circumstance are undifferentiated, he takes imaginative pains to place the episodes of passion in the total structure of the work. Tess and Angel not only feel characteristically, but their acts of feeling are in accordance with the novel's argument and story, with everything that has gone before. Angel's early love for Tess, which he comes to discard as an ignorant love for her shell, is justified as the right reading of integrity, the perfect response to the natural, pure, and whole person. Tess's dreamlike appreciation of the honeymoon interlude is entirely in keeping with her closeness to nature and to her awareness of social constriction. Hardy's methods of dramatizing intense feeling lucidly insists on such continuities.

It is also true that he links the crisis of feeling with a world beyond the work of art. He is not only interested in individualizing feeling, and placing it in the sequence of narration, but he is also constantly aware of the relation of individual feeling to larger traditions and rituals. The force of the episode in Bramhurst Court comes not only from the pressure of all that precedes it in the novel, but from the immediate pressure of a sense of ritual. The coming-together in the empty house is the honeymoon the lovers have been denied, perversely placed after a killing not a wedding. This is clear from the explicit revision of the past, the bed, the return to past feeling, the housekeeper's view of 'A genteel elopement' and the lovers' refusal to think of anything 'subsequent to their wedding-day'. The re-enactment also recalls the previous crossing of ritual, when the wedding-night was marked by Angel's somnambulist laying of Tess in the tomb. Hardy enlarges and solemnizes the individual occasion by relating it to social tradition, but always shows the individual variation. In *Tess*, the ritual enlargements come closer to perversion, for worse and for better, than to renewal. There is a simpler process of ritual enactment when Tess and Angel discover Stonehenge, and she is arrested as she wakes from a sleep on the sacrificial slab. She has been right about history, her nature and her doings 'have been just like thousands and thousands'. Hardy links the moment of passion to the book's past and the historical past beyond the book. The passions are individualized, sometimes through astonishing displacements, but they are related to those ceremonies and rituals through which the individual can express and order feeling. The novelist renews the ritual, as he intensifies and reveals the nature of such feeling and such ceremony.

In *The Mayor of Casterbridge* Hardy's combination of ritual and particularity irradiates the commonplace and domestic scene, but also domesticates and realizes   solemnity and melancholy. Like Dickens, Hardy uses comedy to release and to ground pathos, as in the rendering of Susan Henchard's death. Elegy and eulogy are spoken by the Mistress Quickly-like Mrs Cuxsom in a garrulous, circumstantial, solemn, and delicate narration:

> Mrs Cuxsom, who had been standing there for an indefinite time with her pitcher, was describing the incidents of Mrs Henchard's death, as she had learnt them from the nurse.
>
> 'And she was as white as marble-stone,' said Mrs Cuxsom. 'And likewise such a thoughtful woman, too - ah, poor soul - that a' minded every little thing that wanted tending. "Yes," says she, "when I'm gone, and my last breath's blowed, look in the top drawer o' the chest in the back room by the window, and you'll find all my coffin clothes; a piece of flannel - that's to put under me, and the little piece is to put under my head; and my new stockings for my feet - they are folded alongside, and all my other things. And there's four ounce pennies, the heaviest I could find, a-tied up in bits of linen, for weights - two for my right eye and two for my left," she said. "And when you've used 'em, and my eyes don't open no more, bury the pennies, good souls, and don't ye go spending 'em, for I shouldn't like it. And open the windows as soon as I am carried out, and make it as cheerful as you can for Elizabeth-Jane." '
>
> 'Ah, poor heart!'
>
> 'Well, and Martha did it, and buried the ounce pennies in the garden.

But if ye'll believe words, that man, Christopher Coney, went and dug 'em up, and spent 'em at the Three Mariners. "Faith," he said, "why should death rob life o' fourpence? Death's not of such good report that we should respect 'en to that extent," says he.'

'' 'Twas a cannibal deed!' deprecated her listeners.

'Gad, then, I won't quite ha'e it,' said Solomon Longways. 'I say it to-day, and 'tis a Sunday morning, and I wouldn't speak wrongfully for a zilver zixpence at such a time. I don't see noo harm in it. To respect the dead is sound doxology; and I wouldn't sell skellintons - leastwise respectable skellintons - to be varnished for 'natomies, except I were out o' work. But money is scarce, and throats get dry. Why *should* death rob life o' fourpence? I say there was no treason in it.'

'Well, poor soul; she's helpless to hinder that or anything now,' answered Mother Cuxsom. 'And all her shining keys will be took from her, and her cupboards opened; and little things a' didn't wish seen, anybody will see; and her wishes and ways will all be as nothing!' (Chapter 18)

The Shakespearian echoes are clear, 'as white as marble-stone' recalling Falstaff's death-bed, in the vivid and thematic narrative detail, and the blend of humour and sadness fully drawn from the chief narrator and the chorus. We are moved out of sorrow into robust humour, and back again to pathos in the final invocation of the stubbornly surviving and mercilessly exposed household gods. This intense and balanced invocation of literature and custom is only the poetic conclusion to a long scene, where Hardy contrives to give us the unexpected rather than the predictable and universal. As Mrs Henchard lies dying she is watched by Elizabeth-Jane, her daughter, and the vigil is a fine instance of Hardy's restraint:

To learn to take the universe seriously there is no quicker way than to watch - to be a 'waker', as the country-people call it. Between the hours at which the last toss-pot went by and the first sparrow shook himself, the silence in Casterbridge - barring the rare sound of the watchman - was broken in Elizabeth's ear only by the time-piece in the bedroom ticking frantically against the clock on the stairs; ticking harder and harder till it seemed to clang like a gong; and all this while the subtle-souled girl asking herself why she was born, why sitting in a room, and blinking at a candle; why things around her had taken the shape they wore in preference to every other possible shape. Why they stared at her so helplessly, as if waiting for the touch of some wand that should release them from terrestrial constraint; what that chaos called consciousness, which spun in her at this moment like a top, tended to, and began in. Her eyes fell together; she was awake, yet she was asleep. (Chapter 18)

Hardy neatly displaces the girl's sense of bewilderment and doubt, slightly but sufficiently particularizing the 'things around her' to make them stare at her 'helplessly' as he moves her from metaphysical confusion to sleep. Her mother speaks 'without preface, and as the continuation of a scene already progressing in her mind' as she talks about her wish for Elizabeth-Jane's marriage, and the succeeding dialogue is unmarked by unusual feeling, snatched out of ordinariness and made strange by the circumstances:

> 'You remember the note sent to you and Mr Farfrae - asking you to meet some one in Durnover Barton - and that you thought it was a trick to make fools of you?'
> 'Yes.'
> 'It was not to make fools of you - it was done to bring you together. 'Twas I did it.'
> 'Why?' said Elizabeth, with a start.
> 'I - wanted you to marry Mr Farfrae.'
> 'O mother!' Elizabeth-Jane bent down her head so much that she looked quite into her own lap. But as her mother did not go on, she said, 'What reason?'
> 'Well, I had a reason. 'Twill out one day. I wish it could have been in my time! But there - nothing is as you wish it! Henchard hates him.'
> 'Perhaps they'll be friends again,' murmured the girl.
> 'I don't know - I don't know.' After this her mother was silent, and dozed; and she spoke on the subject no more.
> Some little time later on Farfrae was passing Henchard's house on a Sunday morning, when he observed that the blinds were all down. (Ibid.)

It is strikingly different from the death-scenes in Dickens where every detail is magnified, and extraordinary. Hardy's taste is for a mingling of the ordinary with the extraordinary, sometimes to transform object into symbol, but sometimes in order to register the proximity of low and high feeling. This is to combine expectation with surprise.

Understatement makes its bid for pathos, as in Henchard's will. His death is briefly narrated by Abel Whittle, 'he couldn't eat - no, no appetite at all - and he got weaker; and to-day he died. One of the neighbours have gone to get a man to measure him', to which Farfrae says, 'Dear me - is that so!' and Elizabeth says nothing. Like Susan Henchard's death, this is an off-stage event, Hardy frequently avoiding the actual dying. After this laconic report there follows the reading of the will:

'MICHAEL HENCHARD'S WILL

'That Elizabeth-Jane Farfrae be not told of my
death, or made to grieve on account of me.
 '& that I be not bury'd in consecrated ground.
 '& that no sexton be asked to toll the bell.
 '& that nobody is wished to see my dead body.
 '& that no murners walk behind me at my funeral.
 '& that no flours be planted on my grave.
 '& that no man remember me.
'To this I put my name.
'MICHAEL HENCHARD.' (Chapter 45)

Once more particularity refreshes ritual in the pathetic spelling-
mistakes and the reversal of customary last wishes for ceremony and
memorial. Elizabeth reads the 'bitterness' and responds first with
remorse, then acceptance, 'there's no altering – so it must be'. The
solemn formalizing of bitterness, self-pity, and pride is characteristic of
the man who sold his wife by auction and brought the wedding present
of the caged bird. The act of control is both dignified and indulgent,
like all Hardy's acts. But pathos is dismissed, as the narrator changes
her word 'bitterness' to the compassionate word, 'anguish'. Elizabeth's
response to this request is itself in character:

> She knew the directions to be a piece of the same stuff that his whole life was
> made of, and hence were not be tampered with to give herself a mournful
> pleasure, or her husband credit for large-heartedness.
> All was over at last, even her regrets for having misunderstood him on his
> last visit, for not having searched him out sooner, though these were deep
> and sharp for a good while. From this time forward Elizabeth-Jane found
> herself in a latitude of calm weather, kindly and grateful in itself, and
> doubly so after the Capharnaum in which some of her preceding years had
> been spent. As the lively and sparkling emotions of her early married life
> cohered into an equable serenity, the finer movements of her nature found
> scope in discovering to the narrow-lived ones around her the secret (as she
> had once learnt it) of making limited opportunities endurable; which she
> deemed to consist in the cunning enlargement, by a species of microscopic
> treatment, of those minute forms of satisfaction that offer themselves to
> everybody not in positive pain; which, thus handled, have much of the same
> inspiriting effect upon life as wider interests cursorily embraced. (Chapter
> 45)

We moved from lyricism to narration, and from the isolation and anguish to the tranquil passions of Elizabeth, one of Hardy's conspicuous survivors. The narrative on the last page expands the novel more extensively than the hand-in-hand departure of Angel and Liza-Lu in *Tess*, or the grim arrangements of Arabella at the end of *Jude*. The conclusion to *The Mayor of Casterbridge* wrings out of the narrator the marvellously reluctant admission, 'minute forms of satisfaction that offer themselves to everybody not in positive pain'. The introduction of Elizabeth-Jane's moderate happiness joins but does not diminish the sense of tragedy. It endorses anguish by reluctance and qualification, and also by the insistence that Elizabeth-Jane is aware of the exceptional ease of her case and so refuses to be 'demonstratively thankful'.

One of Hardy's finest uses of ritual comes at the end of *The Woodlanders*, where Marty South visits the grave of Giles Winterbourne. It is a subtly constructed conclusion, rising out of a lower-key passage which creates a strong contrast and a smooth transition. *The Woodlanders*, *The Trumpet-Major* and *Jude* are the only Hardy novels to end on a tragic tone. They have a divided plot, and do not concentrate on a central tragic destiny like that of the last novels, which need, like Shakespearian tragedies, to follow intense anguish with recovery or reordering. A farewell to comedy in a choric discussion of women's wiles, and the climates of courtship, acts as a bridge passage to Marty's elegy. As Upjohn and the other rustics talk, they see 'a motionless figure standing by the gate', recognize her, comment, ''a was always a lonely maid' and go 'homeward', to think 'of the matter no more'. The novel ends with Marty's last speech. It is all ritual, and all character:

> As this solitary and silent girl stood there in the moonlight, a straight slim figure, clothed in a plaitless gown, the contours of womanhood so undeveloped as to be scarcely perceptible in her, the marks of poverty and toil effaced by the misty hour, she touched sublimity at points, and looked almost like a being who had rejected with indifference the attribute of sex for the loftier quality of abstract humanism. She stooped down and cleared away the withered flowers that Grace and herself had laid there the previous week, and put her fresh ones in their place.
>
> 'Now, my own, own love,' she whispered, 'you are mine, and only mine; for she has forgot 'ee at last, although for her you died! But I – whenever I get up I'll think of 'ee, and whenever I lie down I'll think of 'ee again. Whenever I plant the young larches I'll think that none can plant as you planted; and whenever I split a gad, and whenever I turn the cider wring,

I'll say none could do it like you. If ever I forget your name let me forget home and heaven! . . . But no, no, my love, I never can forget'ee; for you was a good man, and did good things!' (Chapter 48)

The traditional flowers of elegy, funeral and vegetation rite are the trees of the local woods, the timber Giles and Marty planted and worked with. The feeling of love and praise is joined to the passion of jealous and triumphant possessiveness. The familiar promise to remember is uttered as a claim to be faithful, and not to forget, as Grace has forgotten. The customary praise of funeral oration and epitaph is individual and justified in the case of this good man. What Marty does is common, as she visits the grave and puts her fresh flowers on it, but it is particular, as she clears away the withered flowers she and Grace had put there together. Its appeal is enlarged and solemnized, but it is wholly individual, remembering the pattern, process, and passions of this novel. It is interesting to see that Hardy's narrator doesn't entirely match the impression of the dramatic speech, as if commentary were outrun by embodiment, the tale wiser than the artist. She had not rejected sex for abstract humanism.

In these instances of passionate drama, comedy co-operates with pathos and tragic awe but is kept distinct from it. In *Under the Greenwood Tree*, Hardy blends the comic and the serious in one medium. He uses exaggeration and irony to poke gentle fun at Dick Dewy's romantic loving, but not destructively. His passionate absorption is amusedly and tolerantly related by a voice speaking from weathered experience like that of the tranter or the shoemaker, who have passed through the first climates of courtship but are never cynical or cruel enough to solve Dick's puzzle about his elders' unromantic attitudes to love. The medium is a steady and consistent one, sustained throughout the short novel, to report and register a range of comic and serious feelings. Hardy's playful registration of serious feeling is like Thackeray's representation of Pen's calf-love in *Pendennis*, which also combines sympathy and nostalgia with a knowing but affectionate irony. Hardy's voice is more subdued than Thackeray's, but achieves a similarly dual effect:

The choir at last reached their beds, and slept like the rest of the parish. Dick's slumbers, through the three or four hours remaining for rest, were disturbed and slight; an exhaustive variation upon the incidents that had passed that night in connection with the school-window going on in his brain every moment of the time.

In the morning, do what he would – go upstairs, downstairs, out of doors, speak of the wind and weather, or what not – he could not refrain from an unceasing renewal, in imagination, of that interesting enactment. Tilted on the edge of one foot he stood beside the fireplace, watching his mother grilling rashers; but there was nothing in grilling, he thought, unless the Vision grilled. The limp rasher hung down between the bars of the gridiron like a cat in a child's arms; but there was nothing in similes unless She uttered them. He looked at the daylight shadows of a yellow hue, dancing with the firelight shadows in blue on the whitewashed chimney corner, but there was nothing in shadows. 'Perhaps the new young wom – sch – Miss Fancy Day will sing in church with us this morning,' he said. (Part 1, Chapter 6)

What is described is hallucinatory reverie, but the language of description is comically intent on unromantic metaphor ('the Vision grilled') and cool self-consciousness ('nothing in similes'). The free indirect style conflates comic detachment and passionate obsession. It shows the double viewpoint of serious passion and the wry knowledge of passionate distortions. Hardy's comic medium is established as a norm in this novel, showing the emotions analytically, always distinguishing the absorption of the character from the knowledge of the narrator. When Dick sees Fancy come into church, there is the same registration of a double point of view, both emotional and detached, hot and cold:

Ever afterwards the young man could recollect individually each part of the service of that bright Christmas morning, and the trifling occurrences which took place as its minutes slowly drew along; the duties of that day dividing themselves by a complete line from the services of other times. The tunes they that morning essayed remained with him for years, apart from all others; also the text; also the appearance of the layer of dust upon the capitals of the piers; that the holly-bough in the chancel archway was hung a little out of the centre – all the ideas, in short, that creep into the mind when reason is only exercising its lowest activity through the eye. (Ibid.)

Innocence, rapture, and transience are represented and appraised. The narrative medium perceives and presents the matter-of-fact wisdom of maturity, and the passionate blindness of youth. Dick wonders 'how it was that when people were married they could be so blind to romance; and was quite certain that if he ever took to wife that dear impossible Fancy, he and she should never be so dreadfully practical and so undemonstrative of the Passion as his father and mother were. The most extraordinary thing was, that all the fathers and mothers he knew were just as undemonstrative as his own' (Part 1, Chapter 8). This is neatly turned inside-out by his father: '"I've walked the path once in my life and know the country, neighbours; and Dick's a lost man!"' and '"The sooner begun, the sooner over"' (Part 2, Chapter 3). Romance is narrated unromantically, and the rare generalizations about feeling are kept appropriately sober: 'There had been just enough difficulty attending its development, and just enough finesse required in keeping it private, to lend the passion an ever-increasing freshness on Fancy's part.' The elastic medium can accommodate stronger irony: 'too beautiful and refined to be a tranter's wife, but not perhaps, too good'. The story draws to a close with the combination of a dramatized confidence and a dramatized lyricism, a bitter-sweet blend very like that of the songs in *As You Like It*, from which the title derives:

> 'Fancy,' he said, 'why we are so happy is because there is such full confidence between us. Ever since that time you confessed to that little flirtation with Shiner by the river (which was really no flirtation at all), I have thought how artless and good you must be to tell me o' such a trifling thing, and to be so frightened about it as you were. It has won me to tell you my every deed and word since then. We'll have no secrets from each other, darling, will we ever? – no secret at all.'
> 'None from to-day,' said Fancy. 'Hark! what's that?'
> From a neighbouring thicket was suddenly heard to issue in a loud, musical, and liquid voice –
> 'Tippiwit! swe-e-et! ki-ki-ki! Come hither, come hither, come hither!'
> 'O,'tis the nightingale,' murmured she, and thought of a secret she would never tell. (Part 5, Chapter 2)

Fancy's question, 'Hark! what's that?', is a way of changing the subject, after she has carefully kept to the letter, but not the spirit, of candour. The novel is full of wry reserve and reservation, and its gently ironic conclusion admits duplicity and deceit, even on the wedding journey. But the irony plays delicately on the scene. Hardy allows his lovers a moon 'just over the full', and the song of the nightingale is traditionally and naturally rapturous, and assimilated to the Shakespearian source through its 'Come hither', which intensifies the notes of amorous solicitation and urgency. Lyrical excitement and beauty curiously co-exist with ironic knowledge. After all, Fancy has only fancied infidelity. The lovers will become middle-aged and unromantic, but this is their moment.

Hardy's *Far from the Madding Crowd* continues this ironic but sympathetic vein, but releasing the narrative medium from a comic consistency which could scarcely be kept up in a long novel. Gabriel's touching courtship of Bathsheba is done very much in the style developed in *Under the Greenwood Tree*. It marks individual scenes and is emphasized by formal symmetry. When Gabriel at the end tells Bathsheba that it is time for her to woo him, we recollect the first comic scene in which she let him elaborate his wooing out of curiosity rather than affection. He was encouraged to go through all the question-and-answer of courtship, by a woman who was enjoying the dialogue as a game:

> 'I'll try to think,' she observed rather more timorously; 'if I can think out of doors; my mind spreads away so.'
> 'But you can give a guess.'
> 'Then give me time.' Bathsheba looked thoughtfully into the distance, away from the direction in which Gabriel stood.
> 'I can make you happy,' said he to the back of her head, across the bush. 'You shall have a piano in a year or two – farmers' wives are getting to have pianos now – and I'll practise up the flute right well to play with you in the evenings.'
> 'Yes; I should like that.'
> 'And have one of those little ten-pound gigs for market – and nice flowers, and birds – cocks and hens I mean, because they be useful,' continued Gabriel, feeling balanced between poetry and practicality.
> 'I should like it very much.'
> 'And a frame for cucumbers – like a gentleman and lady.'
> 'Yes.'
> 'And when the wedding was over, we'd have it put in the newspaper list of marriages.'
> 'Dearly I should like that!'
> 'And the babies in the births – every man jack of 'em! And at home by the fire, whenever you look up, there I shall be – and whenever I look up, there will be you.'
> 'Wait, wait, and don't be improper!'
> Her countenance fell, and she was silent awhile. He regarded the red berries between them over and over again, to such an extent that holly seemed in his after life to be a cypher signifying a proposal of marriage. Bathsheba decisively turned to him.
> 'No; 'tis no use,' she said. 'I don't want to marry you.'
> 'Try.'
> 'I've tried hard all the time I've been thinking; for a marriage would be

very nice in one sense. People would talk about me and think I had won my battle, and I should feel triumphant, and all that. But a husband –'
'Well!'
'Why, he'd always be there, as you say; whenever I looked up, there he'd be.' (Chapter 4)

Hardy describes Gabriel's subsequent constancy in a mixture of matter-of-factness and intensity: 'Separation, which was the means that chance offered to Gabriel Oak by Bathsheba's disappearance, though effectual with people of certain humours, is apt to idealize the removed object with others – notably those whose affection, placid and regular as it may be, flows deep and long' (Chapter 5). Sympathy is scrupulously particularized and generalized. The narration moves out of detachment into Gabriel's inner life, to present feeling in two strong images, the 'secret fusion of himself in Bathsheba' and the 'finer flame'. The modulation of emotional narrative is skilful, language heightening as it moves out of generality to dramatize the subdued force of passion. Gabriel's fortitude and control are shown again when he loses his sheep; Hardy registers his characteristic grip on emotion, and the mixture of that experience. Hardy marks the fluctuations from pity to stupefied despair to loving thankfulness that Bathsheba is not involved, and then to listlessness. The novelist shows the quick turbulence and mixture of feeling in several ways, through action and gesture, through a summary of self-communion and finally through a strong, perhaps too strong, symbolic image, the luridly lit pool; made more sinister by the simile of the dead man's eye:

By the outer margin of the pit was an oval pond, and over it hung the attenuated skeleton of a chrome-yellow moon, which had only a few days to last – the morning star dogging her on the left hand. The pool glittered like a dead man's eye, and as the world awoke a breeze blew, shaking and elongating the reflection of the moon without breaking it, and turning the image of the star to a phosphoric streak upon the water. All this Oak saw and remembered. (Chapter 5)

At the end there is a recall of the whole course of courtship and devotion, calm and humorous:

'I have thought so much more of you since I fancied you did not want even to see me again. But I must be going now, or I shall be missed. Why, Gabriel,' she said, with a slight laugh, as they went to the door, 'it seems exactly as if I had come courting you – how dreadful!'

'And quite right, too,' said Oak, 'I've danced at your skittish heels, my beautiful Bathsheba, for many a long mile, and many a long day; and it is hard to begrudge me this one visit.' (Chapter 56)

The wheel has come full circle, and they both know it. Bathsheba's feelings have changed and settled, but her impetuous and unflattering candour remains. When the narrator sums up the joy of union, it is in a sympathetic but unromantic statement, rational and celebratory:

> They spoke very little of their mutual feelings; pretty phrases and warm expressions being probably unnecessary between such tried friends. Theirs was that substantial affection which arises (if any arises at all) when the two who are thrown together begin first by knowing the rougher sides of each other's character, and not the best till further on, the romance growing up in the interstices of a mass of hard prosaic reality. This good-fellowship – *camaraderie* – usually occurring through similarity of pursuits, is unfortunately seldom superadded to love between the sexes, because men and women associate, not in their labours, but in their pleasures merely. Where, however, happy circumstance permits its development, the compounded feeling proves itself to be the only love which is strong as death – that love which many waters cannot quench, nor the floods drown, beside which the passion usually called by the name is evanescent as steam. (Ibid.)

They are not the only characters in the novel, and Hardy also deals with emotionally violent temperaments, like those of Fanny Robin, Troy, and Boldwood. On one occasion Fanny's tragic affection is compared with Bathsheba's: Troy is startled to feel that both women can be overwhelmed by passion, and makes the recognition in characteristically sexist terms, as 'an unexpected revelation of all women being alike at heart'. Bathsheba's loving and jealousy force her to ask him to kiss her instead of Fanny, but after his rejection, 'I will not kiss you', Bathsheba recovers and 'draws' back into herself again 'by a strenuous effort of self-command'. She is forced out of self, into an emotional storm of need and demand, as if 'Fanny's own spirit' is 'animating her frame'. This is a paroxysm of character, placed and judged. When Hardy shows people stormed by passion, losing the habitual power and command of conscience and intelligence, the event is seen to be exceptional and eccentric. Troy and Bathsheba are surprised by the power of passion to overwhelm identity, and reflective awareness is as marked as the irrational episode.

Boldwood is judged as a case of strongly repressed passion; the control is too powerfully exercised, and too dangerously released, and his violence in love and jealousy is analysed as it is represented. Hardy shows him not only through analysis, but also in action. His irrationality is placed in character, movingly and acutely given a personal style:

> In a locked closet was now discovered an extraordinary collection of articles. There were several sets of ladies' dresses in the piece, of sundry expensive materials; silks and satins, poplins and velvets, all of colours which from Bathsheba's style of dress might have been judged to be her favourites. There were two muffs, sable and ermine. Above all there was a case of jewellery, containing four heavy gold bracelets and several lockets and rings, all of fine quality and manufacture. These things had been bought in Bath and other towns from time to time, and brought home by stealth. They were all carefully packed in paper, and each package was labelled 'Bathsheba Boldwood', a date being subjoined six years in advance in every instance. (Chapter 55)

Troy is remembered for passionate actions and symbols: the spurs catching in the skirt, the swordplay which delights and captures Bathsheba, and the terrible moment when natural catastrophe mocks his memorial and the mud obliterates the flowers he plants on Fanny's grave. But Hardy, like George Eliot, for whom after all he was once mistaken, can follow strong and simple striking symbolic action with introspective analysis, and does so when he displays anguish in its full moral and psychological context:

> Sanguine by nature, Troy had a power of eluding grief by simply adjourning it. He could put off the consideration of any particular spectre till the matter had become old and softened by time. The planting of flowers on Fanny's grave had been perhaps but a species of elusion of the primary grief, and now it was as if his intention had been known and circumvented.
>
> Almost for the first time in his life Troy, as he stood by this dismantled grave, wished himself another man. It is seldom that a person with much animal spirit does not feel that the fact of his life being his own is the one qualification which singles it out as a more hopeful life than that of others who may actually resemble him in every particular. Troy had felt, in his transient way, hundreds of times, that he could not envy other people their

condition, because the possession of that condition would have necessitated a different personality, when he desired no other than his own. He had not minded the peculiarities of his birth, the vicissitudes of his life, the meteor-like uncertainty of all that related to him, because these appertained to the hero of his story, without whom there would have been no story at all for him; and it seemed to be only in the nature of things that matters would right themselves at some proper date and wind up well. This very morning the illusion completed its disappearance, and, as it were, all of a sudden, Troy hated himself. The suddenness was probably more apparent than real. A coral reef which just comes short of the ocean surface is no more to the horizon than if it has never been begun, and the mere finishing stroke is what often appears to create an event which has long been potentially an accomplished thing. (Chapter 46)

Hardy's realization of the life before and after the paroxysm, his sense of the preparations and aftermath of passion, shows itself sometimes in comic language. Timothy Fairway in *The Return of the Native*, for instance, speaks with a joviality tempered by lyricism, about the passing of desire:

> 'Ah, Humph, well I can mind when I was married how I zid thy father's mark staring me in the face as I went to put down my name. He and your mother were the couple married just afore we were, and there stood thy father's cross with arms stretched out like a great banging scarecrow. What a terrible black cross that was - thy father's very likeness in en! To save my soul I couldn't help laughing when I zid en, though all the time I was as hot as dog-days, what with the marrying, and what with the woman a-hanging to me. . . . (Book 1, Chapter 3)

As in *Under The Greenwood Tree*, the contrast and pattern is in essence that of some of the painter Munch's most terrible contrasts between age, middle age, and youth, but shown in Hardy with comic impartiality, wryness, and that light but controlled touch which he shares with Timothy Fairway, Gabriel Oak, and some of his other characters.

Although Hardy can speak and show the clarity and force of passion, he can also relax intensity to show the emotional life between crises, thus shaping the full curve of feeling. He shows the pathways to passion. He shows the interaction of two (and more) people's passionate lives. Sue and Jude are responsive to each other's feelings, and Sue is especially vulnerable, and especially dangerous, through her nervous, doubtful, uneasy susceptibilities, sexually fearful, capricious, vain, affectionate, tender. Hardy, like Lawrence, shows the passions we name with dangerous confidence, and the states of feeling too mixed or complex to be tamed by names. (It is ironic that Lawrence, who so attacked our simplification and classification of feeling, should have so simplified Hardy, but of course it is easier to urge our own complexities of passion than to understand other people's.) Phillotson, Sue's husband, explains to his friend that he cannot say what Sue feels for Jude, 'A curious tender solicitude seemingly'. And he knows that she can perhaps not find a word for it herself, 'though her exact feeling for him is a riddle to me – and to him to, I think – possibly to herself' (Part 4, Chapter 4).

Sue's incapacity for sexual relationships[1] collaborates fatally with her courageous social subversions, and clashes fatally with Jude's needs for a physical and intellectual elective affinity. In some ways they feel together, as in mortification. In some ways they are strikingly different, and Hardy contrasts Jude's emotional solidity and simplicity with Sue's emotional epicureanism:

> They strolled undemonstratively up the nave towards the altar railing, which they stood against in silence, turning then and walking down the nave again, her hand still on his arm, precisely like a couple just married. The too suggestive incident, entirely of her own making, nearly broke down Jude.
>
> 'I like to do things like this,' she said in the delicate voice of an epicure in emotions, which left no doubt that she spoke the truth.
>
> 'I know you do!' said Jude. (Part 3, Chapter 7)

Such epicureanism plays its subtle part in that other novel of strong passion and violent upheaval, where man and nature luridly light each other: *The Return of the Native*. We think of the grand passions of Eustacia Vye, but the only feeling she is really clear about is that of restless longing and discontent, and her tragedy, to some extent like Jude's and Sue's, rests on a lack of grand and ruling passion. These are modern children, self-conscious, analytic, divided, looking over the verge of passion almost before they experience passion, wanting to feel, and over-rehearsing feeling. Hardy, like Forster, knows that human beings are often wrecked and bewildered by feeling that they ought to feel more, or feel differently, from how they actually feel. Like Stendhal's Julien Sorel, Eustacia tries on the fit of different feelings. The rehearsal sometimes moves into genuine action, sometimes not:

She was at the modulating point between indifference and love, at the stage called 'having a fancy for.' It occurs once in the history of the most gigantic passions, and it is a period when they are in the hands of the weakest will.

The perfervid woman was by this time half in love with a vision. The fantastic nature of her passion, which lowered her as an intellect, raised her as a soul. If she had had a little more self-control she would have attenuated the emotion to nothing by sheer reasoning, and so have killed it off. If she had had a little less pride she might have gone and circumnambulated the Yeobrights' premises at Blooms-End at any maidenly sacrifice until she had seen him. But Eustacia did neither of these things. She acted as the most exemplary might have acted, being so influenced; she took an airing twice or thrice a day upon the Egdon hills, and kept her eyes employed. (Book 2, Chapter 3)

This interest in emotional uncertainty reaches its comic, not always controlled form, in that strange novel, *The Well-Beloved*, where Hardy's sense of the fitfulness, arbitrariness, and discontinuity of feeling is shown in the wry instance of a middle-aged man, who – unlike others, observes the novelist's gentle irony – has not sailed past the passions into calm seas.

2   The Trumpet-Major: *A Form for Pathos*

In *The Trumpet-Major*, Hardy's historical sensibility is visibly at work, as he represents and analyses feeling through character and event. Historical consciousness shows itself in his other novels, but since this one is a deliberate attempt to recreate time past, emotions about past and present are central and conspicuous. It is dangerous to generalize about the prevailing feeling of a long novel, but it seems possible to recognize in *The Trumpet-Major* a consistent nostalgia and tenderness, which show themselves through the novelist's treatment of history. He constantly looks back, and looks forwards too, and the stance of an historically alerted narrator forces the feelings of post-Christian melancholy and compassion into a prominent position. He deals with fictitious characters, at least in his central story, but presents them with a double time-sense, as dramatically occupied in the specious present time of the action, and as elegaically lamented in the actual past time which is being recalled. His characteristic joining of the generalization with the particular takes a new and sustained pathetic form. Pity for the unremarkable lives of his ordinary people who rest, as George Eliot would say, in unvisited tombs, becomes a residual feeling for everyone.

Hardy's historical consciousness is compounded of a sense of history and a sense of time. Unlike those historical novelists, Scott or Flaubert, whose interest is primarily social, or even archaeological, he is a novelist of sensibility, a time-haunted man whose attitudes to mutability are personal and emotional. In some ways he is like George Eliot, and with a similar refusal to move from Christian optimism to pessimism, he too calls himself a meliorist. Like her, he takes an intense interest in the individual awareness and unawareness of the conditions that determine life, including the pressures of time, place, heredity and society. He records the changing pattern of custom, ritual and occupation, and returns constantly to a reflection on man's ironical ignorance of the world that makes him. But whereas George Eliot tends to admire people with some sense of history, some sensitive awareness of their own difficulties, and some capacity for action, Hardy is strongly and lovingly drawn to characters who haven't the faintest idea of what is happening to them. This is of course not to say that he confines his attention to limited sensibilities or intellects. Tess, Jude and Sue can stand with Dorothea Brooke or Daniel Deronda as instances of lives made creative and painful by radical imagination. In *The Trumpet-Major*, however, no one is remarkable for mind, passion or creativity, though the Trumpet-Major himself, as his skill and instrument imply, is the most powerful figure. But all the characters, including John Loveday, are ordinary men and women, leading lives over which they have virtually no control. It would not be accurate to call these lives unremarkable, because one of the gifts of a great novel is the proof that all lives are remarkable, if looked at deeply and lovingly enough. These people lack name and fame, and the lack is especially striking because they are placed at a time of historical crisis, are brought up against name and fame. They occupy the same world as people who have made history, the strongly felt though invisible character of Napoleon and the highly visible George III and Captain Hardy. The little people are shown acting out their destinies and dying their deaths alongside the great, whose destinies and deaths are notable and crucial, whose tombs are visited. In *The Dynasts* Hardy incorporated Pitt's historical remark about rolling up the map of Europe because it would not be needed for ten years, but *The Trumpet-Major* uses Hardy's own map of Wessex, memorable not because the place-names are associated with battles and treaties, but because they are associated with the events and persons of his fiction. As usual, there is only a faint veil of disguise, and the association of the Court of George III with Budmouth makes its real name of Weymouth very clear. But there is a sense in which Hardy is dehistoricizing Wessex, masking and displacing maps and dates for his own purposes.

One of his best-known poems, 'In Time of the "Breaking of Nations"', displaces the importance of wars and dynasties by showing the durability of work and love, but its rather challenging defence of the unhistoric life is not entirely typical of Hardy. This attitude is certainly not what we find in *The Trumpet-Major*, where almost everything the people do and say is directly affected by the wars and dynasties. Despite their shared meliorism, Hardy is different from George Eliot in his attitude to the past and the present. While *Middlemarch* and *Daniel Deronda* vibrate with the hope that a knowledge of the past may help us to create a better future (as Dorothea thinks, 'now – in England', anticipating T. S. Eliot's point and perhaps providing a source for his words in *Little Gidding*), Hardy's conclusions are usually sombre, deriving little cheer from bright prospects or sublime deaths. His work is lit with pity, and not only does he frequently show energies checked, frustrated and destroyed, but his affection spreads, un-Victorianly and disconcertingly, over ordinary people as well as extraordinary, weak and strong, moral and immoral.

When he reflects on the future, it is often to observe the disastrously premature careers of those born before their time, like Clym Yeobright, Jude or Sue, and his characters tend to be blighted in their creativity before it really gets started. Hardy leans towards pity, rather than admiration, though esteem and respect are strongly present through the novels. He is like Dickens's powerful anti-Utilitarian, Sissy Jupe, of *Hard Times*, in his refusal to be consoled by statistics and graphs of future improvements. His attitude to history is also like that of Tess, his sense of the shortness of life connected not only with his criticism of society, but also with his doubts about the fairness of nature. This haunting sense of time and death makes his novels especially anxious and melancholy. It may also have something to do with his moral toughness and tolerance.

The Trumpet-Major joins elegaic melancholy with moral tolerance.

Being sharply aware of death's end made Hardy imaginatively permissive. The deaths in the novel do not render life meaningless, but certainly shift our view of success or failure, personal or political. Death in this novel is no entrance to glory, either heavenly or secular. Dickens's last pages often contain the heartening organ-notes of a better world; George Eliot often expects us to cheer up at the thought of joining the choir invisible, and contributing to the larger good of the world by a bit of good road-building, improved woods, or the message of a novel. Hardy refuses to end with these enlargements of vision, though *Tess* and *The Mayor of Casterbridge* end with a limited suggestion of better lives, but only for individuals. *The Trumpet-Major*, like the late novels, ends most startlingly and unreassuringly by assimilating the sense of the fiction's ending to the fact of death.

We are waiting for death throughout the novel. We know we are watching the lives of the dead. The novel's pathos is of a special kind, the pathos of a historical novel which combines elegy with record. *The Trumpet-Major* is unlike most historical novels in its sadness, chronicling the past so reverently and compassionately that history is animated and explained from within.

In *The Dynasts*, Hardy's epic and philosophical poem about the Napoleonic Wars, pity is presented in the large, vague, grandiose abstraction of the Pities. The pitying spirits join with the ironic spirits. The novel also creates a compound of pity and irony, concrete and particular. It is an elegiac novel, but not a sentimental one. Hardy is perhaps the least sentimental of Victorian novelists, unlike Dickens, Thackeray and George Eliot, in never demanding more sympathy from his reader than is legitimately invoked by the particulars of person and event. His language never flattens into melodrama, his rhetoric never wheedles us into stock response. He is steadily, and honourably, a tender novelist. Steadily, because he keeps his head. Honourably, because if he requires a strong response from us he repays us fully, unlike the sentimentalist who traditionally requires something for nothing, pity on the cheap.

The Trumpet-Major tells the saddest story, that common human story which always has the same ending, death. Most Victorian novelists tell happy or unhappy stories which end with emotional, material, or moral success and failure. At times Hardy uses death, as in *Tess* or *Jude*, to emphasize the sadness of the actual life, but in *The Trumpet-Major* death is there to level success or failure. It is beside the point to distinguish or compare the private and the public endings of this novel, as critics sometimes do, because they are subsumed by the remorselessness of the mortal end. Hardy, unlike most novelists, seems to feel that he must include the fact of death because he is writing a historical novel. Perhaps this is to state the case with a pedantry alien to Hardy, so let me put it another way: we might say that Hardy felt a particular compassion for his characters because they were dead. Part of his feeling about history involves the sharp imagining of people dressed differently, in some ways conditioned differently, but exactly like us in their deaths. He could not write about real or imagined people, who lived so long ago, without feeling their mortality. His sense of death is created by his thoroughgoing imagination.

Death is present in the novel in many ways. Hardy employs strict accuracy in showing some dead people alive in memory, like Anne's father, the landscape-painter, and old people afraid of death, like Squire Derriman, the only person to die a civilian death in the present action of the novel. But by far the most impressive and original sense of death is connected with Hardy's special invocation of past and future. In George Eliot's novels, there are occasional distinctions between the reader's and the author's time and the novel's time. Hardy uses the rhetoric of forecast as a method of digression or punctuation throughout the novel. When we use the term 'forecast' we should remember that it is forecast from a retrospective viewpoint: the future of the characters is in the reader's past, familiar as memory or historical chronicle. Hardy's pathos is not just a feature of the historical imagination, but related to traditional floutings of time and poetic illusion. It is like the pathetic moment in Shakespeare's *Antony and Cleopatra* when Cleopatra foresees the time when she may be played by a squeaking boy, or that in *Troilus and Cressida* when Cressida defiantly challenges the future to turn her into the type of infidelity if she should prove untrue. It is like the time-shift at the end of *The Eve of St Agnes* when Keats turns abruptly from the lovers' escape in the poetic present to the death of old Angela and the Beadsman, and then sets a gulf of time between us and his story by telling us that it all happened 'ages long ago'. *The Trumpet-Major* is more precise in its ironies, though perhaps irony is not quite the right word for Hardy's utterly explicit and matter-of-fact admissions of the pastness of the novel's time.

Much of the military detail in the novel makes in practice a theatre for the domestic and amorous action, but there are several moments when Hardy concedes that these were real soldiers who were to die real deaths. Unlike the tension we feel for dramatic characters' innocence of the future, what we feel in Hardy is a double vision of the soldiers' innocence and the author's and readers' wisdom after the events. The two points of view are not implicit as in Shakespeare, but explicitly set side by side. The admission that the simple story of the three lovers, so important and urgent to them, is over is a pathetic truth native to Hardy's historical imagination. It has many effects. One of them is a poignant underlining of the casual moment. The forecast of memory frames the fragile present, for instance, as the soldiers chat to the miller when the cherries are ripe. He gathers bunches and holds them up for the men to take, in their forage-caps or 'on the ends of their switches, with the dignified laugh that became martial men when stooping to slightly boyish amusement'. The moment becomes pregnant as we shift perspective:

> It was a cheerful, careless, unpremeditated half-hour, which returned like the scent of a flower to the memories of some of those who enjoyed it, even at a distance of many years after, when they lay wounded and weak in foreign lands. (Chapter 3)

Hardy has sometimes been compared with Thackeray, whose *Vanity Fair* deals with a slightly later stage in the Napoleonic Wars, and whose *Four Georges* covers the reign of George III. Michael Millgate (*Thomas Hardy: His Career as a Novelist* (1971)) discusses an interesting omission from F.E. Hardy's *Early Life of Thomas Hardy* (1928) of a reference to Thackeray in a letter from Leslie Stephen, and suggests that Hardy was trying to avoid any direct comparison with Thackeray's treatment of Waterloo. This may be so. He certainly followed Thackeray in his methods of displacing historical crisis. Thackeray's treatment of Waterloo is very like Hardy's treatment of Trafalgar. History is more prominent in Hardy, since both the threat of invasion and the naval war play an important part in structuring action, whereas Thackeray's war is only one determining episode in a novel concerned with many other aspects of society. Thackeray speaks amusingly and accurately of his story clinging for a little while 'to the skirts of history' and this was what Hardy's story does too, clinging for a little longer. *The Trumpet-Major* looks like a rural version of the military parts of *Vanity Fair*: both novels place the military preparations and the fighting in the point of view of the civilians who suddenly find themselves in the middle of an encampment, and whose personal lives are changed by war. Michael

Millgate also suggests, I think unconvincingly, that the characters in Hardy resemble the lovers in *Vanity Fair*, but he is right to harp on the association between the novels. By far the most powerful resemblance, I suggest, is found in two crucial sentences. Hardy gave his last sentence much thought, and in the serial version in *Good Words* he intended simply to give his trumpet-major a grand exit, out of Anne's life, out of his father's house, 'to blow his trumpet over the bloody battle-fields of Spain'. The final version took John even further and, impelled by the narrator's imperative sense of period, he goes off 'to blow his trumpet till silenced for ever upon one of the bloody battle-fields of Spain'. The last sound we hear is not a triumphant blast, but silence. This sudden lengthening of the exit, the stepping out of the door into a vast darkness, has a solemn and startling effect, appropriate both to the violence of the death and Hardy's sense of the outrage of those battlefields of the Peninsular War. This shocking narration of death may owe something to that sentence in *Vanity Fair* in which a death in battle also finds appropriately violent announcement, ending the ninth number of its serialization, to resound not quite so long as Hardy's announcement, but until the next instalment:

> No more firing was heard at Brussels - the pursuit rolled miles away. Darkness came down on the field and city; and Amelia was praying for George, who was lying on his face, dead, with a bullet through his heart. (Chapter 32)

Hardy's sense of the past is not wholly unlike Thackeray's, though he attaches it to the narrator's own historical sense. Thackeray preferred to invest and explore a fuller psychological portrait of nostalgia, as he does in *Esmond*, another novel which set out to displace history, by showing great men and historic crises familiarly, from within, often in a deflating and dishevelled domesticity. If Hardy emulated the rhetoric of outraged flourish and elegiac nostalgia of his great predecessor, it is pleasantly ironic, since what he was advised to do by Alexander Macmillan, who had just read 'The Poor Man and the Lady', was to try to emulate Thackeray's 'light, chaffy' style.[2] It should be said that although Thackeray can be the most subtle psychologist of nostalgia in Victorian fiction, he can also lapse into an indeterminate mawkishness about the past, as Hardy never does. Even in his frank authorial elegy, he keeps his eye firmly on that past whose passing he laments. *The Trumpet-Major* is remarkable for earthing nostalgia, for switching from the vivid present to a ghostly sense of the past, justifying elegiac pathos by such transition. The ending does not introduce a momentary melodrama, but finishes something that has been going on throughout the novel. At a fairly early stage we are habituated to Hardy's omniscient reminders of the time and mortal nature of his story. He gives us a steady and personal explanation of his own interest and viewpoint, having not only researched for his novel, as he tells us in the Preface, but listened to the anecdotes and memories of eye-witnesses, in his childhood. It has been suggested by M.G. Edwards that the tones of warm regret and nostalgia may have been promoted by the association of these stories with his boyhood at Higher Bockhampton.[3] There is a vividness about childhood stories which joins historical past with personal past, and Hardy's attitude towards the deadness of history may well be mingled with a nostalgia for real people, real voices and real memories. Hardy's loving tones of recollection make it clear that he was not only a good story-teller but a good listener. Attentive listening went into the making of this tender story. The tone isn't always tender, however, and sometimes its restraint and reticence, like the reserve of the Trumpet-Major himself, makes its effect through understatement, as in this formal statement of the historian's point of view:

> The present writer, to whom this party has been described times out of number by members of the Loveday family and other aged people now passed away, can never enter the old living-room of Overcombe Mill without beholding the genial scene through the mists of the seventy or eighty years that intervene between then and now. First and brightest to the eye are the dozen candles, scattered about regardless of expense, and kept well snuffed by the miller, who walks round the room at intervals of five minutes, snuffers in hand, and nips each wick with great precision, and with something of an executioner's grim look upon his face as he closes the snuffers upon the neck of the candle. Next to the candle-light show the red and blue coats and white breeches of the soldiers – nearly twenty of them in all besides the ponderous Derriman – the head of the latter, and, indeed, the heads of all who are standing up, being in dangerous proximity to the black beams of the ceiling. There is not one among them who would attach any meaning to 'Vittoria', or gather from the syllables 'Waterloo' the remotest idea of his own glory or death. Next appears the correct and innocent Anne, little thinking what things Time has in store for her at no great distance off. (Chapter 5)

The chief characters are not so simply sketched as to lack the life of feeling, and it is chiefly their emotions that animate them. This is true in love, in war, and when love and war come together, as in Bob's mixed reasons for asking to serve with Captain Hardy, or John's comic courtly solicitation of Anne through the arts of martial musicianship. Throughout the military episodes run the amorous feelings, vacillating, steady, capricious, faithful, mixed, never purely rational. The ordinariness of the love-story underlines the abortiveness of the threatened invasion, as the womenfolk flee from the French but end by being annoyed by the militia. The love-story joins with the comedy and farce to domesticate the Muse of history.

The love-story is particularized to create that vivid present which is essential to any good novel, but serves a special purpose in this novel about the past. In order to travel so movingly through time, to take us from the dramatic present to the sense of its history, the novelist renders that present concretely and substantially. Its particularity is not only psychological but sensuous, vivid in descriptions of the scenes and objects which frame or fill the life of the characters. We first see Anne, for instance, on a 'fine summer morning', and the generalized statement of the hour and the season moves quickly into a warmly, affectionately and finely individualized foreground:

> On a fine summer morning, when the leaves were warm under the sun, and the more industrious bees abroad, diving into every blue and red cup that could possibly be considered a flower, Anne was sitting at the back window of her mother's portion of the house, measuring out lengths of worsted for a fringed rug that she was making, which lay, about three-quarters finished, beside her. The work, though chromatically brilliant, was tedious; a hearth-rug was a thing which nobody worked at from morning to night; it was taken up and put down; it was in the chair, on the floor, across the hand-rail, under the bed, kicked here, kicked there, rolled away in the closet, brought out again, and so on, more capriciously perhaps than any other home-made article. Nobody was expected to finish a rug within a calculable period, and the wools of the beginning became faded and historical before the end was reached. A sense of this inherent nature of worsted-work rather than idleness led Anne to look rather frequently from the open casement. (Chapter 1)

Among such scenery the characters move, candid, capricious, strong enough to survive for a time. The depths of the simple story of amorous thwarting are not those of subtle analysis, nor of passionate conflict, but they are sympathetically plumbed. Hardy sends shafts into past time to move feelings of irony, affection, pity and sympathy. The particularities of feeling animate the story and support its moments of abstract comment. The simplicity, the capriciousness and the toughness of the characters stand the historical purpose in good stead. The qualities shown in love are those shown in war, thus linking public and private worlds. They are also animating qualities which insist on the common human nature of Hardy's ghosts, undignified, unsublime, comic, and sadder and more substantial ghosts for all that. Hardy's great achievement, here as in *Under the Greenwood Tree* and *Far from the Madding Crowd*, is to edge melancholy with amusement, toughness with pathos, and blend them together in Shakespearian fashion. Even on that last page, when the novel perhaps challenges what I said about its unsublimity, we feel the particularities of love and survival in sadness and humour. Hardy brings together the courage and sacrifice of John, in his brave acting of the amorous soldier's part, the coarse-grained happiness of Bob, and Anne's wry, thorough sense of the way things are. The last exit into the larger darkness has a complex effect. It makes the fortitude and solitariness of the Trumpet-Major the more striking, gathering together, as Shakespearian deaths often do, all that we know of the man, not forgetting his trumpet. It gives the wry shrug which is a typical gesture of Hardy's irony, as all move into the darkness, foolish and wise, lucky and unlucky, loved and unloved. The last step is felt, as a thrill at the imagination of the novelist, and then as a chill in the heart, as we recognize in the shift from life to death a last and personal home truth. This conclusion is a climax long prepared. The high points of passion in Hardy's novels are never local intensities or appeals out of place or out of character. The crises of passion are accompanied by recognition and reflection. Feeling in Hardy's novels is placed as part of a developed representation of characters, relationships and action, visibly moving with all the continuities, appropriate growths of the total form.

NOTES

1 The best discussion of Sue Bridehead is John Goode's 'Sue Bridehead and the New Woman', in *Women Writing and Writing about Women*, M. Jacobus (ed.) (London, 1979).

2   Alexander Macmillan, letter to Thomas Hardy, 10 August, 1868, quoted in
    C.L. Morgan, *The House of Macmillan* (London, 1943).

3   M.G. Edwards, 'The Making of Hardy's *The Trumpet-Major*', M.A. thesis,
    University of Birmingham (1967).

7

HENRY JAMES
Reflective Passions

In *The Portrait of a Lady* Henry James uses an omniscient narrator, even more reticent than George Eliot's, to pronounce on the author's arousal of the reader's feelings. Lengthy analysis of Isabel Archer's consciousness is succeeded by the comment, 'she would be an easy victim of scientific criticism if she were not intended to awaken on the reader's part an impulse more tender and more purely expectant' (Chapter 6). This remark cannot be accepted at face value. The novel provokes criticism – though scarcely of a scientific kind – as well as solicitude. Isabel is to fall victim to her own vagueness of emotion as well as to the 'natural' if not reasonable emotions of others, such as envy, greed, and possessiveness. But the narrator draws attention to an important element in James's form and subject. Like Dickens and George Eliot he solicits or stirs tender feelings for his fictions, as he scrupulously and centrally presents what Isabel calls 'natural and reasonable emotions', and the efforts to comprehend the affective life. He is the first novelist to concentrate action within the consciousness of the character, though many of his predecessors in fiction had achieved such a narrative shift, on a smaller scale and in a less sustained form. James's characters are like Robinson Crusoe and Clarissa in their attempts to define what they feel, and what they think they feel. They are like Dombey and Will Ladislaw as they select and symbolize. They are like Paul Dombey and Jo as objects of sympathy. They are like Sophia Western, Lucy Snowe and Gwendolen Harleth in their inner theatre of passion. But they are also the fictional elements in James's experiment in limited focus. The individual character's responsibility for analysis is constricted, and shown to be so limited, but it is sustained and developed over a long and elastic stretch of narrative.

The chief sufferer and analyst in James's first long novel, *Roderick Hudson*, is Rowland Mallet, patron and spectator, who reflects and reflects on his own emotions and on the emotions he imputes to others. Though ostensibly only a spectator, it is he rather than Roderick who is the paradigm of the artist. He undergoes the strain of observation and imagination. He also brings out the oddity of fictional emotion. He constantly forces the reader to observe with him, and feel with him, but in a narrative form which does not break the fiction and return us to fact, or enlarge the particularity by moving into generalization in the manner of George Eliot. James is averse to the formal intricacies of the multiple Victorian novel, and diagnoses a sophisticated interplay of fictional modes and models as 'a leak in the interest', but his misunderstanding of contemporary art, like many artistic and scientific misunderstandings, is fruitful. Dickens, Thackeray, and George Eliot, who appear to James aesthetically naive in their multiplication of subject and omniscient narrators, devise forms which force the reader to recognize that 'Really, universally, relations stop nowhere' (Preface to *Roderick Hudson*). James's 'first attempt at a novel, a long fiction with a "complicated" subject', was an attempt to draw 'by a geometry of his own', the circle in which relations 'shall happily *appear* to do so'. His omniscient narrator, whose presence is felt in varying degrees in all the novels, never imposes those abrupt transitions in feeling which mark *Bleak House*, *Vanity Fair*, and *Middlemarch*. The interpositions of his narrator can be seen as a formal change of key, but do not radically dispel or challenge the reader's attitude to fictional character.

Guidance is given through the 'view and experience' of Rowland, as he promotes, assists, observes, and suffers Roderick's adventure. James's Preface shows the aim to contrive that view and experience in emotional terms, connecting Rowland's consciousness 'intimately, with the general human exposure, and thereby bedimmed and befooled and bewildered, anxious, restless, fallible'. The novelist insists on the 'joy' – the novelist's creative emotion, identified in matter-of-fact, yet Coleridgean terms – 'of such a "job" as this making of his relation to everything involved a sufficiently limited, a sufficiently pathetic, tragic, comic, ironic, personal state to be thoroughly natural, and yet at the same time a sufficiently clear medium to represent a whole'.

The emotional records in the novel often displace our expectations. We may expect from the title a story like *Roderick Random*, but the adventures of the eponymous hero are refracted through Rowland's impassioned and individualized analysis. Rowland's affection for Mary Garland is registered, with her feelings, as he watches and waits. The novelist shows Rowland lovingly observing her affections, which are not directed towards him:

> the ineffable charm of Rome at that period seemed but the radiant sympathy of nature with his happy opportunity. The weather was divine; each particular morning, as he walked from his lodging to Mrs Hudson's modest inn, seemed to have a blessing upon it. . . . He found Mary sitting alone at the open window. . . . She always had a smile, she was always eager, alert, responsive. She might be grave by nature, she might be sad by circumstance, she might have secret doubts and pangs, but she was essentially young and strong and fresh and able to enjoy. . . . Rowland felt that it was not amusement and sensation that she coveted, but knowledge – facts that she might noiselessly lay away piece by piece in the fragrant darkness of her serious mind, so that under this head at least she should not be a perfectly portionless bride. She never merely pretended to understand; she let things go in her modest fashion at the moment; but she watched them on their way over the crest of the hill, and when her attention seemed not likely to be missed it went hurrying after them and ran breathless at their side and begged them for the secret. (Chapter 18)

Rowland registers the exquisiteness of her 'pious desire to improve herself', which he encourages 'none the less that its fruits were not for him'. The free indirect style, though punctuated by the occasional 'Rowland felt' or 'cried Rowland', emphasizes his appreciative excitement, as he observes her observation and feels her feelings. It is a tranquil way of judging his emotions, as we see him judging hers. His style is dramatized as tender, generous, and elated; the characteristic images James provides are gentle correlatives of his loving: 'the fragrant darkness of her serious mind' and 'begged them for the secret' are metaphors which speak his alert and enamoured praise. Rowland is the Pygmalion who sculpts Mary Garland's character, though for the reader's benefit, not his own. The registration of his consciousness works quietly because his love is secret, restrained, self-effacing, renouncing the publicity of exclamation and protestation.

For larger stretches of the novel, Rowland is occupied with Roderick, and the representation of Roderick's feelings is located in his consciousness. On one occasion Rowland registers Roderick's renewed susceptibility to Christina Light with 'infinite impatience': 'And why the deuce need Roderick have gone marching back to destruction?'

After this clear mark of indignant adjuration and question, a complex
course is charted:

> Rowland's meditations, even when they began in rancour, often brought
> him comfort; but on this occasion they ushered in a quite peculiar quality
> of unrest. He felt conscious of a sudden collapse in his moral energy; a
> current that had been flowing for two years with liquid strength seemed at
> last to pause and stagnate. Rowland looked away at the sallow vapours on
> the mountains; their dreariness had an analogy with the stale residuum of
> his own generosity. At last he had arrived at the uttermost limit of the
> deference a sane man might pay to other people's folly; nay, rather, he had
> transgressed it; he had been befooled on a gigantic scale. He turned to his
> book and tried to woo back patience, but it gave him cold comfort and he
> tossed it angrily away. (Chapter 25)[1]

Rowland's meditations on the emotions of Christina and Roderick
lead to self-observation: there is a fine transition from one cause of
anger to another, as the stream of passion swells his impatience with
Christina and Roderick, and bursts through irony and anger to an
impatience with himself. There is continuity, psychologically acute
and narratively sustaining, in the varied motions of emotion, from 'He
felt conscious' and the direct statement that follows, through the
provisionality of the metaphor of the current which 'seemed . . . to
pause', to the 'literal' landscape, which is also interpreted tentatively:
'had an analogy'. The metaphor of arrival makes its point, but is
qualified, 'nay, rather'; the final gesture of impatience is done through
behavioural drama, on the literal level of action: 'turned to his book'
and 'tossed it angrily away'. Action is joined to personification, which
characteristically delights in refreshing the proverbial 'cold comfort'
with the inventive 'tried to woo back'. The rhetoric registers inner
feeling and outer action in a form which is fast-moving, intense,
various and self-questioning. Rowland is the observer who tires, too
late, of the spectator sports of sympathy.

James sometimes moves us suddenly into crisis, as he does here,
when emotion swerves and surprises. At times he uses a lavish set-piece,
carefully constructed as an entire scene. This is his method in the scene
in a Franciscan garden at Fiesole (Chapter 16), where landscape is
ordered as the theatre for an emotional drama with prologues, conflict
and resolution. The conflict begins when Rowland arrives in Florence,
where he has gone to 'more freely decide upon his future movements'. James uses strong personification as a prologue: 'Reflective

benevolence stood prudently aside, and for the time touched the
sources of his irritation with no softening side-lights'. There follows a
summary account of feeling; Rowland's irritation is not soothed by the
Arno or the galleries: 'He was sore at heart, and as the days went by the
soreness deepened rather than healed.' Straightforward description of
feeling lasts for a sentence or two, then moves into self-conscious and
introspective analysis, coloured by the prevailing mood. He takes an
irritated but not humourless look at irritation and its causes, feels sore
about his increasing soreness. The meditation on the nature and causes
of feeling is generative:

> He had tried to be wise, he had tried to be kind, he had engaged in an
> estimable enterprise; but his wisdom, his kindness, his energy, had been
> thrown back in his face. He was disappointed, and his disappointment had
> an angry spark in it. The sense of wasted time, of wasted hope and faith, kept
> him constant company. There were times when the beautiful things about
> him only exasperated his discontent. He went to the Pitti Palace, and
> Raphael's Madonna of the Chair seemed in its soft serenity to mock him
> with the suggestion of unattainable repose. He lingered on the bridges at
> sunset and knew that the light was enchanting and the mountains were
> divine, but there seemed to be something horribly invidious and
> unwelcome in the fact. He felt, in a word, like man who had been cruelly
> defrauded and who wishes to have his revenge. Life owed him, he thought, a
> compensation, and he should be restless and resentful until he found it. He
> knew – or he seemed to know – where he should find it; but he hardly told
> himself, and thought of the thing under mental protest, as a man in want of
> money may think of certain funds that he holds in trust. In his melancholy
> meditations the idea of something better than all this, something that might
> softly, richly interpose, something that might reconcile him to the future,
> something that might make one's tenure of life strong and zealous instead of
> mechanical and uncertain – the idea of concrete compensation in a word –
> shaped itself sooner or later into the image of Mary Garland. (Chapter 16)

James's narrator ironically relieves the intensity of his meditation
by addressing the reader, admitting that it may seem 'odd' that
Rowland should be brooding over a girl 'of no brilliancy', glimpsed
two years before, and dryly remarking, with a sharp registration of
literary authority, 'We must admit the oddity, and remark simply in
explanation that his sentiment apparently belonged to that species of
emotion of which by the testimony of the poets the very name and
essence are oddity.'[2] There follows a turn in the inner drama; the
narrator declines to be explicit, but tells us that Rowland's thoughts

take a turn which 'excited him portentously'. Like Dorothea, he spends a night of waking conflict, and the morning finds him 'less excited':

> It seemed to him that he saw his idea from the outside, that he judged it and condemned it; yet it stood there before him, very distinct, and in a certain way imperious. During the day he tried to banish it and forget it; but it fascinated, haunted, at moments frightened him. He tried to amuse himself, paid visits, resorted to several violent devices for diverting his thoughts. If on the morrow he had committed a crime, the persons whom he had seen that day would have testified that he had talked strangely and had not seemed like himself. He felt certainly very unlike himself; long afterwards, in retrospect, he used to reflect that during those days he had for a while been literally *beside* himself. His idea persisted; it clung to him like a sturdy beggar. The sense of the matter, roughly expressed, was this. If Roderick were really going, as he himself had phrased it, to 'fizzle out', one might help him on the way – one might smooth the *descensus Averni*. (Ibid.)

Personification is structural, reminiscent of the internal but external-seeming figures of Gwendolen Harleth's passion-play. Equally reminiscent of *Daniel Deronda* is the combination of hallucinatory suggestion (*'beside* himself') with demonic force. Internal analysis and drama are transformed into a distanced view, as we follow Rowland's movements in the garden from noon till late afternoon. He wanders about, then stretches himself on a bench, hat over eyes. Place and persons are suggestive. The garden is tangled, old, wild, and assumes personality: 'you ramble from terrace to terrace and wonder how it keeps from slipping down in full consummation of its dishonour and decay'. He is watched by a monk, 'a pale gaunt personage', grave, ascetic, 'and yet of a benignant aspect', who sees on his face 'the traces of extreme trouble'. Narrative becomes tentative: 'It can hardly be determined whether his attitude, as he bent his sympathetic Italian eye upon Rowland, was a happy incident or the result of an exquisite spiritual discernment', though Rowland 'under the emotion of that moment' finds it 'blessedly opportune'. In the ensuing dialogue religious associations thicken; Rowland tells the *frate* that he has been tempted by the Devil: 'He was here . . . in this lovely garden, as he was once in Paradise, half an hour ago. But have no fear; I drove him out.' After the friar praises him for resisting the 'hideous' temptation, and promises a mass, Rowland gives alms, having 'had what is vulgarly called a great scare; he believed very poignantly for the time in the

Devil'. Internal drama is externalized and mythologized by the traditions of religion; the intensity of the conflict is matched and contrasted with the dialogue in which Rowland initiates theological language. The rhetoric of inner events, stamped and animated by personification, meets resonant and particularized place and persons.

Another similar scene of double action is used again at the climax of the novel, in the last chapter, when Rowland and Singleton search in the mountains and find Roderick's body. Extreme agitation is registered through the collaborative action of inner and outer life. The chalets have 'low foul doors' on which Rowland thumps 'with a kind of nervous savage anger'; he challenges the 'stupid silence to tell him something about his friend', but it is 'horrible' and 'seemed to mock at his impatience and to be a conscious symbol of calamity'.[3] The only human being in the cabins is 'a hideous *crétin*' who grins and cannot help (recalling the cretin in *Villette*). The sun shows him 'nothing but the stony Alpine void – nothing so human even as death'. The narrative accretes images of emptiness and unresponsiveness until, 'He stopped looking; he was afraid to go on', 'sick to the depth of his soul', his mind engaged with 'several things, chiefly trivial, that had happened during the last two years and that he had quite forgotten'. There is an appropriate displacement of reasonable feeling. We see him passionately reading the symbols, and the process generates fresh feeling. Analysis is impassioned and analytic; places and objects come to act as metaphors in a thoroughly elucidated transformation.

After Roderick's body is found, Rowland stays with it for seven hours, in the last scene of solitary and intense feeling:

> his vigil was for ever memorable. The most rational of men was for an hour the most passionate. He reviled himself with transcendent bitterness, he accused himself of cruelty and injustice, he would have lain down there in Roderick's place. . . . At last he grew almost used to the dumb exultation of the cliff above him. (Chapter 26)[4]

The straightforward naming of passions gives place to the imaginative fusion of feeling and environment in the 'dumb exultation of the cliff': the cliff could tell, if it were not dumb, and the exultation is that of sublime nature. (A subdued pun on 'exaltation' is confirmed by the preposition 'above'.) Rowland tries to reconstruct his friend's last adventure, even gauging the height from which he has fallen. The feverish application of reason gives way: 'Now all that was over

Rowland understood how exclusively, for two years, Roderick had filled his life. His occupation was gone.' The echo from *Othello* magnifies emptiness and remorse.

The flexible register of Rowland's consciousness is adapted to present his feelings as a medium for the feelings of the other characters. It is a form of representation which presents simple and ordinary, as well as complex and extraordinary, characters. Roderick's mother, for instance, is dramatized in depth – the depth of Rowland's ability to observe and plumb her characteristic passions, acutely, sympathetically, and humorously. We see, through James's double perspective, his view of her, and his view of himself, as he wittily registers the limits of her intensity: 'There was no space in Mrs Hudson's tiny maternal mind for complications of feeling, and one emotion existed only by turning another over flat and perching on top of it' (Chapter 21). Since Roderick is transformed in this tiny mind, outstripping 'her powers of imagination' and making her too scared to blame him, the only comfortable thing for her is to blame Rowland: 'Rowland felt as if his trials were only beginning.' His attentiveness and analysis are always sharp and excited, as he feels guilt, aspiration, frustration, love, jealousy, energy, accidie, and pain. The passions of the novel are refracted through his impassioned intelligence, as he acts, responds, and meditates upon meanings. The form is a triumph of indirection.

In *The Portrait of a Lady* Isabel Archer is heroine and chief observer; from the outset she is represented as aware of the emotions she feels and may feel. She is critically conscious of her own vagueness, eagerness, and pride. After Lord Warburton proposes marriage, she questions the very ease with which she contemplates refusing the magnificent 'chance', seeing it as setting her apart from her sex. She questions her ambitiousness, pride, and even sympathy, to feel 'really frightened at herself'. She talks to her uncle, in order to 'feel more natural, more human', and after their conversation, reflects that it has assured her 'that she was concerned with the natural and reasonable emotions of life and not altogether a victim to intellectual eagerness and vague ambitions' (Chapter 13). Isabel is the first Victorian heroine to have been brought up on George Eliot, and may benefit, in her awareness of vague and undefined feelings, from a knowledge of her ancestors and sisters, Janet, Maggie, Dorothea, and Gwendolen, some of whom James mentions in the Preface as belonging to the tradition to which his heroine is attached: that of the 'frail vessel . . . charged with George Eliot's "treasure" of human affection'.

Like Gwendolen, Isabel resists the destiny. We see her resisting both Caspar and Warburton, rejoicing, as their figures seem to grow dim, that she has not given 'her last shilling, sentimentally speaking' to either of them. Like Catherine Linton, she subversively rejects conventions of love at great expense of spirit. She is agitated by her agitations, which move her away from defining conventions, but disturbingly take no definite form. Like Dorothea, she needs to feel a more than personal feeling, is sentimentally ambitious for emotions which will connect her life with the larger movements of mankind, instead of imprisoning her in personal relationships. She is the reverse of Gwendolen, whose unawareness of political contexts makes even her rejections of a woman's conventional destiny facile and pathetic. Isabel has read George Eliot, knows the wear and tear of carrying the treasure of human affections in the nineteenth century. She tutors her imagination to expect and desire pain, and see the need and the indulgence of a planned personal Bildung: to desire perfection, plan progress, and enlarge moral consciousness involves the question 'What should one do with the misery of the world?', which preoccupied Bunyan's pilgrim and George Eliot's Dorothea Brooke.

Isabel's analysis of her feelings is more perceptive than that of the heroines she has read about in novels. Unlike them, she is alive to the dangers of emotional vagueness and introspection, but after her marriage to Gilbert Osmond, the sterile dilettante, the emotions she feelingly inspects are far from vague, and self-examination becomes urgent and painful. In the effort to break with convention, she is trapped by convention. Like *Roderick Hudson*, *The Portrait of a Lady* builds a pattern of inner and outer events, and the environments James creates for Isabel, as for Rowland, are metonymies which merge with metaphors of thinking and feeling. The houses, furnishings, and gardens of the novel's surface are animated, never statically described. They are matrices for figures of feeling. The imagery of gardens is plucked from Gardencourt, to shape Isabel, and her act of shaping. Her nature is described as having 'in her conceit, a certain garden-like quality'. She quickly connects the image with its opposite: 'she was often reminded that there were other gardens in the world than those of her remarkable soul, and that there were moreover a great many places which were not gardens at all' (Chapter 6). Isabel's mode of analysis is dynamic; she adapts the environment for imagery, quickly catches on to the implications of that imagery, and extends it scrupulously to existences outside herself. The solipsism and indulgence

of imaginative conscience is figured and recognized, though the
narrator sees the rebuke to introspection becoming dangerously
ponderous and labyrinthine, and restores us to the sense of the limits of
self-analysis: 'She was too young, too impatient to live, too unacquainted
with pain.'

When her acquaintance with pain is improved by marriage,
introspection becomes more sustained, and we are drawn into its
labyrinths. The style is established, the conceits still drawn from the
outer world, but the field has expanded to mark a sensitivity to the
multiple meanings of that world. The reader reads ironies better than
Isabel when she first innocently enters Gilbert Osmond's masked,
uncommunicative house, with those massively crossbarred windows,
'jealous apertures'. But she comes to her night-vigil; she has caught up.
Now she draws imagery from houses as well as gardens, from artefacts
instead of flora, from enclosure rather than spaciousness. The mood
which provokes and animates the long analysis is fear: 'her soul was
haunted with terrors which crowded to the foreground of thought as
quickly as a place was made for them' (Chapter 42). The vehicle of
imagery is changed, and so is its form: allegory takes over from the
more static trope of metaphor. Like Rowland and Gwendolen, she is
terrorized by her terrors. The process of being forced into concentration
marks the first entry of personified fear, set in motion by the famous
scene where slight occurrence weighs like lead – she has seen Osmond
sit while Madame Merle stands. Her vigil creates scenery, properties,
and person. The décor is taken from the environments we know, but
space is replaced, as it was for Dorothea and Gwendolen, by
narrowness and darkness: 'she had suddenly found the infinite vista of
a multiplied life to be a dark, narrow alley with a dead wall at the end.'
The old passions were located in 'the high places of happiness', from
which 'one could look down with a sense of exaltation and advantage,
and judge and choose and pity', but the new ones find an appropriate
locale in 'realms of restriction and depression'. Darkness is imputed to
an emotional cause, 'It was her deep distrust of her husband – this was
what darkened the world', and the generative power of passion leads to
the contemplation of its unplumbable, unnameable aspects. We move
from named feelings to those less easily classified, but there is no
vagueness any more.

It was her deep distrust of her husband – this was what darkened the world.
That is a sentiment easily indicated, but not so easily explained, and so

composite in its character that much time and still more suffering had been needed to bring it to its actual perfection. Suffering, with Isabel, was an active condition; it was not a chill, a stupor, a despair; it was a passion of thought, of speculation, of response to every pressure. She flattered herself that she had kept her failing faith to herself, however - that no one suspected it but Osmond. Oh, he knew it, and there were times when she thought he enjoyed it. It had come gradually - it was not till the first year of their life together, so admirably intimate at first, had closed that she had taken the alarm. Then the shadows had begun to gather; it was as if Osmond deliberately, almost malignantly, had put the lights out one by one. The dusk at first was vague and thin, and she could still see her way in it. But it steadily deepened, and if now and again it had occasionally lifted there were certain corners of her prospect that were impenetrably black. These shadows were not an emanation from her own mind; she was very sure of that; she had done her best to be just and temperate, to see only the truth. They were a part, they were a kind of creation and consequence, of her husband's very presence. They were not his misdeeds, his turpitudes; she accused him of nothing - that is, but of one thing, which was *not* a crime. She knew of no wrong he had done; he was not violent, he was not cruel: she simply believed he hated her. (Chapter 42)

The figure here is not personification, but works like it, through sustained images of darkness, emerging from the originating emotion of distrust. Her account of the composite character of that distrust combines irony with accuracy, and demonstration takes us to another emotion, also composite, called suffering. Suffering, too, is individualized, described through alternatives and negations, 'Not a chill, a stupor, a despair', and then demonstrated in a passion of speculation and response. Her inner discourse is marked by the generation of feeling and thinking, as meditation feverishly elaborates images and continuously creates new ones. There is also a movement of careful, qualifying, thought. The definiteness of metaphor, 'the shadows had begun to gather', is revised to become a simile, 'it was as if Osmond', followed by a list of images for darkness, 'gathering shadows', 'extinguished lights', 'deepening dusk'. We are kept aware of the activity of that suffering mind, 'a passion of thought, of speculation'.

We are also kept aware of Osmond, and the 'real world' of the novel's times, places and objects. The putting out of lights is a grim domestic image. Though there is a sense that distrust darkens the world, there is a revision of this interpretation too, through the permutations of image: 'These shadows were not an emanation from her own mind'. Darkness marks Osmond's activity and her passiveness. He is one of the haunting terrors, as he 'almost malignantly' puts out lights; his mind is personified, through a sinister and reductive synecdoche. The image of darkness comes to be identified and particularized in images of house, walls, and windows already familiar in the 'external' environment of the novel:

> But when, as the months had elapsed, she had followed him further and he had led her into the mansion of his own habitation, then, *then* she had seen where she really was.
>
> She could live it over again, the incredulous terror with which she had taken the measure of her dwelling. Between those four walls she had lived ever since; they were to surround her for the rest of her life. It was the house of darkness, the house of dumbness, the house of suffocation. Osmond's beautiful mind gave it neither light nor air; Osmond's beautiful mind indeed seemed to peep down from a small high window and mock at her. (Ibid.)

The imagery of haunting, darkness, and enclosure are presented generatively and analytically, from within Isabel's point of view, to elucidate the past through the play of passionate intelligence, fearfully and distrustfully analysing fear and distrust. The play of feeling advances the novel in leaps: the experience marks the distance Isabel has travelled since we first saw her courage and curiosity, and acts out, in memory, assessment, and prediction, what she has hitherto not faced. She has called for lights, as she sits alone, to meditate in 'the still drawing-room', to become enlightened about the nature and causes of growing darkness. The vigil also marks an explanation so far withheld by the novelist: the reader sees her reasons for marrying Osmond: he 'had talked . . . about his renunciation, his indifference, the ease with which he dispensed with the usual aids to success; and all this had seemed to her admirable.' She had learnt that his sense of the world is far from indifferent, but threatens her open and passionate curiosity in its enclosure and intolerance. The image of the garden returns, significantly reduced, and no longer leading, as it had done earlier, to a sense of other gardens and other places which were not gardens at all. It returns as a landlord's property:

> Her mind was to be his - attached to his own like a small garden-plot to a deer-park. He would rake the soil gently and water the flowers; he would weed the beds and gather an occasional nosegay. It would be a pretty piece of property for a proprietor already far-reaching. (Ibid.)

Through images she analyses Osmond's hatred, scorn, contempt, inferring his view of her emotions, which 'he believed he should have regulated'. She assesses her present feeling, which is not hate: 'She didn't hate him, that she was sure of, for every little while she felt a passionate wish to give him a pleasant surprise.'

At the end the figure of personification marks division. Isabel has to hide her misery: 'She concealed it elaborately; she was perpetually, in their talk, hanging out curtains and arranging screens'. In the final paragraph there is a return to the physical facts of time and place. Like George Eliot, James is always aware of the environment of feeling, and makes his characters similarly aware. Like Dorothea in her boudoir, after Casaubon's rebuff, Isabel is indifferent to physical surroundings, 'in a fever', in no danger of feeling the cold even though the fire goes out. Hearing the hours strike, 'her vigil took no heed of time'. Her indifference is communicated, and communicates the precise details of place and time to the reader. The last figure for feeling personifies her visions, and her creation of visions, 'Her mind, assailed by visions, was in a state of extraordinary activity, and her visions might as well come to her there, where she sat up to meet them, as on her pillow, to make a mockery of rest.' She is imaginatively active, but the personification represents passiveness, as she tries to make sense of what assails her.

The scene stands perfectly in relation to the larger narrative, in its combination of energized outer environment and energized inner theatre, merged yet distinct. It is also a summary rendering of the novel's subject, the imprisonment of love and imagination. The woman's openness is enclosed by the man's restriction, both demonstrated in persistently self-correcting analysis.

Isabel's second passionate reverie comes towards the end of the novel, on the train from Italy to England. For Dorothea, the scene of meditation is usually an interior, but for Isabel, the still drawing-room is matched by the moving journey, which allows for the solitude and enclosure of the railway carriage. James makes the physical facts of the journey work for his representation, as Dickens does with Dombey and Tolstoy with Anna Karenina. The scene is framed by being narrated retrospectively: the opening sentence delivers Isabel, at her journey's end, into 'the hands . . . of Henrietta Stackpole', and the narrative returns to the emotions and thoughts of the journey. The mood is established as one of vagueness, a state of fluidity dreaded as much by James as by Flaubert.

On her long journey from Rome her mind had been given up to vagueness; she was unable to question the future. She performed this journey with sightless eyes and took little pleasure in the countries she traversed, decked out though they were in the richest freshness of spring. Her thoughts followed their course through other countries – strange-looking, dimly-lighted, pathless lands, in which there was no change of seasons, but only, as it seemed, a perpetual dreariness of winter. She had plenty to think about; but it was neither reflexion nor conscious purpose that filled her mind. Disconnected visions passed through it, and sudden dull gleams of memory, of expectation. The past and the future came and went at their will, but she saw them only in fitful images, which rose and fell by a logic of their own. It was extraordinary the things she remembered. Now that she was in the secret, now that she knew something that so much concerned her and the eclipse of which had made life resemble an attempt to play whist with an imperfect pack of cards, the truth of things, their mutual relations, their meaning, and for the most part their horror, rose before her with a kind of architectural vastness. She remembered a thousand trifles; they started to . life with the spontaneity of a shiver. She had thought them trifles at the time; now she saw that they had been weighted with lead. Yet even now they were trifles after all, for what use was it to her to understand them? Nothing seemed of use to her to-day. All purpose, all intention, was suspended; all desire too save the single desire to reach her much-embracing refuge. Gardencourt had been her starting-point, and to those muffled chambers it was at least a temporary solution to return. She had gone forth in her strength; she would come back in her weakness, and if the place had been a rest to her before, it would be a sanctuary now. She envied Ralph his dying, for if one were thinking of rest that was the most perfect of all. To cease utterly, to give it all up and not know anything more – this idea was as sweet as the vision of a cool bath in a marble tank, in a darkened chamber, in a hot land. (Chapter 53)

This is a scene of inner action which balances the earlier vigil, related to it by contrast as well as comparison. Vagueness replaces energy, the uncertainty replaces speculation, inertia replaces fever. Like Dickens in Dombey's railway journey, James uses the shifting scenery to bring out emotional vision. Dombey ignores and selects, Isabel ignores and evades. The external images of spring ironically bring out the dreariness of her winter, the physical journey becomes a metaphor to emphasize tracklessness, obscurity, and hateful defamiliarization. Isabel is no longer purposeful. She receives memory and impressions, in the vague generality of 'things' and 'trifles', deadly in their refusal to specify. Personification returns, to show her passiveness as the 'fitful images . . . rose and fell with a logic of their own'. Vividly particularized are the clashing similes representing lack of meaning, a game played 'with an imperfect pack', and 'a kind of architectural vastness'. The dislocation of category and scale forms and states her incoherence. The feeling for Ralph is not even melancholy: 'She envied Ralph his dying'. This is a psychologized despair, a loss of identity like that of Marlowe's Dr Faustus.

The second paragraph balances the first. The sense of passiveness is repeated, through the facts of the journey: 'She sat in her corner, so motionless, so passive, simply with the sense of being carried'. Confusion and emptiness are registered through the juxtaposition of a modern woman alone in a train with funereal art and history: 'she recalled to herself one of those Etruscan figures couched upon the receptable of their ashes'. The emotions are enlarged and mytho-logized, but still specific. The narrator uses the indirect style, but the creative effort is Isabel's, tired, disordered, and inturned. There is a movement, as she comes to question the way ahead, but she sees without volition, clarity, or form, 'the future, of which from time to time she had a mutilated glimpse'. At the end of the meditation there is another animating movement, as she feels 'Deep in her soul – deeper than any appetite for renunciation . . . the sense that life would be her business for a long time to come'. This is briefly inspiriting, but the dominant emotion recalls her from comfort:

> And at moments there was something inspiring, almost enlivening, in the conviction. It was a proof of strength – it was a proof she should some day be happy again. It couldn't be she was to live only to suffer; she was still young, after all, and a great many things might happen to her yet. To live only to suffer – only to feel the injury of life repeated and enlarged – it seemed to her she was too valuable, too capable, for that. Then she wondered if it were vain and stupid to think so well of herself. When had it even been a guarantee to be valuable? Wasn't all history full of the destruction of precious things? Wasn't it much more probable that if one were fine one would suffer? It involved then perhaps an admission that one had a certain grossness; but Isabel recognised, as it passed before her eyes, the quick vague shadow of a long future. She should never escape; she should last to the end. Then the middle years wrapped her about again and the grey curtain of her indifference closed her in. (Ibid.)

The novel does not leave Isabel with nihilistic feeling, but her renunciation of freedom, after Caspar's embrace has given her something definite to renounce, is coloured by the visionary dreariness of the railway scene. It is not for nothing that the heroine of this novel has read, and understood, the renunciations in George Eliot. The frail vessel is not sublimely described; frailty and burden are imagined from the inside, with a painful sense of fatigue, disintegration, and waste.

The patronizing term is revised and doubted. James sometimes forgoes the interiority of such representations of feeling. The triumphs of *What Maisie Knew*, *The Awkward Age*, and *The Tragic Muse* are those of an ironic drama of understatement and implication. In the late novels, the inner theatre returns, creating the same brilliant conjunction of inner and outer scene, the same concentration and dynamism of images, the same generative processes of impassioned reason. But James develops the transformation of surface to symbol in a new figure, all his own. In Book 5, Chapter 4 of *The Wings of the Dove*, he presents Milly Theale's unnameable emotions, after she has been given the ambiguous prognosis that she can live if she will, in a great set-piece, the episode in Regent's Park, in which every physical movement and every appearance becomes emotionally symbolic. James achieves perfect economy and concentration of form. Emotional nuance and motion find correlatives in the outer scene, to bear out perfectly James's rhetorical question, 'What is incident but the determination of character? What is character but the illustration of the incident?' ('The Art of Fiction', 1884).

Every incident brings out emotions which are private, hard to admit, and inaccessible to naming. Milly leaves the enigmatic doctor, Sir Luke Strett, feeling 'literally' that she must have an impersonally peopled isolation: 'her only company must be the human race at large.' Every thought and feeling carries her further, and each step is pictured. She thinks of 'the grey immensity of London', then relates the grey immensity to herself, as 'her element'. She feels the need to rush, and knows that company would slow her down. She feels loss, gain, fear and courage: the 'mixture of her consciousness' is imaged in a simile of the ornament plucked 'off her breast', then replaced by 'some queer defensive weapon, a musket, a spear, a battle-axe'. The weapon generates the allegory of battle, 'the first charge had been sounded', and the battlefield becomes the park, which she enters for the first time, on foot:

> she had come out, she presently saw, at the Regent's Park, round which on two or three occasions with Kate Croy her public chariot had solemnly

rolled. But she went into it further now; this was the real thing; the real thing was to be quite away from the pompous roads, well within the centre and on the stretches of shabby grass. Here were benches and smutty sheep; here were idle lads at games of ball, with their cries mild in the thick air; here were wanderers, anxious and tired like herself; here doubtless were hundreds of others just in the same box. Their box, their great common anxiety, what was it, in this grim breathing-space, but the practical question of life? They could live if they would; that is, like herself, they had been told so; she saw them all about her, on seats, digesting the information, recognising it again as something in a slightly different shape familiar enough, the blessed old truth that they would live if they could. All she thus shared with them made her wish to sit in their company; which she so far did that she looked for a bench that was empty, eschewing a still emptier chair that she saw hard by, and for which she would have paid, with superiority, a fee. (Book 5, Chapter 4)

The scene announces emotional significance through the innuendo of 'going into it', the image of tired and anxious wanderers, the generalizing metaphors, 'their box' and 'this breathing-space', and the symbolic act of choosing a seat for which no fee is necessary. The ordinary motions and places are transformed into metaphors and metonymies by emotional obsession. Environment is magnified into personal symbol through an act which requires sympathy. Indeed James is rewriting the concept of sympathy: Milly's interpretation of the outside world as a sign of her consciousness of life and death involves the understanding that the outer world is populated by those up against the same question and reduced to the same state. Hence the attempt to discard superiorities of purse and position. The sense of feverish activity advances the acts of imagining. A little later, the notion of poverty returns:

It reduced her to her ultimate state, which was that of a poor girl – with her rent to pay for example – staring before her in a great city. Milly had her rent to pay, her rent for the future; everything else but how to meet it fell away from her in pieces, in tatters. This was the sensation the great man had doubtless not purposed. Well, she must go home, like the poor girl, and see. There might after all be ways; the poor girl too would be thinking. It came back for that matter perhaps to views already presented. She looked about her again, on her feet, at her scattered, melancholy comrades – some of them so melancholy as to be down on their stomachs in the grass, turned away, ignoring, burrowing; she saw once more, with them, those two faces of the question between which there was so little to choose for inspiration. It was perhaps superficially more striking that one could live if one would; but it was more appealing, insinuating, irresistible, in short, that one would live if one could. (Ibid.)

The passage shows the rhythm of James's handling of outer and inner imagery. It reverses the previous process, in which scene and persons became grist to the mill of imagination. In this episode, the image of the poor girl emerges from Milly's reflections on the doctor's compassionate question about her friends; she thinks of an image, regards it, extends it, 'with her rent to pay for example', developing image into story, and story into personal interpretation and generalization, 'her rent for the future' and 'she must go home, like the poor girl'. She returns to the outer scene with its examples of anonymous poverty, isolation, and misery, which need no explicit language of comparison but speak for themselves. In another economical stroke James registers fertile inventiveness and symbol-making emotion.

A similar scene of exteriorized passion takes us into the reverie of Merton Densher, after Kate has fulfilled their contract by going to bed with him and then left him to the false and tacit courtship of the dying Milly. His passionate obsession shows itself in a similar activity of imagination which dissolves barriers between inner and outer space, past and present time. Like Dick Dewy, he is passion-haunted.

> It played for him – certainly in this prime afterglow – the part of a treasure kept at home in safety and sanctity, something he was sure of finding in its place when, with each return, he worked his heavy old key in the lock. The door had but to open for him to be with it again and for it to be all there; so intensely there that, as we say, no other act was possible to him than the renewed act, almost the hallucination, of intimacy. Wherever he looked or sat or stood, to whatever aspect he gave for the instant the advantage, it was in view as nothing of the moment, nothing begotten of time or of chance could be, or ever would; it was in view as, when the curtain has risen, the play on the stage is in view, night after night, for the fiddlers. He remained thus, in his own theatre, in his single person, perpetual orchestra to the ordered drama, the confirmed 'run'; playing low and slow, moreover, in the regular way, for the situations of most importance. (Book 9, Chapter 1)

The free indirect style cleverly blurs the origin of image-making, but the provisionality of language – 'it played for him . . . the part' – does not impute imaginative action to Densher, but initiates the scene and the passionate reverie. The image of treasure elides with the objects of

Densher's room, door, and key. There is ironic judgement in the image of sanctified treasure, since this act has been unhallowed, brought about by blackmail and transaction. The simile of the theatre expresses passionate repetition and absorption, and quietly but firmly admits evaluation. Once more, there is a change of gear, as we move from one level of rhetoric to another: the treasure is metaphorical, but brought close to the represented reality of locked and private place. There is continuity, as we move into the elaborated dramatic metaphor of 'act', in another of James's exquisite exploitations and revivals of dead metaphor, 'the act of intimacy'. 'Hallucination', kept tentative by the modifier, 'almost' creates a scrupulous discrimination and a hyperbole. The imagery brings out obsession, concentration, repetition, and enclosure, with a suggestive, implicit motion of sexual memory. The symbol-making is fertile, as it shifts from metaphor to surface, and from the image of treasure to theatre, functionally blurring illusion and reality.

In the next chapter Densher is refused access to Milly's palazzo, and stands outside in the damp loggia with Eugenio:

> It was a Venice all of evil that had broken out for them alike, so that they were together in their anxiety, if they really could have met on it; a Venice of cold lashing rain from a low black sky, of wicked wind raging through narrow passes, of general arrest and interruption, with the people engaged in all the water-life huddled, stranded and wageless, bored and cynical, under archways and bridges. (Book 9, Chapter 2)

The scene continues in the Piazza San Marco:

> The wet and the cold were now to reckon with, and it was to Densher, precisely, as if he had seen the obliteration, at a stroke, of the margin on a faith in which they were all living. The margin had been his name for it - for the thing that, though it had held out, could bear no shock. The shock, in some form, had come, and he wondered about it while, threading his way among loungers as vague as himself, he dropped his eyes sightlessly on the rubbish in shops. There were stretches of the gallery paved with squares of red marble, greasy now with the salt spray; and the whole place, in its huge elegance, the grace of its conception and the beauty of its detail, was more than ever like a great drawing-room, the drawing-room of Europe, profaned and bewildered by some reverse of fortune. He brushed shoulders with brown men whose hats askew, and the loose sleeves of whose pendent jackets, made them resemble melancholy maskers. (Ibid.)

Like the scene in Regent's Park, everything tells. Weather, canals, architecture, people, shops, clothing, are transformed into emblems, which speak for themselves; Densher is stranded, wageless, exposed, expelled, melancholy, unmasked as a masker. Some details fill in the physical particularities of place but in language so conceptual as to magnify the crisis: the words 'a Venice all of evil', and 'profaned and bewildered', decorously limit the implications of moral crisis, reserving full disclosure until Densher discovers Lord Mark in Florians, and understands that he has been to Milly and told her, in a breach of faith, about the breach of faith. The few instances of emotional naming, 'together in their anxiety' and 'as if he had seen the obliteration', fix the feelings of bewilderment and suspicion.

Such scenes are more frequent in the late novels than in *Roderick Hudson* and *The Portrait of a Lady*, and mark a movement away from the typical Victorian rhythm of separated scene and inner reflection. In *The Wings of the Dove* James fuses scene and reverie, making the whole action of the novel emotional and physical, in a totally relevant form. In *The Golden Bowl* the scenes of emotional crisis are clustered in the second volume, presided over by Maggie's awakened consciousness. The characters perform their actions and arrange their scenes with a full sense of symbolism and creativity. Nothing is casual, innocent, or superficial. James records scene and passion with a constant elision of distinctions between inner and outer life. At the end of the first volume Fanny Assingham begins to read Maggie's feelings from her actions; she has gone home to wait for her husband, instead of following recent routine, and waiting for him in the Ververs' house. Volume 2 takes us inside that interpreted action, to confirm Fanny's reading. The high felicity of the working relationships between the two married couples has come to an end, and Maggie is forced into the unease and action of consciousness. She feels excitement and the need to conceal excitement; James moves from dead metaphor to live conceit:

> She could at all events remember no time at which she had felt so excited, and certainly none – which was another special point – that so brought with it as well the necessity for concealing excitement. This birth of a new eagerness became a high pastime in her view precisely by reason of the ingenuity required for keeping the thing born out of sight. The ingenuity was thus a private and absorbing exercise, in the light of which, might I so far multiply my metaphors, I should compare her to the frightened but clinging mother of an unlawful child. The idea that had possession of her would be, by our new analogy, the proof of her misadventure, but likewise

all the while only another sign of a relation that was more to her than anything on earth. She had lived long enough to make out for herself that any deep-seated passion has its pangs as well as its joys, and that we are made by its aches and its anxieties most richly conscious of it. She had never doubted of the force of the feeling that bound her to her husband; but to become aware almost suddenly that it had begun to vibrate with a violence that had some of the effect of a strain would, rightly looked at, after all but show that she was, like thousands of women, every day, acting up to the full privilege of passion. (Book 4, Chapter 1)

This is unlocated feeling, presented entirely through the narrator's imagery. Feeling is clearly expressed, but in generalized terms, eloquent of nuance, emphasizing Maggie's sense both of 'a violence that had some of the effect of a strain' and of its vagueness. The agitation cannot be defined or explained, the emotion is 'semi-smothered'. Just as feeling is unparticularized, so Maggie's sense of dealing with crisis involves a purely symbolic act and change, which can be communicated without disclosure, concealing dangerous meaning. It is a signal, put out with the greatest care, delicacy, and tact. It is an act of symbolic import, a return to her own fireside, a marking of territory. It is a clandestine act, which her innocence and simplicity has hitherto been unequipped to make, a dangerous move, a provocation, and a challenge:

For it had been a step, distinctly, on Maggie's part, her deciding to do something just then and there which would strike Amerigo as unusual, and this even though her departure from custom had merely consisted in her so arranging that he wouldn't find her, as he would definitely expect to do, in Eaton Square. He would have, strangely enough, as might seem to him, to come back home for it, and there get the impression of her rather pointedly, or at least all impatiently and independently, awaiting him. These were small variations and mild manoeuvres, but they went accompanied on Maggie's part, as we have mentioned, with an infinite sense of intention. Her watching by his fireside for her husband's return from an absence might superficially have presented itself as the most natural act in the world, and the only one, into the bargain, on which he would positively have reckoned. It fell by this circumstance into the order of plain matters, and yet the very aspect by which it was in the event handed over to her brooding fancy was the fact that she had done with it all she had designed. She had put her thought to the proof, and the proof had shown its edge; this was what was before her, that she was no longer playing with blunt and idle tools, with weapons that didn't cut. There passed across her vision ten times a day the gleam of a bare blade, and at this it was that she most shut her eyes, most knew the impulse to cheat herself with motion and sound. She had merely driven on a certain Wednesday to Portland Place instead of remaining in Eaton Square, and – she privately repeated it again and again – there had appeared beforehand no reason why she should have seen the mantle of history flung by a single sharp sweep over so commonplace a deed. (Ibid.)

Jamesian characters, at their fullest power of intuition, learn to behave in conformity with Jamesian artifice. For them as for the reader, surfaces are symbols, accidents are essences, forming a taciturn communication of feeling. The scene is recorded indirectly, like the retrospect of Isabel's train journey, presented as an inner act, narrated by memory: 'It fell for retrospect into a succession of moments which were *watchable* still; almost in the manner of the different things done during a scene on the stage.' The theatrical simile emphasizes portentousness, strangeness, design, performance and control. Maggie emphasizes the detail of her symbolic production, where set and properties have a message to convey: the house she returns to, the drawing-room where she sits, the pale novel she cannot read, and the newest frock, worn for the first time: 'It was a wonder how many things she had calculated in respect to this small incident'. She has to strike a delicate balance between clarity and suggestiveness in order to convey a sense of change without committing herself to gross communication. She makes a scene in order not to make a scene in the vulgar sense. That scene is set by a 'tension of spirit in which she was afterwards to find the image of her having crouched' but she tries 'to banish any such appearance'. Surfaces are decorously still, but expressive, and it takes an effort to achieve such stillness and expression. The entrance of Amerigo is marked, for character and reader, by one of James's remarkable elisions of register. Maggie remembers how she anxiously contemplated the new dress, and moved to a contemplation of Charlotte's disguised disapproval of her clothes. We move from the particular meaning of appearance and dress to something more general, as she thinks of the possibility of producing a surprise, 'something a little less out of the true note than usual'. The sense of appearance, and the sense of not knowing, take us from the outside to inside, as Maggie puts one more suspicion, and one more unanswered question, into 'her accumulations of the unanswered':

They were *there*, these accumulations; they were like a roomful of confused objects, never as yet 'sorted', which for some time now she had been passing and re-passing, along the corridor of her life. She passed it when she could without opening the door; then, on occasion, she turned the key to throw in a fresh contribution. So it was that she had been getting things out of the way. They rejoined the rest of the confusion; it was as if they had found their place, by some instinct of affinity, in the heap. They knew in short where to go, and when she at present by a mental act once more pushed the door open she had practically a sense of method and experience. What she should never know about Charlotte's thought – she tossed *that* in. It would find itself in company, and she might at last have been standing there long enough to see it fall into its corner. The sight moreover would doubtless have made her stare, had her attention been more free – the sight of the mass of vain things, congruous, incongruous, that awaited every addition. It made her in fact, with a vague gasp, turn away, and what had further determined this was the final sharp extinction of the inward scene by the outward. The quite different door had opened and her husband was there. (Ibid.)

Maggie's tension and the reader's are broken at a stroke; we move, with the explicit and emphatic differentiation of 'The quite different door', out of the image into the scene, out of the privacy of imagination into the publicity of relationship. The vagueness of excitement, and the sense of crisis, are acted out in a narrative equivalent of what Maggie articulates as 'the abrupt bend in her life'.

The planned action succeeds, as a scene of revelation for both characters, which maintains equilibrium. Surface teems with meaning, but is preserved as surface:

She had given him no help; for if on the one hand she couldn't speak for hesitation, so on the other – and especially as he didn't ask her – she couldn't explain why she was agitated. She had known it all the while down to her toes, known it in his presence with fresh intensity, and if he had uttered but a question it would have pressed in her the spring of recklessness. It had been strange that the most natural thing of all to say to him should have had that appearance; but she was more than ever conscious that *any* appearance she had would come round more or less straight to her father, whose life was now so quiet, on the basis accepted for it, that the least alteration of his consciousness, even in the possible sense of enlivenment, would make their precious equilibrium waver. *That* was at the bottom of her mind, that their equilibrium was everything, and that it was practically precarious, a matter of a hair's breadth for the loss of the balance. It was the equilibrium, or at all events her conscious fear about it, that had brought her heart into her mouth; and the same fear was on either side in the silent look she and Amerigo had exchanged. (Ibid.)

This scene of crisis in the action, and in the consciousness of the characters, is followed by another stroke of James's inventive art, an unspoken speech, openly expressing anxiety, need, and love:

It would have been most beautifully therefore in the name of the equilibrium, and in that of her joy at their feeling so exactly the same about it, that she might have spoken if she had permitted the truth on the subject of her behaviour to ring out - on the subject of that poor little behaviour which was for the moment so very limited a case of eccentricity.
' "Why, why" have I made this evening such a point of our not all dining together? Well, because I've all day been so wanting you alone that I finally couldn't bear it and that there didn't seem any great reason why I should try to. *That* came to me - funny as it may at first sound, with all the things we've so wonderfully got into the way of bearing for each other. You've seemed these last days - I don't know what: more absent than ever before, too absent for us merely to go on so. It's all very well, and I perfectly see how beautiful it is, all round; but there comes a day when something snaps, when the full cup, filled to the very brim, begins to flow over. That's what has happened to my need of you - the cup, all day, has been too full to carry. So here I am with it, spilling it over you - and just for the reason that's the reason of my life. After all I've scarcely to explain that I'm as much in love with you now as the first hour; except that there are some hours - which I know when they come, because they almost frighten me - that show me I'm even more so. They come of themselves - and ah they've been coming! After all, after all—!' Some such words as those were what *didn't* ring out, yet it was as if even the unuttered sound had been quenched here in its own quaver. It was where utterance would have broken down by its very weight if he had let it get so far. (Ibid.)

What is not said - and cannot be said until the last sentences of the novel - has been implied. James offers the crude alternative, and the inner pressure, in the restrained release of an *occupatio* ('what *didn't* ring out') which draws attention to its own art. He develops and changes the analysis and expression of feeling, taking us out of the nineteenth into the twentieth century, preparing for new modes of understatement, indirection and silence.

NOTES

1 James's elaborations of language in the revision for the New York Edition (the text of Percy Lubbock's edition of *The Novels and Stories of Henry James*) are well known. He makes marked changes in figures of feeling, usually adding and extending metaphor and personification. In this passage, he replaces the 'quite peculiar quality of unrest', which describes the effect of Rowland's meditation, by the defined imagery of painful things, like 'sharp-cornered objects bumped against in darkness'.

2 A fine example of James's topos of inexpressibility, consciously placed in literary tradition, as 'that species of emotion of which by the testimony of the poets the very name and essence are oddity' is replaced in the revised text by a generalized comment: 'such impressions show a total never represented by the mere sum of their constituent parts'.

3 In the revised text the personification of 'the silence' is extended. Instead of 'a conscious symbol of calamity', it is said to be 'charged with cruelty and danger'.

4 In one of James's most striking changes, the subdued personification in 'the dumb exultation of the cliff' is developed to become 'The great gaunt wicked cliff' and 'almost company to him'. It is elaborated by simile, 'as the chance-saved photograph of a murderer might become for a shipwrecked castaway a link with civilisation', and finally implicated, 'for it had done *its* part too, and what were they both, in their stupidity, he and it, but dumb agents of fate?' The brief statement, 'The most rational of men was for an hour the most passionate' is transformed into metaphor, 'The most rational of men wandered and lost himself in the dark places of passion, lashed his "conduct" with a scourge of steel, accusing it of cruelty. . . .' The tendency is to elaborate, particularize, and intensify but not, in my opinion, to improve on the 1879 text, conveniently available in the Penguin edition. My references to *Roderick Hudson* have been taken from this text.